Lessons from Privilege

Lessons from Privilege

THE AMERICAN PREP SCHOOL TRADITION

Arthur G. Powell

HARVARD UNIVERSITY PRESS

Cambridge, Massachusetts
London, England

For Ida Powell, Bayard Schieffelin,
and Virginia Schieffelin

Copyright © 1996 by the President and Fellows of Harvard College
All rights reserved
Printed in the United States of America

Library of Congress Cataloging-in-Publication Data
Powell, Arthur G., 1937–
Lessons from privilege : the American prep school tradition /
Arthur G. Powell
p.   cm.
Includes bibliographical references (p.) and index.
ISBN 0–674–52549–3
1. Preparatory schools—United States.   2. Preparatory school
students—United States.
3. Upper class—Education (Secondary)—United States.   I. Title
LC58.4.P68 1996
373.2'22—dc20
96–9157
CIP

Second printing, 1997

Contents

Preface

This book originated in a memorandum I wrote in 1988 on the occasion of the twenty-fifth anniversary of the National Association of Independent Schools (NAIS) and its decision at that time to discontinue its quasi-autonomous, foundation-supported Commission on Educational Issues. The memo suggested that an appropriate valedictory for the Commission might be a contributed volume about independent schools. As the idea evolved it seemed more feasible to have only one author.

The Commission was a 1970s response to the NAIS's belief that independent education was too isolated from innovative developments in public education. Its mission was to link prep schools to outside practice and research, with financial support separate from the dues member schools paid for regular NAIS services. I was privileged to direct the Commission during its last decade, and to work with unusually distinguished commissioners drawn from almost every corner of the American educational landscape. Although this book's Appendix emphasizes research methodology, much of what I know about independent schools I learned during my work with the Commission between 1978 and 1988. My debt to the commissioners and the NAIS board of directors is immense.

By far our largest project was an inquiry into American secondary education, A Study of High Schools, which was directed by the

Commission's chairman, Theodore R. Sizer. By 1986 the high school study had produced three books and one of the largest school-reform projects in American history, the Coalition of Essential Schools. But it was unarguably a study mainly of public schools. Public education by then seemed less notable for the solutions it offered than for the problems it confronted. The Commission gradually became less germane to the emerging priorities of independent schools, and by the late 1980s its time had passed. It was instead timely to ask what lessons independent schools may have to offer other schools, just as in the mid-1970s independent schools asked the question in reverse.

The greatest single force behind getting this book off the ground was the commitment of John Esty, then president of NAIS. He believed the study was important and should be done independent of any NAIS direction. He secured much of the foundation support that sustained it for half of its life. In addition, he remained a close, constructive, and engaged critic following his retirement from NAIS.

Unlike A Study of High Schools, this project was very much a personal effort. There was never any secretarial or regular staff, and only five part-time consultants participated for brief periods of time. I deeply appreciate the contributions of Anne Chase, Faith Dunne, Bob Hampel, Barbara Powell, and Nelson Treece, even as I exonerate them from errors of fact or judgment that are mine alone.

Foundation support was crucial for the study to exist at all, and was especially indispensable for the quantitative investigations and the field studies. I thank the Geraldine R. Dodge Foundation, the Edward E. Ford Foundation, Gates Foundation, the Esther A. and Joseph Klingenstein Fund, Inc., the New York Community Trust, and the Rockefeller Brothers Fund. In particular, I thank John Klingenstein and Claire List for a second grant from the Klingenstein Fund that enabled much of the quantitative work to go forward.

During the more than three years that the project received no direct funding, the Consortium for Policy Research in Education (CPRE) and its allied Finance Center provided support for the development of ideas. This helped me formulate my initial ideas on independent-school governance, in a paper commissioned for the CPRE Finance Center, and ideas about incentives and external assessment first outlined in Susan H. Fuhrman, ed., *Designing Coher-*

ent *Education Policy* (San Francisco: Jossey-Bass, 1993). NAIS gave no financial support in order to preserve the project's independence, but nevertheless helped in many indirect ways.

Access to most of my sources involved courtesies of many kinds. NAIS opened its archives and those of its predecessor organizations. Morton Owen Shapiro helped me think about prep school financial aid in the context of financial aid in private higher education. Gretchen Rigol of the College Board's Admissions Testing Program authorized release of SAT:90, and Wade Curry and Walter B. MacDonald of the Advanced Placement Program made available many documents that I otherwise would not have found. Barbara Schneider (whose advice on many points I should have taken) and Steven J. Ingels of the National Opinion Research Center at the University of Chicago, and Jeffrey Owings of the National Center for Education Statistics, were helpful guides to NELS:88. Mary Rollefson and her colleagues at the National Center for Education Statistics were endlessly patient in providing data that allowed me to make maximum use of SASS:88. None of these numbers might have been crunched without the timely intervention of Doc Howe of the Harvard Graduate School of Education. His many personal kindnesses were easily the equivalent of an additional foundation grant.

It is always difficult to acknowledge properly the contributions of students, parents, teachers, and administrators to field research. There are too many of them to list individually, and the practical benefits that accrue to schools from inquiry committed to confidentiality are usually meager. I am especially indebted to parents like "Sam's" mother, who made sure I received her son's written comment with salient passages highlighted. The perceptive observations of veteran teachers like "Mr. Evans" and "Mr. Posner" provoked much thought. Students like "Jessica" were astonishingly candid. It isn't easy to talk gracefully about the frustrations of working hard and getting Cs. Administrators and their staffs went out of their way to organize our visits. No one symbolized this selfless cooperation better than Hilary Carlson, the assistant head of Kent Denver School, and her late husband, John, who opened their home to this project as warmly as the school opened itself.

These symbolic examples must suffice. On behalf of their communities I thank Mike Teitelman (the Bishop's School), Peter Gunness

(Buckingham Browne & Nichols School), Chris Babbs (Colorado Academy), Jerral Miles (Francis Parker School), James Connor (Germantown Academy), Redmond Finny (Gilman School), Tom Kaesemeyer (Kent Denver School), John Chandler (Pingree School), Earl Ball (William Penn Charter School), and Carolyn Peter (the Winsor School). In addition, I am grateful to the Stanford Center for Research on the Context of Secondary School Teaching, under the direction of Milbrey McLaughlin and Joan Talbert, for making available relevant field notes.

During this project I interviewed dozens of private school leaders, chiefly during meetings or on the sidelines of athletic games. These brief chats were wholly informal and remarkably useful. Some individuals took the time, between 1988 and 1993, for more formal reflections on the independent-school tradition. With apologies to those I have inadvertently omitted, I thank for these interviews Richard Cowan, Adele Erwin, John Esty, Wellington V. Grimes, the Rev. F. Washington Jarvis, David Mallery, Cary Potter, Robert Smith, and Dean K. Whitla.

No one helped more than colleagues who, in a busy world where time to read others' work is scarce, nevertheless made thoughtful comments on various drafts of the book. I am especially indebted to Don Erickson, John Esty, Bob Hampel, Alan Peshkin, Cary Potter, Barbara Powell, John Ratté, Nancy Faust Sizer, and Ted Sizer. Members of the personalization working group of the ATLAS Seminar affiliate of the ATLAS Communities project, and especially Mindy Kornhaber, gave valuable feedback on the personalization section. Christine Thorsteinsson edited the manuscript with patience and professionalism. Carter Umbarger was a steadying force throughout.

I am grateful to my family for sticking with this project even though it is far from the "Murder in the Classroom" bestseller that my son Ben argued should be my logical and lucrative next step. My mother, Ida Powell, and my father-in-law, Bayard Schieffelin, died within a span of ninety days just before the work began in 1989, and my mother-in-law, Virginia Schieffelin, died when the full manuscript first saw the light of day at the end of 1994. They were all teachers in their different ways. Ida was a teacher of fifty years in fact, Bayard and Virginia were teachers at heart, and all three were important teachers of mine. Their lessons are on every page.

INTRODUCTION

Sam's Comment and the Prep School Tradition

Sam's sixth-grade social studies progress was described in a routine school practice called a "written comment." Teachers wrote comments about each of their students three times a year. Faculty advisors also wrote summary comments about advisees based on teachers' observations and their own knowledge of students. Sam's comment revealed nothing especially dramatic. He had experienced neither triumph nor tragedy during the winter trimester. The first part of the comment recounted his homework, quiz, and writing development: "His writer's workshop piece was edited well, edited carefully."

Then the teacher's tone suddenly changed—"However, there is something else"—and the primary audience being addressed shifted from Sam's parents to Sam himself. The teacher noted that Sam, although attentive and in no academic difficulty, was speaking up less in class. He was "sitting out some of the rough and tumble of discussion. I'm getting no 'relevant' jokes, and see less of his panned smiling." Probably it was nothing at all, "but Sam, it might be worth your while to consider the matter. Why? Strong opinions go soft in too much silence or reserve. And I miss your voice."

Sam's mother was moved by the feeling and the feedback. She especially appreciated the graceful tone of respect and concern. By his interest in her son's "voice," the teacher expressed interest in Sam as a unique person. He cared about Sam and was working hard to help him learn. The school was special, the mother emphasized, because all its teachers "want to hear each child's voice."

Most schools have sixth-grade social studies, but not all have teachers who are expected to know and be interested in all their students. The school's admissions director explained that parents who sought out personal attention often had children who did not stand out as much as others. They were neither superstars nor burdened by handicaps—the kinds of uniqueness that automatically command special attention in most schools. They were simply regular students.

Sam's comment was meant to advance distinctly academic purposes. Caring was valued, but it was not the only value. The school's educational methods assumed students' active participation in their studies and the entirety of school life. The warning that silence in class could breed mental softness and the punch line "And I miss your voice" made gently clear that class participation was expected. Doing well on tests and writing assignments was not enough. Sam was nudged to do more for the sake of his own intellectual growth. The school's public commitment to high standards meant a commitment to push every student to engage with the learning opportunities available.

The comment was not a voluntary, spontaneous gesture by a single teacher, but rather a direct expression of school policy, a time-consuming responsibility built into every teacher's job description. Sustaining a system of high-quality written comments was an exhausting affair involving multiple policies ranging from faculty hiring to small teacher loads to quality control over drafts of the comments themselves. Schools that expected teachers to know students and adopted consistent policies to achieve that end were likely to be decent communities for adults and students alike.

Sam attended Colorado Academy, a private day school pleasantly sited in southwestern Denver, where the city thins out and the plains approach the Rockies' eastern slope. CA, as it is locally known, typifies the sort of private school that calls itself "independent" and is usually called "prep" or simply "private school" by everyone else. Such places proudly cultivate distinct personalities while forming a national community of rather similar institutions.

They are nonprofit, self-governing entities, espouse a central academic purpose geared toward preparation for four-year colleges, and are usually secular in spirit, even though many originated in the more elegant Protestant denominations. Only rarely are they Catholic, and hardly ever conservative Christian.

They are also very costly to attend. By the mid-1990s, the median national ninth-grade tuition for day students exceeded $10,000. CA's tuition was very close to the median. These are privileged schools; they number few more than a thousand, and most are members of the National Association of Independent Schools (NAIS).

Like its colleague schools nationwide, as well as most private colleges, CA is not part of a school system but is an incorporated nonprofit institution governed by its own board of trustees. Founded in 1900, the school is relatively small, with only 40 or so seniors. Because it encompasses prekindergarten through twelfth grade, its student enrollment of 660 is larger than grade size alone would suggest. Independent schools often include more grades than public schools—preK–9 and 7–12 patterns are common in addition to preK–12. But grades are usually clustered into smaller organizational units. CA, for example, has lower, middle (where Sam was enrolled), and upper schools, each with its own principal but all located on the same campus. The average independent school is much smaller, but a majority of prep students attend schools with more than 500 students.

Originally CA's mission was highly specialized. It was a military boarding school for boys, about as specialized a school environment as one can imagine. But like most independent schools that began with specialized purposes, its mission broadened considerably over the years. In the 1960s it dropped the military aspect and became college preparatory. In 1971 it abandoned boarding and became coeducational. These changes paralleled changes occurring elsewhere; many other prep schools stopped boarding students, and by the early 1990s only 11 percent of independent-school students were boarders. Once mostly single sex, independent schools also became overwhelmingly coeducational.

Nearly all CA graduates progress to four-year colleges. The school's core mission is to prepare students to gain admission to colleges that have more qualified applicants than available slots. More graduates in recent years have enrolled in the state university at Boulder than in any other institution. But most venture out of state to liberal arts schools, especially in the Northeast and on the West Coast. CA students become keenly aware of the national community of selective colleges and universities, wherever their location.

CA and other independent schools have made determined efforts to provide financial aid to help offset their very high costs. Their labors have had real but modest effects. CA awarded more than $500,000 annually to assist 11 percent of its students in the early 1990s. But almost 90 percent of CA families paid the full tuition. Costs have clearly limited the growth of independent education nationwide. NAIS schools enrolled about 400,000 students in the mid-1990s, less than 1 percent of the total school population and less than 8 percent of the entire private school population. Total independent-school enrollments have increased gradually since World War II, but these percentages—the schools' "market share"—have remained quite stable. New York City's public schools alone have three times the number of students in all prep schools combined.[1]

It is therefore not surprising that issues of economic privilege have traditionally overshadowed issues of educational practice in public consciousness of independent schools. When success or scandal gets them in the papers, their names are usually preceded by "exclusive" or "elite." Their existence symbolizes both the advantages conveyed by privilege and the insulation of privilege from the presumed melting pot of public education.

Scholars and critics, for example, have pondered the extent to which independent schools contribute to social processes such as the power, decline, reproduction, or preservation of the upper and upper-middle classes. Others defend or attack private schools on policy or philosophical grounds—the claims of individuals against the claims of society. Still others deliciously dissect the eccentricities of privilege—elegant tea service immediately following punishing athletic contests, the habit of wearing boxers instead of briefs.

But what high tuition actually buys educationally—the school experience of young Sam—remains something of a mystery. Few people get excited about practices like written comments, and therefore the legacy of independent education, the uses that other schools might make of some of its traditions, remains somewhat mysterious as well.

I first noticed this imbalance of attention when studying CA and two other independent schools during 1981 and 1982. Up to that time I knew virtually nothing about privileged private schools. I grew up in a different world—Staten Island, a remote region of New York City where for fifty years my mother gallantly taught public school at P.S.1 in Tottenville. I was raised in the 1940s and 1950s to believe that my New York public schools were the best in the country, that private school meant Catholic school, and that Catholic school meant rigid religiosity for students too unambitious or untalented to succeed in public school. I became aware of expensive non-parochial private education only when my college's freshman football team happened to play the varsity of a boarding school.

Many years later, privileged private schools quite suddenly entered my life. In 1978 I became director of the NAIS Commission on Educational Issues. In 1981 our family moved to the campus of a private boarding school when my wife became its headmistress. My oldest son enrolled in an independent day school after an unhappy year in our elite suburban public school. At the same time, my work for the Commission involved field research in fifteen schools, upon which *The Shopping Mall High School* was eventually based. Although that book was primarily concerned with public education, three of the schools examined were independent day schools.

Looking closely at CA was an especially instructive experience. Its statistical location in the middle of independent schooling nationally—and its actual location in the heart of the West—freed it from many rigid stereotypes that often sidetrack discussions of privileged private schools. CA presents itself more as an educational place than as an institution weighed down by traditions and burdens of social class. It invites educational more than social examination. Privilege is there but does not overwhelm. It is not a heavily endowed boarding school intimately associated with the old Protestant establishment, nor is it the most socially desirable prep school in Denver. It is as secular and coeducational as any public school. And when economic recession struck Denver soon after we concluded our visits in the 1980s, CA revealed itself as poignantly vulnerable to declines in enrollment and morale. It was by no means manicured, confident, or insulated perfection.

Most important, the school was impressive educationally to all our research staff who spent time there. Some of its traditions, like Sam's comment, are typical of schools of its type but rare elsewhere. CA was also struggling with many of the issues central to the national school-reform movement then gathering steam. How do schools build community without the moral authority of some religious orientation? What do high standards mean in the context of diverse students, and how does one know they have been adequately met? Does freedom from the constraints of being one unit in a larger system increase school morale and effectiveness? Although high tuitions isolated prep schools from most American families, it was clear that these institutions were not isolated from many issues facing all American schools as the century ended.

The focus of this book is the education that privileged schools provide and not privilege itself, the schooling experience and not the social system that permits independent schools to exist. Of what constructive use is the American prep school tradition, now more than a hundred years old, to all American schools? What positive lessons do such schools offer the country? If they offer any lessons, why not learn them? And if money or other barriers make applying their lessons difficult or perhaps undesirable, the public should know what most American schools are missing—and why.

To the greatest possible extent, I attempt to avoid the debates for and against private schools, and the various claims of the individual against those of society. These issues are obviously important and can never be entirely avoided, but an abundant literature already exists on them. Americans may love or loathe private schools for many reasons but still wonder which of their qualities might make their own schools better. Everyone can learn much that is constructive from prep schools without endorsing them or embracing the privatizing of schooling as wise public policy.

I believe that many school types are valuable in a free country. Privileged private schools claim they are truly public in their purposes if not in their funding and governance, and my experience suggests that this is very often the case. But public education demands more national attention today because it serves many more students and is far more troubled. Still, the fates of public and private schools are intertwined. Strong public schools are good for privileged private schools because they force them to be creative to justify their high prices. When public schools are perceived as weak and uncompetitive, independent schools often become complacent.

The notion that there are "lessons" to be learned from private schools does not assume that good practices found in many of them are exclusive to private schools. Public governance is not a barrier to any of the ideas discussed in this book. Nor does this notion assume that independent schools have most of the answers. Rich schools do not show other schools a clear path to guaranteed success. Indeed, very advantaged schools cannot guarantee success anywhere close to a dentist's guarantee that he can fix a toothache. Humility about education's complexity is one of the first lessons prep schools teach.

Nor do lessons always mean practical, concrete, and replicable programs. Of equal value are fresh perspectives on school possibilities, barriers, and limits. Lessons can also be warnings about what to avoid. The most powerful features of independent schools are often their most controversial. Unlike a cure for a dread disease, which the whole society applauds, many lessons from these schools are admired by some but condemned by others.

The task of identifying useful lessons suggested a series of interpretive chapters about key problems facing all American schools rather than a comprehensive "study" of independent schools. Each of the book's main sections and most of the chapters begin by describing these problems. Only then are prep schools brought into the discussion. The ideas of community, standards, and personalization are the heart of the independent-school tradition, and the book is therefore organized in three sections around these ideas. The chapters aim to be pointed reflections. Although grounded extensively in research, they are not research reports. This approach required me to combine widely varied sources of information in order to see how very different materials informed an understanding of common problems. These written, quantitative, and in-school interview sources are described in the Appendix.

I

COMMUNITY

1

The Vulnerability of Educational Communities

The power of schools to develop culture and intelligence in the young was challenged by increasingly potent "avenues of escape" from mental exertion after World War II. But the administrator of a leading private school association was confident in 1952 that serious learning would defeat its escapist competition. Television had joined radio, comics, and the movies as diversionary forces to be reckoned with, but she thought they could all be contained. "The little boy buying a comic book and the children watching Milton Berle are not monsters," she stated reassuringly. "They are the reasons schools exist. They are the reasons teachers exist." High-quality schools were society's organized antidote to the dubious temptations of youth culture. The values of school would surely prevail in the never-ending battle for the loyalty of the young.[1]

How poignant such confidence seems at century's end! All schools today are vulnerable to relentless competition from forces far stronger and pernicious than the benign diversions of Uncle Miltie and Captain Marvel. The avenues of escape from mental exertion and the cultivation of intelligence have multiplied remarkably. Schools and the values of learning now face formidable and heavily financed enemies.

The most obvious evidence of schools' vulnerability is the direct insertion of weapons, drugs, and violence into many of them. But a more telling indicator, because it is so pervasive across geographic regions, economic classes, and ethnic groups, is the great competition schools face simply to hold students' attention. The educational impact of the youth consumption industry and especially of the youth-oriented media is enormous and growing. The tremendous purchasing power of American youth has created numerous businesses that challenge the educational function of schools by offering entertainment and pleasure requiring no mental effort at all.

These businesses aim to "educate" just as surely as do schools, but with very different motives. Greed for profit, not healthy child development, is the incentive. The long-range business plan is to inculcate consumption habits that almost by definition are anti-educational.

At the center of the industry is the movie-music-video complex. It is largely antiread, antiwrite, antithink, and antitalk. It celebrates and rewards instant gratification and short attention spans. It loathes complexity and thoughtful reflection. Time spent consuming the media is time lost from school and learning. The income-producing youth employment essential to consumption takes additional time from school and learning.

When the Nickelodeon cable channel decided to expand into preschool programming dominated by public television, its president explained, "We recognize that if we start getting kids to watch us at this age, we have them for life. That's exactly the reason why we're doing it." Nickelodeon's activity is benign compared with others' exploitation of violence, promiscuity, and other anticommunity behavior designed purely to grab the interest and dollars of children. Some kids re-enact in real life horrendous images they have seen or heard because those images are so compelling.[2]

Undeniably, pop culture designed primarily for the youth market is sometimes of high quality. Some rock or rap groups or songs, some movies, some of almost all forms of entertainment have much lasting value. They open rather than close the American mind and heart. In addition, much that has no lasting value beyond entertainment is educationally harmless. Given such realities, *ad hominum* harangues about youth's descent into cultural barbarism at the hands of the evil media empire lack constructive effect. Critics easily become typecast as dour old fogies, patronizing elitists, or cultural absolutists who presume that some expressions of experience are better than others.

Furthermore, the profit motive will not disappear. First Amendment protections that permit youth pop culture to thrive without much interference will remain. And the lines between good pop culture and enduring culture will continue, as always, to be blurry and in flux. It is instructive that no new American museum of the early 1990s, aside from the Holocaust Museum, received more respectful critical praise than the Rock and Roll Hall of Fame.

The practical educational task is not pompous and useless condemnation of greedy youth predators; it is strengthening the power of all schools to make good on their distinct public mission to develop culture and intelligence. Schools are special places whose mission is very often at odds with that of the pop culture industry. Schools should understand the cultural struggle they are part of and be committed to battle for educational values.

But against this competition most schools fight back weakly or not at all. They seldom attack the industry and the violent, calculating, and prurient advertising that shares in the profits. Although schools actively oppose many nasty "isms," the one they touch least is the anti-intellectualism of youth pop culture. They play into the hands of the competition by emulating it. They try to make learning more entertaining, show more movies (sometimes as visual-literacy substitutes for reading books), permit homework to be done in class because it will not be done at home, and at times invite the competition inside their walls by showing students TV news with commercials.

Why this reluctance to fight back? One reason is that the enemy is harder to know than traditional ones. Public schools are more familiar with school-board crazies bent on book censorship or penny-pinching voters defeating budget referenda. The latter opponents present clear and immediate educational dangers. The new enemies are usually physically distant from schools, employ talented public relations firms to defuse criticism in the name of freedom of speech, possess huge economic resources, and contribute to worthy causes. They gain from media apologists who praise pop culture's capacity to entertain over old-fashioned mastery of ideas, and who confuse the brilliant potential of modern communications technology with its less-than-brilliant present content.

Another reason is that education's enemies are frequently more popular with students and many teachers than is education itself. Criticism
of them becomes awkward when educators rarely regard them as enemies and in fact consume them almost as much as their students do.

For schools to compete they must become purposeful educational
communities that know an educational enemy when they see it. But
reaching agreement on a schoolwide pro-education offensive is difficult in the face of changes in school authority relations since the
1960s. The ability of most schools to shape their destiny has been
reduced by legislative mandates, court orders, lobbyist pressures,
bureaucratic rules, and teacher unions. Many parents have become
more opinionated, more single-issue oriented, and more demanding
consumers. Other parents have become more apathetic and withdrawn, not only from school but from parenting. Students are more
diverse, schools more inclusive, and advocates for student groups
more influential. Students confront fewer moral, cultural, or legal
sanctions from behaving in whatever manner seems most pleasurable. The idea of general educational standards, much less moral
ones, is widely challenged as cultural oppression.

None of these developments has been conducive to sustaining
purposeful—educationally focused—school communities. Public
schools, because of both deliberate and accidental public policies,
are less independent from all these forces than they were a generation ago. Schools are more democratic, egalitarian, and sympathetic
communities. But they are also weaker communities in their capacity to take educational stands and embrace pervasive and visible
ideals about what education should be. They are diverse but divided, inclusive but fragmented.

This plays into the hands of their competitors. Too many notions
of purpose compete with and cancel each other, and no accepted authority exists to make difficult choices among them. People rarely
talk about most schools as if they should be united communities
with a distinct institutional purpose. Instead, a good school is often
regarded as a place that offers many different opportunities and programs. The program is expected to have the impact, not the school.
The more opportunities, the argument goes, the better the school.

It is hard to criticize opportunities for students to learn. If some
elementary schools offer foreign-language instruction and others do

not, high school students drawn from the first group will have a foreign-language advantage. But the disconcerting reality in most schools is not the absence of opportunities but the unwillingness of students to take advantage of those that exist. In a society where pro-education values are at risk, schools cannot merely provide opportunities; they should be pervaded by shared, visible, and consistently expressed educational purposes. These purposes should be translated into policies that constantly press students to engage seriously in some of the opportunities offered. Schools influence student engagement by the messages they send about what school is for, how students should behave in school, and what is worthy of respect and commitment.

Inevitably and properly, our schools are influenced by the world around them. But we should expect them to be safe for and devoted to serious learning. They should command enough authority over children's and parents' lives to hold anti-education behavior sufficiently in check while they exemplify pro-education values. They must be *decent* communities and *educational* communities. This does not imply monasteries or moated castles. But schools do have walls—physical and metaphorical—which properly separate them from those parts of the outside world hostile to their work. Today those walls are breached far too easily.

Decent Communities, Educational Communities

The maddeningly vague word "community" means more than merely a group of people associated by common traits, ties, or rules. The most urgent meaning of community in most schools, and especially many public schools, is gaining shared agreement that students will be decent and civil to one another. It is hoped that they will be tolerant and respectful as well. All schools long for decent community in the sense of a safe, courteous, and supportive atmosphere. At minimum all members should peacefully coexist. The problem of school community is widely regarded as mainly a problem of good human relations.

The popularity of school community defined as decent community comes not just from the need to preserve harmony and keep the peace. If it did, the idea would not be nearly so popular as it is in well-off and safe schools. By the 1980s, getting along together, labeled "teamwork," was everywhere celebrated as a necessary workplace skill and hence a desired educational goal. Getting along together was also transformed into a popular educational method called "cooperative learning."

Further, Americans generally place a high value on the happiness and psychological well-being of their children, a value that has certainly grown with increasing education and the popularizing of self-improvement, self-esteem, and self-absorption. Teachers are affected by the same trends. They regard noneconomic conditions of their work life—their relations with colleagues and superiors, their sense of how their work is valued by students, parents, and the outside community, their beliefs about how much they are in control of their work—as crucial elements of job satisfaction and personal dignity.

Defining community as the creation of decent human relations, in short, addresses more than just the administrative problem of persuading large and sometimes diverse groups of young people to get along amicably. This notion of community also addresses the educational goals parents have for their children and teachers have for themselves. The characteristics desired for the community are the same as those desired for its members.

Highly organized efforts to create school communities based on decent human relations typically take the form of distinct and specialized programs. Respect for others, especially those who are regarded as different in politically charged respects, is promoted through school programs that focus on appreciating differences, repudiating hatreds, and confronting abuses. Developmental issues like growing up or growing old are addressed through programs ranging from coping with adolescence (from both student and parent viewpoints) to gaining freedom from chemical dependency (by both students and their parents). The most elaborate programs are often found in more privileged public and private schools, where the need for them is arguably less urgent than in less privileged schools but the resources to mount them are greater.

Creating decent school communities is very difficult work that is never completely accomplished. Like most school work it is a continuing struggle with some small victories but no final triumph or recognizable end-point. It is sometimes fashionable to stereotype "sharing and caring" efforts as sentimental psychobabble, attempts to accommodate feel-good student and teacher preferences that have nothing to do with academic learning and are often undermining of it. But this critique needs tempering. Far from attempts to recover a lost cooperative age, begin a communitarian assault on individualist excess, or simply make everyone happy, the desire for decent community is a practical judgment about good workplace conditions. Many schools wish to be more supportive, safe, and caring simply because they are alienating, unhappy, and dangerous. For them, respecting diversity is purpose enough.

But a decent school community, though necessary, is not sufficient to provide a large boost to schools' competitive position against anti-education forces. The idea of decent community emphasizes helping students get along, work together, and grow as persons. It rarely gives explicit attention to education in the sense of intellectual skills, knowledge, and long-term serious interests or habits.

These basically cognitive qualities constitute what schools exist uniquely to cultivate in a society often indifferent or hostile to them. They are the tools—or sometimes weapons—that enable adults to be intellectually free and committed, qualify for jobs that are not mindless, become constructive citizens, and deepen their understanding of the human condition. These intellectual tools enable those who possess them not only to compete in the job market, but also to withstand the onslaught of the movie-music-video complex. Cultivating them is what all schools must ultimately be judged on—although they are by no means the only important human qualities. It is essential for schools to strive to be educational communities with the same passion that they now devote to tolerating differences, attacking isms, and creating self-help and social service programs.

This is not easy. Decent school communities are rarely controversial. No one is against safe schools, although they are sometimes hard to create, and most people value respect and tolerance within them. But there is much less consensus about what an educational community should be and more than a little suspicion of schools that become too aggressive in their intellectual commitments or demands.

Throughout the twentieth century critics have consistently found that American schools reflect rather than challenge local anti-intellectual or anti-academic attitudes. They do not fight back. Although the sociologist David Riesman once hoped that schools might become "countervailing" pro-education forces against provincial values, this was rarely attempted or attained. Even among educational reformers there is considerable sentiment that local schools should express local values. If some schools value learning and the life of the mind, it is usually because the geographical communities they represent want schools of that sort.[3]

Another difficulty in creating schoolwide educational communities is that serious educators often disagree with one another about what a good educational community is. Battles throughout the century between "progressive" child-centered advocates and "traditional" subject-centered proponents have often been more bitter than battles between either group and those hostile to both approaches (or any serious approach). Internal squabbles have divided pro-education reformers and weakened reform.

Despite their differences over means, most reformers agree on many key objectives. These include the importance of understanding what one studies (as distinct from mindless memorization); the importance of knowledge as one key to understanding (knowledge really is power); and the importance of cultivating serious long-term interests and habits (as distinct from forgetting material the moment an exam is over). Because together they are a minority, reformers must respect one another. Educational communities lose focus when weakened from within by disagreements among those who are most committed to education.

A further problem is that islands of community with shared educational values already exist within many schools. Pro-education students usually find one another, and teachers do, too. They get what they want in specialty shops within shopping mall schools. They do not need to fight for a schoolwide sense of purposeful community. Part of the brilliance of most American schools is their capacity to provide something for everyone. This has been, so far, the best way to accommodate our belief in universal and often endless schooling with the absence of any agreement about what the substance of education should be. Americans' satisfaction with their local schools suggests that this approach has had some success.

So why push for a schoolwide sense of educational community? What is wrong with islands of focused purpose within less purposeful institutions? Why force serious education on everyone if it is there for those who want it?

One answer is based on the practical needs of the country and the moral responsibilities of a democracy. Many educators, politicians, and businesspeople have recently argued that basic and advanced intellectual skills for all young Americans—or at least almost all of them—need ratcheting up to compete in a global economy where decent jobs require a skilled workforce.

At the same time, the insistent egalitarianism that continues to characterize schools much more than most other institutions has co-existed, more than in the past, with demands for excellence, quality, and standards. The national goals developed by the governors and two presidents at the beginning of the 1990s, for example, nicely express an overly ambitious conception of excellence deliberately intended to apply to the many and not the few. If an educational community is perceived as being hostile to equity—which can very easily occur—neither excellence nor equity will likely prosper.

This simultaneous embrace of equity and excellence is strikingly different from the previous great surge of support for academic reform in the late 1950s and early 1960s, when the nation seemed at risk because of Soviet leadership in science and technology. Then the solution was to identify and educate the gifted in tough technical disciplines. This could be done by encouraging enclaves of purposeful educational community within schools. The development of Advanced Placement (AP) academic courses for high-end students perfectly expressed that position.

But if it is now agreed that most students, and not just a few, should be pressed to develop intellectual habits and cognitive skills, then the logic seems clear that islands of purposeful community are insufficient. Entire schools must be suffused with commitment to learning, because entire student populations must become seriously engaged in learning.

Another reason to press the idea of schoolwide educational community is that it is a very powerful but surprisingly neglected educational force. A purposeful school community actively educates students and energizes teachers. It is a positive force and a condition of work for everyone comparable in many respects to courses, programs, teachers, and facilities. Schools can struggle to create and sustain it through deliberate policies.[4]

A thoughtful parent admitted that the constantly invoked sense that his daughter's school was a truly special community might be no more than a "creative fiction" constructed by the school over the years. But that did not matter if belief in the school's specialness made its entire membership "rise to that mythical quality" and bring an "added jolt of energy each day." Artful cultivation of some myth of special community has always been a preeminent objective of most good public or private schools. Such myths give schools distinct identities, and students and teachers a strong sense of community obligation. Students become "fiercely proud, even borderline arrogant" about their school and driven on to live up to its ideals.

Without some overarching sense of purpose, it is difficult for schools to put in place procedures, expectations, and traditions that together send a clear and constructive message to all students, teachers, and families. Schools are imbedded in society but are also places apart from it. They are havens where educational values in jeopardy on the outside are not only respected but lived.[5]

Character, Decent Communities, and Independent Schools

Independent schools have long committed much energy to creating decent school communities even though their problems of student safety and friction are far fewer than in most schools. Fights in independent schools are unusual, and the national symbol of bureaucratic mistrust known as the hall pass is largely unknown. One student observed that in his school "chewing gum and sticking it on a table is a big deal." You could get into trouble for leaving your bag outside your locker, not because it might be stolen, but because it looked messy. Some schools have no lockers at all, just open cubbies.

Until the 1950s brought intense academic pressure on prep schools to secure admissions to selective colleges, the development of character was their most important professed objective. They have valued decent communities not because internal tensions needed resolution, but because they have aimed to develop decent young people. "The essential purpose of our kind of school," wrote Frank Hackett of Riverdale Country School, above Manhattan, in 1941, "is not an intellectual purpose, but a moral and spiritual purpose."

Decent communities are inextricably linked with the struggle to build decent individual character. Many prep schools, for example, have honor codes of various kinds. Sometimes students can write exams at home, and sometimes exams are given in unproctored classrooms. One headmaster talks all the time to students about the code. "He tries to rally us around it," they say, but admit that "sometimes it's in one ear and out the other." When evidence mounted that some students were abusing the code, student pressure rose to abolish it. But after a lengthy discussion—assisted by the fact that students were on the honor board, making it their project and not just the grownups'—they voted to expand it to include nonacademic dishonesty such as locker-room theft. The code symbolized decent community expectations. Everyone knew that living up to it was a never-quite-successful struggle. But the students decided to continue the struggle rather than settle for the presumption that dishonesty was the inevitable norm.[6]

Further, decent communities are valued not just as instruments to other ends but as ends in themselves. A thoughtful headmaster argued, in the midst of prep schools' preoccupation with academics in the 1960s, that decent community alone could make them "shining places" regardless of whether they produced much academic achievement. The most important outcome of schooling, according to David Aloian of Concord Academy in Massachusetts, was the quality of the lived experience day in and day out.

Schools were not just delivery sites for academic services, like doctors' offices, but communities where people spent long periods of time together. Time was the key. Students did not just come to school for periodic appointments; they were there hour after hour, day after day. What elicited loyalty and satisfaction from them and their families was whether school, in Aloian's words, was a "humane community . . . based on reason, restraint, decency, and a just regard for each person's point of view." The struggle to develop decent people and decent communities took no back seat to academics.[7]

Religion and Sports

The oldest tool prep schools have used to build character and decent community is religion. As late as 1954, paid advertisements promoting independent education in *Harper's* and *The Atlantic Monthly* began, "We teach that true learning begins with faith in God and a basic, ingrained belief in the universal brotherhood of man." More than a third of prep schools existing in the 1930s were established by or closely affiliated with some denomination (usually Protestant and usually Episcopal). Until the 1960s even nonsectarian schools typically required daily chapel attendance and Bible study, and supported lively extracurricular religious clubs. The clergyman head of St. Paul's School in New Hampshire argued in the 1920s that its job was "not to conform to the rich and prosperous world which surrounds us, but rather, through its children, to convert it." Hackett of Riverdale was no clergyman, and Riverdale had no denominational ties, but his popular morning chapel talks were published as a book.[8]

To those who believed that religion was the "rock on which the whole program of our schools should be set," a school's moral and spiritual impact depended on more than required services or courses. Religion not only had to be part of a school's official life, but also had to suffuse the entire institution. In 1951 Allan Heely of New Jersey's Lawrenceville School distinguished school morality based on a "body of corporate conviction" from that based on the "arithmetical total of the moral convictions of members of the faculty." Only the first had bite and power. But Heely was well aware how rare such shared "corporate conviction" was in independent education. The difficulties grew as secular and material values increased and out-of-school supportive traditions like family prayer declined.[9]

Little evidence existed that prep students were more devout, moral, or decent than others despite the prominent role religion played in most schools. In 1952, for example, the deeply religious dean of admissions at Amherst College, Eugene S. Wilson, scathingly attacked private school claims to develop faith and character. He examined independent-school catalog assertions as well as statements from the National Council of Independent Schools

(NCIS) such as "Independent Schools are vital strongholds of religious faith in the United States." He then interviewed prep students and observed prep graduates who attended Amherst and other colleges.

Religion, Wilson concluded, was for most prep students an empty school ritual. The mealtime grace "Bless this food to our use and us to Thy Service" meant "Now we eat." Students had no idea why they said it except that the headmaster liked it. They attended chapel because the head liked chapel, because of tradition, and because it was supposed to be good for them. It was easy for them to regurgitate the Lord's Prayer on command because they didn't think about the words they were saying. Wilson believed the prayer should be difficult to say, not easy.

Even more disconcerting was behavior he observed afterwards in college. Public school graduates who had experienced no school religion participated more in campus religious groups than prep school alumni. Wilson also checked the records of Amherst students who broke college rules of "decent community living" or committed less punishable but no less cruel offenses like bullying. Eighty percent of the offenders were prep school graduates.

Because Wilson was a friend of independent education, his devastating observations were taken very seriously by its leaders. He had no easy answers and admitted the near-impossible job schools faced in a society friendly to churchgoing as social custom but indifferent to religious commitment. Prep schools seemed willing neither to invest greater effort and resources in the religious struggle nor to reduce their extravagant claims about character-building.[10]

Wilson's blunt observations are not unique. School histories, if they discuss religious behavior at all, often note the gap between school ritual and student behavior. When Massachusetts's nonsectarian Phillips Academy (usually called Andover) was forced by student protests in the late 1960s to abandon required religious services, attendance at voluntary services dropped precipitously. Given a choice, the vast majority of students ceased any connection with formal religion.

By 1988, 73 percent of prep school eighth-graders reported no required religious studies of any kind. Only three of ten day secondary schools examined in 1992 required any instruction about the Bible or world religions; an art history teacher complained that hardly any ninth-graders had even heard of the Crucifixion. When a student in a school that still required weekly chapel was asked what chapel was for, he replied hesitantly, "They may be trying to put the God figure in your life. They are hinting that He is out there." In 1990, 73 percent of prep schools had no formal or informal ties to any religion.

Faith itself is not a distinctive feature of prep students today. In 1990 roughly 33 percent of prep school sophomores asserted that they held no religious beliefs at all. They were less likely to think of themselves as religious than were sophomores in either privileged public or all public schools, and far less likely than Catholic school or other private school sophomores. Twenty-three percent of prep school seniors claimed in 1990 to have no official religious affiliation, compared with 18 percent of college-bound privileged public school seniors and 17 percent of all college-bound public seniors.

The ability of prep schools to be bodies of corporate religious conviction has been eroded not just by secularism but by religious diversity. Schools that once were religiously homogeneous now deliberately seek students from all or no faiths. Old prejudices against Jews and sometimes Catholics are generally a thing of the past. Catholics are the largest denomination among prep students; at 24 percent, their representation is about the same as it is in public schools. Jews constitute more than 8 percent of independent-school seniors, compared with 3 percent of college-bound public school seniors. A large and academically committed student applicant pool is valued much more than one with shared religious beliefs. This distinguishes independent schools from most other private schools.

Religious diversity has transformed the traditional problem of developing moral character into one of accommodating different traditions without offense. Many prep schools agonize over such questions as "Should we have wreaths on the doors at Christmas when we are over 20 percent Jewish?" Christmas assembly gets renamed "winter" assembly and the music becomes less traditionally Christian and often conspicuously more secular and commercial. "And what about the Hindus? What do we do with their holidays?" Despite the dilution of school-sponsored religion, very few veteran teachers believe that prep school communities of decades ago were more decent places than prep school communities of today.

Religion's role in directly promoting moral character in schools today is modest. Only 14 percent of prep school sophomores in 1990 regarded themselves as very religious. Most schoolpeople of deep faith seem to prefer the greater voluntarism of the present to the rigid prescription of the past. Postwar secularism provoked more lively thinking about religion's relevance to youth than occurred earlier in the century, when religious authority was taken for granted. The religious tradition of many schools has kept the moral-character issue alive even after religion itself waned as a distinctive prep school force. In these schools the legacy of religion is an active commitment to keep struggling with the character issue, rather than abandoning it in despair for the safer groves of academic achievement.[11]

Among other methods to build character and community over the years, sports hold an old and cherished place. Sports and religion have close school ties, although the former has been better financed. Through sports, personal salvation is recast as a fulfilled inner life expressed by self-confidence, integrity, courage, or robust good health. Sports also emphasize decent human relations in the context of teamwork rather than brotherhood. The claim is that sports remedy students' personal and social deficiencies. A headmaster once argued that "combative" sports like wrestling were especially suited to the "timid, the exclusive, the reserved." The selfish aloofness of privilege needed a democratic counterweight. "Football is that democratizer." On the gridiron students learned teamwork and fair play.

In prep schools these classic arguments are almost always made without reference to the talents students bring to athletics. The character value of sports is portrayed as inversely related to athletic skill and directly related to personal participation. This does not mean that most prep schools are averse to athletic success; athletic achievement is excellent advertising for most day schools. It does mean that prep school sports give virtually all students, especially average athletes, the chance to play. Spectatorship can be fun and can help build decent community in the sense of school spirit, but watching others play builds not character but the habit of watching.

Prep school students participate much more in sports than privileged public or all public school students. Only 6 percent of prep school seniors in 1990 reported no high school sports at all, compared with 13 percent of privileged public college-bound seniors and 23 percent of all college-bound public seniors. Fifty-four percent of prep seniors participated in at least four school sports, compared with 39 percent of privileged public seniors and 30 percent of all public seniors.[12]

But just as Dean Wilson questioned character-building claims for religion, others have questioned similar claims for sports. No one doubts that sports are enjoyable, but athletic achievement for talented players can cultivate arrogance as well as virtue. Often (as in academics) students with good skills coast rather than try hard to improve. Working together as a team does not necessarily teach players to work together as a community in their school or in later life, when the prizes to be gained for team play are more elusive. Weak athletes play on prep school teams, but sit on the bench when games are on the line. Sports have had far more staying power than religion in modern independent education, but they are no panacea for character education.[13]

Self-Esteem and Caring

Between the 1960s and 1980s, independent-school character concerns were dominated by newer ways to preserve and invigorate the inner self. In 1951, in a harbinger of things to come, Lawrenceville's Heely gave almost equal treatment to the character-building possibilities of psychotherapy and religion. Traditional moral infractions like lying, cheating, and stealing, he claimed, were emotional maladjustments caused by the "tormented world" of depression and war that Americans had endured for two decades. Bad student behavior was not an expression of sin but a psychological "cry for help." Foreseeing a hard and unpredictable future for America, he regarded personal insecurity as inevitable. Punishments were useless, but therapy could answer the cry.

Although Heely was wrong about the postwar years—they were not hard and unpredictable but comfortable and stable compared with the 1930s and 1940s—affluence itself seemed to beget its own torment and insecurity. Growing up privileged meant being bombarded with unprecedented temptations for pleasurable consumption that previous restraints such as religion, sports, adult authority, and tradition no longer kept in check. To many independent educators, the surrender to consumerism produced passive, unproductive, and rootless students. The heightened college admissions competition increased what were soon called problems of "identity" or "self-esteem." When John Esty of Taft School in Connecticut argued in 1965 that the "fragile psyche" of adolescents required schools to "stop worrying about building character" and start worrying about building self-esteem, three thousand extra copies had to be printed to meet the prep school demand.[14]

The mental health movement was kept at arms length by most prep schools until the 1960s. Students who needed help got it through private counseling outside schools. In most cases they still do. Psychological ideas often first penetrated schools through required religion courses striving to be relevant to student needs. Sometimes these courses introduced literature about personal identity, such as *The Catcher in the Rye,* well before English departments. One course still starts with the Bible and ends with the "self-concept" theory of the psychiatrist Harry Stack Sullivan.

When personal problems—sexual freedom, drug abuse, rage at adult authority—began to affect large groups of their students, prep schools began to invest time and money on them. NAIS received favorable publicity in 1966 when its advocacy of sex education won front-page attention in the *New York Times.* NAIS also offered student programs based on "affective education" techniques like sensitivity training and encounter groups. But the most illustrative prep school response to fragile psyches and low self-esteem in the 1960s was developing an American version of Britain's Outward Bound schools.[15]

Outward Bound was created by Kurt Hahn, an eminent German progressive educator who fled Hitler in the 1930s to found Scotland's Gordonstoun School. Outward Bound offered a programmatic approach to self-esteem that neither religion nor sports seemed able to provide. Take soft, unchallenged, identity-confused youth away from their privileged (or even underprivileged) homes for a month. Put them amid the challenge of nature at its most unforgiving—the Rocky Mountains, the Atlantic Ocean, the lakes and forests of the Upper Midwest. Create an intense and dangerous experience in which they are forced under careful supervision to confront formidable physical obstacles. Under these conditions, students accomplished what they never believed possible. Their self-esteem shot up dramatically, as indicated by self-reports and parent satisfaction.

The Outward Bound idea was imported and developed almost entirely by independent-school people, notably Joshua Miner of Andover and Charles Froelicher of Colorado Academy. The first American Outward Bound summer school was built in Colorado by prep school boys in 1961 and publicized mainly at private school meetings. Within a decade more than five thousand teenagers had attended Outward Bound programs, and the ideas behind it affected countless others. Numerous offshoots included Peace Corps training, urban replications, much "experiential education," and the prep school habit of student-faculty retreats to the great outdoors.

This private school sponsorship was no accident. Hahn was an old-fashioned advocate of manly individual character without religious trappings as the end of education, a combination especially appealing to many independent schools in a secular age. He had only modest use for academics, no use for academic meritocracy, accepted to Gordonstoun students with below-average intelligence or emotional problems, and assessed performance on nonacademic dimensions such as public spiritedness, sense of justice, and conscientiousness. This appealed to many prep school teachers committed to character, disaffected with the academic emphasis of the postwar years, and dubious about the overly competitive aspect of team sports.[16]

In theory, Outward Bound was supposed to affect not only the inner life of individuals but also their relations with others. It was a group experience, and its objectives included learning human interdependence and concern for those in danger or need. But in the 1960s and 1970s these more relational dimensions of character were submerged in favor of personal self-esteem. Outward Bound was effusively praised for helping young people get "in touch with themselves." One study concluded that the group coalesced only because it was task-oriented and had to. Individuals rarely got to know one another. The ethic of "service" was defined as rescuing others from immediate danger, not as a caring or compassionate attitude toward them. And since it was devoid of much political content, Outward Bound avoided aspects of character such as citizenship and its demands.[17]

Increasingly, independent schools recognized that this valuable approach to character neglected important social virtues such as compassion, respect, and courtesy. By the 1980s, the ambitious individualism of the "me generation" seemed a greater character problem than the absence of self-esteem. The issue was what students believed important besides themselves. To redress the balance, schools emphasized "caring" individuals and "caring" communities. Students should "respect one another" and "work harder together."

By 1985, for example, 56 percent of independent schools had formal community-service programs, and of these 41 percent required student participation. Since then the percentage of schools requiring some form of service has increased. Community service was a passion for some schools, was accepted by most as a useful educational opportunity, but was not a high priority if it meant a serious redistribution of student time or school resources.

Most schools also offered programs to encourage caring within their own walls. Although virtually no hostility existed among students or student groups in one school, an administrator decried insufficient togetherness and mutual respect. A crucial dimension of personal character and decent community was absent. "We've got to help these kids form a larger picture to make this community here as special as it can be. It can't be just groups getting along. It has to be that the school values each other's contributions, whether that is the quarterback on the football team or the artist in the photography lab."[18]

Valuing differences as a central attribute of decent character and decent community has been further propelled into the forefront because student bodies in independent schools are more diversified in the 1990s than ever before, and because respecting differences is a national virtue among the more privileged. Respecting differences previously ridiculed as inferior or deviant—differences based on race, ethnicity, gender, religion, sexual orientation, family background, or handicaps—became the goal of special assemblies, daylong events, and other programs designed to teach respect.

In one school an entire ninth grade of more than a hundred students spends nearly two weeks camping in the woods before ever attending a class. During the opening week of a middle school, all students and teachers in each grade go off to different outdoor settings to live and work together. Seniors in other schools have dinner together monthly, while other senior classes embark on three- or four-day retreats. Such programs—uncomplicated in conception but nightmarishly hard work to execute—have become staples of modern independent education.

Another technique is to mount consciousness-raising programs on potentially awkward and controversial subjects. Such programs are often presented by outside vendors who specialize in particular topics. One school's annual "Ism Day" addresses sexism, racism, antisemitism, alcoholism, ageism, or homophobia. During one such day Jewish students resisted the outside facilitator because they felt too much attention was given to a problem that did not exist in their institution. Some parents opposed the session on homophobia by the local Gay and Lesbian Alliance because they feared it would celebrate behavior they deplored. The headmaster reassured them that the agenda was understanding, not advocacy, and that the program would go on regardless of their feelings. In the most successful session, a teacher emotionally revealed the dilemmas he faced as the child of an alcoholic, prompting extensive discussion of alcohol abuse by parents and students and the establishment of a student Alateen chapter. Understanding and often celebrating differences is at the heart of this school's notion of decent community.

Still, nothing could be taken for granted. In the early 1990s one school stressed "what they call community and it's all based on ethics and morals. Where you can leave your jacket and school bag out with nothing getting stolen. It's pretty much like the honor system." Although jackets are sometimes stolen, the school is so successful in being a decent community that some students complain it is a "false community." To them its decency is counterproductive. It gives no practical preparation for the cutthroat nastiness of real life outside.

One day the school's drama society performed a play before a captive student-body audience. From the darkened auditorium a few students used rubber bands to shoot a handful of paper clips at the actors. No one was hurt (the clips had been bent to sharpen them), most in the room were not even aware of the incident, and the show went routinely on to its conclusion. In many schools the response to such an incident would have been confined to the few individuals involved: find the culprits and comfort their targets.

But here the upper-school head, supported by many teachers and parents, immediately defined the problem as a crisis of decent community. "As a community we had failed," he concluded, "and so we all had to make amends." He demanded that those responsible come forward according to the school's extensive statement of objectives regarding tolerance and honesty. There was no mystery about who they were, since some had boasted of the act afterwards. He was amazed when no confessions were forthcoming.

The school then took things "to the nth degree." It went out of its way to "call attention to this terrible incident and reinforce that this was a bad thing . . . We won't stand for it." All campus privileges were revoked for the entire student body until the case was solved, including a cherished mid-morning break, and special meetings of advisory groups were held. After two weeks enough evidence was obtained to confront the perpetrators, and the case finally was on its way to being closed. The head was happy he had stuck to his beliefs but shocked by the student attitude of "I didn't do anything wrong unless I'm caught." His whole semester had been "poisoned," even though parents thought that his strong reaction had guaranteed that students would think twice about similar discourtesy for a long time to come.

Some furious students claimed that removing everyone's privileges because of the dumb actions of a few was wholly unfair. But many emphasized the need for community that the incident exposed. "It should be on the honor code. This community as a whole should respect that. That's part of the school." To many in the drama society, the issue was more personal: it was an example of the tendency of some students, often athletes, to "dump on anyone who is different, especially people involved in the arts." Sometimes they were called "art fags," as if the arts were the private preserve of homosexuals.

The fissures exposed by the paper-clip incident are a warning to anyone who believes that maintaining a decent school community is easy. Familiar adolescent tensions flare up like firestorms hard to extinguish. Cruelty and meanness, often grounded in either personal insecurity or just immature thoughtlessness, are not readily eliminated by special assemblies, special days, or dramatic administrative gestures. Dealing with them is a constant struggle.

The school's dogged commitment to pursue and dramatize the incident—to make it a "teaching event"—suggests how seriously it took issues of institutional decency. Decades of self-conscious attention to the importance and difficulty of building character—by religion, sports, therapy, outdoor education, community service, or specialized in-school programs—had revealed no single method or panacea. Above all else, the schools had learned that the surest way to promote individual character and decency was to sustain decent communities. A decent atmosphere did not guarantee decent individual character, but it was a useful first step.

Educational Clarity and Consistency

Before the 1960s most prep schools embraced rather specific conceptions of educational purpose that helped differentiate them not only from suburban public schools but from each other. Church schools (mostly Protestant) were denominational and took religion very seriously. Many prep school students boarded. Most schools were single sex, and most students attended single-sex schools.

Pedagogical and curricular differences added to the variety of school personalities. Legendary headmistresses and headmasters with quirky notions of educational purpose ruled their small fiefdoms. Deerfield Academy's Frank Boyden rode around the Massachusetts countryside in a horse-drawn buggy and fielded enough football teams so that every boy enrolled could play a real schedule against other schools. Putney School's Carmelita Hinton pressed her idiosyncratic version of progressivism, which married coeducation with her distaste of sexuality and rejected urban sophistication for farming, the Vermont outdoors, and folk singing.

Lawrenceville's Allan Heely did not hesitate to lambaste publicly America's "anti-intellectualism" and love affair with "the mediocre, the trivial, and the meretricious in recreation and amusement." Without embarrassment he stood firm for Brahms and against boogie-woogie. Independent schools were one of the few places, a teacher observed in the 1960s, "where the already standardized American child can escape from his standardized culture."[19]

But economic and social forces since the 1960s have reduced this variety. Schools sought to broaden their market appeal at the very time their emerging market wanted less arcane versions of school community. Fewer school heads possessed their predecessors' power, longevity, or certainty about personal visions. Single-sex schools and boarders are now exceptions within independent education instead of defining elements of it. Schools are far more secular even if they maintain some historic affiliation with a church. They have typically become more generic or "standard" independent schools. Decent human relations and an academic work ethic are their most common denominators.[20]

Since prep schools by definition strive to provide academic preparation for high school and college, it is not surprising that educational purpose and academic achievement seem almost synonymous. "Academics runs on autopilot," concluded a middle-school head. He explained that an academic mission is such a "given" in his school in the 1990s that no one talks about it, defines it, defends it, or critiques it. It is simply "part of the place." Most of the school day is "spent doing academics, so that's a value statement right there."

In the seventh grade, for example, students attend five academic classes each day. They are told to expect homework in each subject every school night—a total of about two hours per night. The "jolt" experienced by new students, the head explained, is "not so much that they did two hours of homework Monday night, but that they also had it Tuesday night and then Wednesday night and now it's Thursday and we're going to do it again."

The keys to sustaining this kind of educational community, most teachers agree, are clarity and consistency. In another school a teacher emphasized that "a sense of expectation creates unity within the school. Consistency and follow-up is what helps and inconsistency and absence [of follow-up] is what holds us back from the level of community we can reach." Educational community depends on many little things. "If you don't do what you say then nothing else makes too much difference." Community was like a bed of nails: "If you have enough of those little things all operating on the same level, it is absolutely amazing what they can support. If some are at uneven levels, the pain is just terrible."

For years, this teacher recalled with a sense of shame, young students on their way to lunch passed by a room used as a study hall by older students. The furniture, lighting, and sound were all terrible.

Folding chairs used for an afterschool day-care center were jammed against long tables. The room gave the appearance of a "holding pen." When the young students walked by they sometimes saw, depending on which teacher was in charge of the study hall, older students "strolling on the tables and chatting and throwing tennis balls back and forth." On other days another teacher would tell them they had to do schoolwork and could not read *People* magazine. The absence of consistency sent the young students, in this teacher's judgment, a clear anti-educational message. "When they got into this building, they didn't have to be quiet in the halls. There was nothing important going on." The perception that nothing important is going on can easily defeat the idea of educational community.

Some teachers find a substantive flaw in the notion of hard work and academic achievement as the centerpiece of prep educational purpose. It does not seem especially ambitious educationally, it does not aim to transform or remake students, and it does not suggest unique educational methods. Students or parents rarely speak, without considerable prompting, of academics in terms that suggest passion, immediacy, interests, engagement, or intellectual curiosity. Independent schools present elaborate programs, assemblies, or whole days on issues bearing on decent community—respect for differences, handling developmental crises, and so on. These events are numerous, costly, and well promoted. They are meant to affect behavior, and an air of urgency is never absent from them. It is much less common for prep schools to explore with similar urgency and depth themes drawn from the academic curriculum, such as the problematic futures of genetic engineering, U.S.–Mexican relations, or American drama.

Sometimes teachers complain that students do not convert academic achievement into intellectual interest or passion. One noticed how often graduates come back and say, "I'm having a great time" in college. Hardly ever do they mention anything about what they are learning and what in the college curriculum excites them. Their interests are grades, social life, and careers.

Teachers accept with a certain stoicism that the educational communities they preside over are far more academic than intellectual. Students work, but too often dutifully and bloodlessly. They care much about academic achievement as measured by grades, scores, and college placement. They care much less about intellectual enthusiasm as measured by voluntary interest in what they are studying.

In one school teachers characterize most students as "doers" and "achievers"—they are involved in classes and in every sort of extracurricular activity. But they are not viewed as an "intellectual" group. The head admitted, "You don't really see kids sitting around playing with ideas." He wanted more playing with ideas, learning to make wise judgments, using education to talk and argue about the large issues that affect their lives. But it rarely happened on a broad scale. A few students, one boy reported, have "really cool conversations about ideas or the philosophy behind a historical movement or something." But most others would curiously ask, "Why are you talking about that? We're not in class right now."

Such laments must be seen in context. There is no peer pressure against cool conversations about ideas for those who want to have them. The commitment to doing academics well, if not necessarily loving academics, is consistently valued and enforced across the schools. Students with prior experience in less academic schools even dispute that students are unengaged with their subjects or serious life issues. Everything is relative. "They have more to do with the world," observed a newcomer to prep school students, "and they're more intellectual than asking what mall is the best."

Trying to express what she thought her son's independent school fundamentally stood for, a mother in the early 1990s recalled a moment at the beginning of sixth grade. Her son had never forgotten his teacher's injunction that the classroom had only one general rule: "Be nice and work hard." That summed up, she thought, what the entire school attempted to teach.

"Be nice and work hard" captures well the two notions of decent and educational community most independent schools struggle to sustain. It is a simple and general phrase, but it suggests the accommodations independent schools make to attract a broad range of families while still preserving some serious sense of purposeful community. Safe, civil, and academic purposes appeal to a much more inclusive potential constituency than the specialized purposes these schools typically espoused in the past.

These values suggest a modest paradox. On the one hand, they appear somewhat unambitious to those teachers, parents, and reformers who notice the many advantages of independent schools and the many social problems they do not have to solve. Kindness in schools is not the same thing as good character. Hard academic work is not the same thing as active intellectual engagement. One rarely finds prep school communities characterized by widespread student excitement or passion about issues in the curriculum.

On the other hand, most American schools find decency and an academic work ethic very challenging objectives to realize. They cannot take for granted that the values symbolized by "be nice and work hard" will dominate their institutions. The struggle for them is often an uphill battle. A majority of American high school graduates go on immediately to some kind of postsecondary education, and nearly half the age cohort eventually does. In this situation the broad injunction to work hard at academic learning seems a proper public purpose. It is no less important than the more widely accepted idea that decent human relations are one pillar of a good school community.

So prep schools that actually embody kindness and hard work as central community elements do not usually feel any need to apologize. They have much of what others want. They do not feel unambitious. Many people will pay high tuitions for communities that embody these virtues. The head of an upper school noted in 1992 that "the market is satisfied—the school is full and the parents are happy with what they regard as a desirable commodity. Why change it?"

2

The Family School

Perhaps the most painful American dilemma that private schools help clarify, although certainly not resolve, is the enormous impact that students and their family backgrounds have on schools. The composition of any school's student body is a powerful educational force. It often determines whether or not a school becomes a decent community or an educational one. Students are a major reason some schools are avidly sought out while others are avoided at almost any cost.

The values, motives, dilemmas, and capacities students bring daily to school clearly shape what they learn just as decisively as the learning opportunities schools officially provide. Students also help educate or diminish the education of *other* students, and are probably the most important working condition teachers experience. So it is misleading to see students merely as clients, consumers, or recipients of services provided by others, although in part they are that. They are not merely raw material that "school" attempts to mold. They are not like patients in a waiting room who seek a medical service but go their separate ways unaffected by and oblivious to the other patients' presence. Students are not just members of a school community; they help create it.

American students and their families possess such unusual power in large part because the American educational system actively encourages it. It is part of our national heritage. Compared with many other industrialized nations, most American public schools have little authority to mandate or even strongly encourage student effort and commitment. Relatively little state and no national consensus exists on what the substance of education should be. Our extremely decentralized system, with few high-stakes examinations or other requirements to influence the behavior of individual students and teachers, is exquisitely sensitive to the characteristics of local populations. Whatever the merits of the argument that American parents are not involved enough in school governance, parents and their children already have enormous impact on their school communities. They are intensely involved not by the amount of their power but by the quality of their parenting.

Democratic localism, a value held deeply by most Americans and many of the best contemporary school reformers, has enhanced the power of family (and thus student) characteristics to shape school communities. Even if the well-documented savage financial inequalities that flow from democratic localism are reduced, savage value inequalities will certainly remain. The power of student bodies is an understandable result of the way Americans have chosen to organize schooling.

Some reformers criticize the uniformities that make the organization of American schools seem very much the same. These include forty-three-minute periods, Carnegie units, central office direction, and a few textbooks that are used everywhere. But the on-site impact of different students and different families makes American schools very different from each another despite these uniformities. Within the same framework of the forty-three-minute period, the same Algebra I textbook is experienced differently in various schools depending on student backgrounds.

We ignore and even suppress this awkward reality because it is so hard to address. We resist the full implications of student-body composition because they challenge deeply held egalitarian and professional convictions. It is much more comfortable to imagine students as essentially neutral in the workings of a school. They aren't supposed to affect school, school is supposed to affect them, regardless of their backgrounds. That is the democratic ideal. Shared civic values have always been imagined as a proper result of good education, but shared pro-education values have less often been regarded as a crucial cause of it.

Educators themselves sometimes downplay the educative power both of family background and of individual students on their classmates because it implies that their own professional power is limited. It is hard for any profession to accept the idea that clients have much more power to help or hurt themselves than they are thought to have. Only recently have medical doctors better understood this reality.

Less self-centered reasons also explain why educators downplay the power of students. School-board budget-cutters, as well as enemies of equality of opportunity, have often seized upon this issue to avoid improving programs, facilities, and teaching. If family background and other students are so important, why waste money on good teachers or good facilities? The argument is disingenuous, because the importance of one factor does not negate the importance of others. Even in the hands of education's friends, the idea of students as an educational force can be troublesome to school finance. If the educative power of families is ever seriously recognized and converted into well-funded, profamily social policies, the result might be that money is taken away from school budgets.

In 1966 the sociologist James Coleman demonstrated authoritatively in a monumental research report how much families and students contribute to education, and was roundly denounced by many educators for the policy implications they feared could be drawn from his work. "An important part of a child's school environment," he concluded with admirable clarity, "consists not of the physical facilities of the school, the curriculum, and the teachers, but of his fellow-students. A child's fellow-students provide challenges to achievement and distractions from achievement; they provide the opportunities to learn outside the classroom, through association and casual discussions."

What stood out in the Coleman Report was the statement that "schools bring little influence to bear on a child's achievement that is independent of his background and general social context." This overgeneralization weakened his case among readers who knew from experience that good schools were often influential precisely because they exposed unsophisticated youth to sophisticated new environments. Still, the general policy point held true for most students in most schools. Society had placed too many of its youth-development eggs into the one basket of schools, and needed to address the educational functions of institutions like the family. This remains a hard message for many educators to swallow.[1]

We behave in contradictory ways toward the awkward power of student-body composition. On the one hand, we often maintain what we know is not really true: that innovative, adult-developed programs or adult-organized restructured schools can, almost alone and unaided, transform students regardless of the motivations, values, and capacities they bring to school. We burden schools with a herculean task that wholly underestimates the cultural and contextual aspects of student learning. We exaggerate the power of in-school professional skill while attending insufficiently to nonschool forces that more directly affect whether students will sustain or destroy decent or educational communities.

On the other hand, educators and laypeople are by no means naive about student-body composition. Everyone privately understands how explosive it is. We are always ready, for example, to dismiss the superior results of a school we don't much like by saying that the students and families make the school look good. The superior performance would have occurred anywhere. Just look at who the kids are! And we often explain away poor school performance by reference to dysfunctional families, dangerous neighborhoods, and negative peer groups. Just look at who the kids are! The problem is not that we are wrong about the power of student-body composition; the problem is that the issue is so awkward to discuss that we dodge it by falsely defining "school" without including students.

Actual public school practice, furthermore, takes student-body composition very much into account. This is primarily done by separating and grouping students in various ways while they are in school. When schools initiate grouping, by assigning students to programs, courses, or sections of courses based on assumed ability or past performance, the procedure is often called "tracking." In the 1990s tracking became anathema to many educational liberals, despite the irony that homogeneous grouping originated as a liberal reform to recognize and address individual differences.

But in recent years students have been offered unprecedented public school options to group or track themselves within schools or among schools. These include variations on age-grading such as combined first and second grades; ambition grouping, where demanding courses such as AP are available to those who want them; greater across-the-board curriculum variety and greater student choice (including choices of less demanding subjects); and sub-schools, magnet schools, exam schools, schools of choice, and charter schools. The list goes on even when confined to choices within a school district. Sometimes these options are defended as providing new opportunities and individual attention, and sometimes they are attacked as aiding only informed students and families.

Knowledgeable parents clearly understand the realities of student-body composition and try to make it work constructively for their own children. Although choice possibilities like those just mentioned are familiar to these parents, the most common family-choice strategy is residential relocation. Time and again realtors must answer questions about schools when families with children consider moving to a new town or a new neighborhood. At least within the metropolitan areas where most Americans live, it is probably true that there has never been as much concern among all economic and racial groups about who their children's school-mates will be as there is in the 1990s. When parents move to communities for good schools, they define good schools in part by the friends their children will make and by the associations they hope to avoid.

Realtors often document claims to good schools by quoting student test scores. They never mention teacher scores. Consumer guides to colleges also assert that the quality of students is an excellent indicator of college quality. The guidebooks provide much better information on this issue—student test scores, ratios of applications to admissions to enrollments—than they do on faculty quality, curriculum quality, or facilities. In the 1950s, college guides took seriously how many books a library contained or how many faculty members had doctorates. Technology and the proliferation of doctorates have made these indicators obsolete. They no longer meaningfully discriminate among institutions. Student bodies do. They are what give the "better" colleges their reputations today.

Accepting the view that students help *make* schools and do not just *attend* them places a large and direct burden of responsibility on students and their families for whether a school becomes a decent and educative community. Since their impact is inescapable, students from all backgrounds have as many moral obligations to school as they have needs that school must morally meet. Responsibility for the quality of school community is inherently reciprocal.

This belief is a crucial part of the prep school tradition. Given the way these schools are funded, it could hardly be otherwise. Small numbers of families have been responsible for the establishment, survival, prosperity, or demise of independent schools to a degree that has few parallels in public education. If most revenues come from parents, the parents will be heard.

The idea of the "family school," a prep school phrase from the late nineteenth century that still resonates loudly in today's private school rhetoric, captures two large themes regarding how family and school are ideally expected to relate. The first theme is gathering together like-minded families. Schools have been magnets, attracting and repelling families depending on what sorts of places they are. Like-minded constituents tend to reinforce one another's values and tend to pull the minority of outsiders toward those values. Schools fully committed to becoming decent and educative communities have the best chance of attracting families who value such communities. The presence of those families, in turn, makes the schools more likely to succeed in their aim.

The second theme is the deliberate blurring of sharp, compartmentalized distinctions between family and school. The emphasis instead is on continuity and congruence of institutional purpose. Sometimes it is hard to see exactly where school stops and family begins, because school is like an extended family.

Like-Minded Families

Often the initiative to start an independent school has come directly from a family or a group of families. A group of close-knit Cambridge, Massachusetts, parents, for example, had a problem and a dream in 1915. They worried that their satisfactory public elementary school would be ruined by the construction of a new building, the retirement of a beloved principal, and rapid negative changes in the city's schools and politics, which they attributed to immigration. Many also dreamed of a school with "plenty of fresh air, no matter how cold" as a healthy alternative to overheated regular schools.

Thus the Cooperative Open Air School (later called Shady Hill) began, dominated by Harvard faculty families as parents and part-time teachers, as well as by very cohesive purposes not easily obtainable elsewhere: cold instead of warm air, a self-proclaimed intellectual atmosphere in which learning was done for pleasure and not out of dutiful necessity, and coeducation. Such an unconventional mix of purposes could not be sustained on a daily basis without utterly committed parents. Few principals then and fewer today could have forced them on a captive and diverse audience without revolt.

Many prep schools did not originate with parents. The time between roughly 1880 and the Depression was the great age of educational entrepreneurship, when women and men could become captains of education instead of industry by founding schools and promoting their personal visions to potential customers. Entrepreneurs as different as the upwardly mobile Frank Hackett, the founder of Riverdale Country School, and Endicott Peabody, the superbly connected founder of Groton School, west of Boston, were similar in the effectiveness with which they advertised their respective educational visions. They relied especially on personal friends and friends of friends to find early cohorts of students who often knew one another and were drawn from similar backgrounds. As families sought out schools and schools sought out families, the tradition of close bonds between family and school grew.

This tendency was also apparent in the attempts of floundering existing schools to reinvent themselves. A venerable New York institution, Collegiate School, had been founded in 1638 by the Dutch Reformed Church. Until 1887 Collegiate was an obscure and impecunious free elementary school operating as a charity for poor children. Then, sensing the opportunity that rising New York affluence provided, Collegiate transformed itself by transforming its student body. Within a few years it had fired its entire faculty, moved uptown, added secondary grades with an emphasis on college preparation, employed its first college graduate ever as principal (Williams College, Class of 1870), changed his title to headmaster, eliminated girls (it had been coed), and instituted high tuition fees. As a result, Collegiate became a cohesive and successful school community with a distinct appeal to certain families.[2]

The shared values of these and similar schools sometimes reinforced educational values that lacked widespread support in the larger community. But sometimes the values shared were more social than educational. Especially before World War II, prep schools were often places of arranged acquaintanceship. A desired outcome was lifelong social relations—personal friendships above all else, but business connections and marriages, too. A headmistress complained in 1940 that social pressure forced girls out of local day schools like her own. "Many girls must go to certain big, socially important boarding schools, or else not meet the socially important people and become social successes." Schools were often as well known for the families who used them as for the educational objectives they tried to instill.

Recalling the 1950s, a veteran prep school teacher concluded that the sense of tight community in his school derived from the fact that its members were "very much alike." "They lived in the same few neighborhoods and went to the same summer camps. They belonged to the same group of clubs . . . There was a standard of accepted performance and behavior." Many prep schools were links in a chain of institutions—camps, country and city clubs, colleges, fraternities and societies, summer places, churches—where like-minded affluent groups mingled. This was how schools, churches, jobs, and families created like-minded social communities all over America. In prep schools it was just done on a more expensive and deliberate scale.

Inevitably, the schools were also places of arranged exclusion. They were desirable in part because of those who were not present. In 1908 the head of Horace Mann School in New York was asked by Columbia College authorities why more of the school's graduates did not enroll there. Virgil Prettyman bluntly replied that Columbia didn't attract enough undergraduates of the right sort to interest Horace Mann boys. It contained a "prepondering element of students who have had few social advantages and . . . in consequence, there is little opportunity of making friendships of permanent value among them." It was naive to believe, he continued, that students sought only academic learning from school or college. No less important were "associations and friendships which may be formed within the student body." Columbia had too many newly arrived East European Jews. A Harvard president who grew up in Boston at the turn of the century, James B. Conant, remembered that the prep school dictum of "educating for life" often translated into "It isn't what you learn but the friends you make that matters."

These qualities of the family school—its financial dependence on families, the conjunction of family and school educational purposes, the social connections created or solidified—had the cumulative effect of making most prep schools before the 1960s quite homogeneous in student-body composition. Since then religious, racial, and other kinds of social homogeneity have vastly decreased. But families still understand that some kinds of shared values are an invaluable school resource.[3]

Students as Educators

In 1915 the first book-length consumer guide to American private schools went out of its way to emphasize that the impact of any school depended in no small measure on who attended it. Its author, Porter Sargent, was a former teacher in Cambridge's Browne & Nichols School whose second career, leading European tours for privileged adolescents, was abruptly cut short by World War I. Sargent then decided to write about what he knew most for the market he knew best. His annual "handbooks" became the standard and nearly the only source of information about independent schools for half a century.

The earlier editions were pungent and incisive, loathed or loved by schoolpeople according to individual school write-ups, which often included acerbic comments on the families who started or sustained them. For example, "St. Paul's made a somewhat snobbish appeal to the new economic class that was rapidly acquiring wealth from the development of water power, textile mills, and the exploitation of Irish 'mill workers.'" Sometimes he mentioned whether schools accepted Jews. Nothing like Sargent in his prime exists today.

Sargent stressed that a unique advantage of private schools was "the larger influence that the classmates and school associates exert upon the adolescent and developing personality." He approvingly quoted Emerson: " 'You send your boy to the schoolmaster but 'tis the schoolboys who educate him.' " When parents compared schools their duty was to learn not just of traditions, leadership, and teaching staffs but about "the class of the patronage—that is, the kind of families from which the pupils come and the consequent atmosphere that your children's associates will create."

Sargent's practical advice to parents anticipated what Coleman analyzed with statistical rigor a half century later. Get a critical mass of families with similar purposes, match their children with institutions whose purposes coincide with theirs, and a good school community will probably result if the purposes are worthy ones. A veteran headmaster years later urged schools to continue selecting students from "homes in which old-fashioned concepts such as integrity, duty, manners, and responsibility are still inculcated." After all, reasoned Frank Ashburn of Brooks School in Massachusetts, "there is no student more welcome at a school than one who from infancy has been exposed to high ideals, good books, good talk, and interesting people." An admissions director in 1992 contended that parents wanted most from his school the sense of community that arises from "being with people who have like values."[4]

What changed after World War II was not the idea that student-body composition mattered, but rather the idea of what an ideal student body should be. The postwar American revolution of rising college expectations filled preferred colleges to overflowing and permitted them to become much more choosy or "meritocratic" in admissions. If prep schools wished to retain the reputations associated with getting their graduates admitted to these colleges, they needed students who possessed what the colleges wanted. Increasingly, selective colleges wanted bright students who would work hard once there.

The postwar baby boom providentially created a new market for prep schools when they most needed it. A sizable generation of families with means wanted some advantage in the new and frightening college admissions race and hoped private schools would provide it. Their numbers swelled the applicant pools of many schools. They held out the intriguing possibility that schools' academic achievement could be changed most directly not through curriculum or teaching but through the academic composition of their student bodies.

The increasing tendencies of schools to appoint full-time admissions directors and college counselors, to increase financial aid, and to expand public relations and advertising were thus not mere administrative additions; they were educational additions designed to have educational effects through the students they would attract and place, effects analogous to those of curriculum and teaching. The ability to select students in the first place, as distinct from the capacity to expel a tiny number of misfits later on, was one of the most significant developments in many independent schools after 1945.

By the 1980s a school trustee, speaking in that decade's unapologetic consumerist voice, indicated that parents could "buy a competitive edge for their children and improve the quality of their lives." What independent schools had most to sell was their students. "Children who come from successful families tend to transmit heightened expectations or aspirations to their classmates. This 'borrowed background' may be one of the most significant characteristics of independent schools, and one that parents most keenly seek." Student bodies became a centerpiece of modern prep school marketing strategy.

Schools learned that they needn't apologize for attracting good raw material, as if admitting this would diminish the schools themselves, but should celebrate such students as vital elements in their effectiveness and reputation. Praising their good students was a way of praising themselves. If they did not have reputations as schools where good students were happy and successful, the students would not have enrolled in the first place. One school's college counseling handbook bluntly announces, "We say without a twinge of arrogance that we are a great school—because we know that our greatness comes from our students; it is their praises we sing, not ours." An administrator from another school struggling to achieve that kind of self-assurance could never forget that its SAT scores were a "marketing instrument," for better or for worse.

Marketing tools (if student bodies are strong enough to market) include publicizing college acceptance and attendance lists, SAT means and medians, AP participation rates and scores, National Merit winners, semi-finalists, and commendations. At the end of the twentieth century it almost seems as if the quality of prep schools is determined mainly by how hard it is to get into them and at which colleges their graduates matriculate. When any school or college wants to "prove" its success over time, it usually lists prominent graduates (preferably celebrities) as its bottom-line indicator. This is one area in which public and private institutions behave in exactly the same way.[5]

Thus like-minded families and shared family values have remained crucial, but have become less dominated by social background and more by educational attributes and beliefs. These beliefs are characteristically very general. Few families in the 1990s speak of a particular philosophical commitment, a preferred method of instruction, or the importance of denominational religion. Sharp-edged ideologies like fresh air are rare in today's prep school world. Many parents say that their schools' "common bond" is supportive families whose children will attend college. A typical mother asserted that "kids here are all fairly highly nurtured whatever background they come from, because the parents want them to be in a good school, they want them to be exposed to good teaching, to the environment that's here." What was most attractive about her school was the "lack of diversity of kids coming from backgrounds that have different levels of nurturing." Families value being nice and working hard.

This more generic homogeneity has produced, in the judgment of participants, educational benefits comparable or superior to those of more socially homogeneous student bodies of the past. School atmospheres are relatively decent and civilized because students are that way. "One of the best things here," noted one boy, "is the kids. We don't have any real slimeballs to ruin things. It must be the atmosphere, maybe it is their upbringing, but the kids here are overall respectful." Another explained that the school was "like a family, a community where we have respect for each other. We look out for each other, and there aren't necessarily a lot of rules around us. We kind of go by that code. We are all aware of it."

Another important benefit is that the attitude of working hard and doing well at academics "rubbed off" on them. "A lot of people work so you also want to work. So it's not like you're a dork if you're studying hard, because everyone's doing it. You kind of use your friends to keep motivated." One boy succinctly concluded that "all your peers are motivated the same way you are and most people are like you. Good chemistry."

Teachers agree that both individual family backgrounds and the collective impact of the peer group are important sources of a purposeful school community. "Initially," an English teacher explained, "what brings kids here is that their parents place that strong value on education and on college. But once kids are here, you know what they say? 'What a relief to be in a place where it's cool to do your homework, to not have to deny that you spent the whole evening working on it, where everybody does his or her homework.' " She admitted that students stayed up late to read *Hamlet* partly because they were motivated to gain admission to selective colleges, but she thought their main motivation was the fact that "the other kids in the class are going to do it, and they want to have something intelligent to say."

Peer pressure in such schools can work in unusual ways. When the teacher's junior English class got excited about *The Scarlet Letter*'s point that love and hate were at bottom the same, everyone wanted to talk about love and hate. As two students began to speak, they were confronted by classmates who asked, "Did you read the chapter?" When they admitted that they hadn't, they were told, "Well, don't talk. If you haven't read the chapter, don't talk." A "collective attitude" prevailed in the class. Preparation was a prerequisite for participation.

This was the same school in which seventh-graders had been "jolted" by consistent expectations of two hours of homework per night. The principal did not believe the school simply imposed those expectations; he understood that adults alone had no such exclusive power. "I think the kids want those expectations," he concluded. "They're expecting us to expect these things. The vast majority of the kids anticipate us saying, 'Okay, now you're going to work hard.' " The students permitted the school to operate as it did, but the school's commitment to do so was a magnet to draw willing students in the first place. "The school values academics," the principal said, "and so we attract families who value academics."

School as Extended Family

Schools can create family-like experiences and rituals when children
are not with their actual families. This supportive rather than func-
tionally distinct role of school was especially attractive to many affluent families around 1900. The idea of school as a nurturing and
protective haven—a larger and in some ways more resource-laden
version of what many families imagined themselves to be—proved
appealing when affluence and urban immigration were both growing. Moreover, some families' only earlier experience with schooling
had been with private tutors who came to homes and sometimes
lived there. Sending children to separate day or boarding schools
was an unfamiliar, unsettling experience. More recently, the idea of
school as extended family has drawn new strength because dual-career and single-parent families with means want help in providing
high-quality, safe experiences for their growing children.

School as extended family has generally meant that students,
teachers, and school heads are expected to know one another and
treat one another like children and parents, brothers and sisters.
The extended family school provides personal attention, although
this did not necessarily mean warm attention earlier in the century.
Formal and traditional models of distant caring were often embraced by heads who astutely cultivated surrogate patriarchal or matriarchal roles.

This might entail shaking hands with each student daily or, in
boarding schools, creating sleeping spaces that neither isolated students in wholly private spaces (as if they were unrelated) nor
lumped them together barracks-style (for the same reason). Even
boarding schools that never much emphasized the family school
idea, such as Phillips Exeter Academy in New Hampshire, gradually
moved in that direction. Boarding houses where students lived independently were replaced by school-owned dormitories run by resi-
dent masters.

The family school was often viewed as a small and humane alternative to the "factory school," where hordes of students were allegedly lumped together as anonymous and interchangeable raw
material. Family-like relations were also encouraged by a broad
grade range; K–12, 5–12, and 7–12 models became typical in prep

schools. Even boarding schools often began in seventh grade as late as the 1950s—six years away from home before college. A broad grade range gives students more human continuity and institutional stability. Changes of schools and of established relationships are kept to a minimum. Even the support staff doesn't leave, a mother said admiringly of maintenance workers and bus drivers who knew her children as toddlers and now as high schoolers. The wide age range also makes it more likely that siblings will be together in the same school at the same time.

Although boarding schools represent a literal family substitute—the students live there for months on end—the family school idea was most fully expressed by the "country day school" movement. Country day schools became the most popular version of prep schools in the twentieth century, and respect for the educational impact of families was a crucial part of the country day idea. A student might be the "product" of his school, argued the head of the Country Day School of Boston, "but in disposition, mind, spirit, will, and aptitudes, he is the son of his parents and the influence they provide for him out of school hours." School should not dilute that family influence, but reinforce it.

A feisty, civic-minded, and affluent young Baltimorean, Mrs. Francis K. Carey, invented the country day idea in the mid-1890s. She had concluded that going to school in the middle of the city was neither healthy nor educational (not a new idea among the well-off), and that sending sons away from home to distant New England boarding schools was equally unappealing. She had great sympathy with boarding school ideals as she understood them, but wanted her son to grow up surrounded by the "cultivated influences" of her own home.

Mrs. Carey set out to create a school with all the rural and family-like trappings of boarding schools, but without the beds. She gathered together like-minded mothers (and their husbands) who shared her beliefs and could pay the bills, found a lovely site on the city's outskirts, and hired a young teacher from Phillips Exeter to start in 1897 what became known as Gilman School. Even the original school building looked more like the gracious family home it had recently been than like an institution.

The lure of house-like structures has remained a major theme in prep school architecture over the decades. The fact that families

have always preferred small-scale and well-maintained physical facilities incidentally provided facilities for teachers that, though
rarely lavish, were rarely shabby or neglected. One school still has
bathtubs in small offices that had been bathrooms when the building was a family estate. To many the bathtubs symbolize the family-
like informality of the place. So do the "bookbags all over," the ba-
bies that teachers sometimes bring when sitters fail to show, and the
dogs ("God knows, one time we had a pack leaping on all of us").
School is "just like a normal household—a mess."

Elsewhere, a teacher recalled that while interviewing for jobs in
the early 1990s, she visited a locked urban public school where an
armed guard let her in after she rang the doorbell and passed through
a metal detector. Later that day she walked through the door of a
nearby independent school and was warmly greeted by a maid in a
black uniform with a white apron. Being welcomed to this school
was like being welcomed to an elegant family home. The school later
decided that its welcoming tradition was as dated as it was for most
affluent families. It was dropped, but not without discussion.

Other features of country day schools had more lasting appeal. A
school on the outer edge of a city could be fully rural but still accessible to student commuters. The outdoors was a laboratory to explore nature—good habits of observation, memory, and thoughtfulness were automatically associated with rural but not urban life. The
country also permitted physical activity, especially organized sports,
which were perceived as healthy, manly, and character-building.
The fact that students liked sports and large grassy fields further justified their centrality in institutions needing customer loyalty. Perhaps most important, the country was away from the city, serene
and safe instead of crowded, dirty, dangerous, and worldly. Disen-
chantment with urban environments for youth remains a strong
prep school tradition, and an appealing one for much of affluent
public education as well.

The most important organizational feature of country day schools
was their schedule. Even though students went home at night for
supper and family life, they spent large amounts of time at school.
That was the point. School was intended to fill their weekday hours
when they were not actually at home. A typical program early in the
century was study and recitation periods in the morning, a hot din-

ner in the middle of the day, a two-hour period for sports and activities, followed by a longer study period. The hope (rarely achieved) was for homework to be completed in school by the end of the afternoon so that evenings might be free for wholesome family life.

These advantages so impressed Porter Sargent that he recommended that urban public schools relocate to accomplish the same thing. "Instead of the city high school in crowded and densely populated sections," he asked, "may we not look forward to a time when they will be located on the city's outskirts with ample grounds and playing fields about them, where something of country life may be enjoyed." In achieving a "prolonged school day" filled with varied activities, a school's location made a significant difference. Sargent did not know that one day large cities would indeed be ringed by public country day schools, but that these would be reserved for suburban students and be largely inaccessible to those who lived in the heart of the cities.

Sargent also discerned one of the most troubling aspects of the country day idea. Parents were presumed to be as educationally influential as schools. That was well and good if parental impact was beneficial. But suppose family background instead was "antagonistic or uncultured." Many parents read Sargent or purchased his counseling services precisely because of problem children or problem homes. It seemed obvious to him that even the best day schools could not "in the twelve hundred hours that make the school year neutralize the unfortunate influence the home may exert in the other seven-eighths of the year's hours."

Sargent's straightforward solution to inadequate family background was boarding school. Removing children from the source of the problem seemed commonsensical, especially since his readership could usually pay the bills. In the years before the Great Depression, Sargent and many others expected boarding schools to become the most typical school choice for privileged Americans, just as they were in England. (A 1925 study reported that 70 percent of American coed or boys prep schools maintained boarding departments.) One reason Sargent emphasized students as a potent educative influence on one another was his assumption that many would board. In residential settings peer influences would be even stronger than in day schools.

The issue could become tricky, since Sargent was preaching boarding school for troubled youngsters at the same time he was urging parents to evaluate the "class of the patronage" when they examined prospective schools. A school could not take too many students from antagonistic or uncultured circumstances without risk to its atmosphere. Schools changed when their clients changed. It was just such uncertainties that justified the annually updated school descriptions that Sargent's publishing business provided.

Just as he imagined that city public schools would copy the country day idea, Sargent also foresaw a large public role for boarding schools in the future. After all, the negative impact of family background was most pervasive among the great majority who could never afford boarding school. But the boarding idea had never been tried in the public sector except with special populations such as orphans and delinquents. "Either the private boarding school must be recognized as a public necessity," Sargent insisted, "or the public will have to provide a public boarding high school."

This was among the more radical policy proposals the prep school tradition could make regarding a problem that later grew to proportions Sargent never imagined. Yet Americans have never found publicly funded residential schools to be a solution to any of their major youth problems. The modest exceptions include some schools for Native Americans, a few boarding departments in rural high schools before World War II, some public financing for handicapped and troubled youth needing institutional care, and a few states' support of residential science and math academies for gifted students in the 1980s.

Within the private sector only a few boarding schools were established with distinct missions to help students from troubled or nonexistent families, and fewer still for such students without money. The most important private-sector exception, numerically small but significant for the schools and people involved, was an organized effort to recruit inner-city black students with academic promise to established white boarding schools after 1963. Although this effort was designed more to remove students from troubled neighborhoods than from troubled homes, it seems closer to the spirit of what Sargent had in mind than any other major example from private or public education.

Disinterest in boarding schools should not be surprising. Such a solution would have been expensive to implement and intrusive on parental rights. It would have been a tacit admission that families educate in an advanced society often as powerfully as schools, an admission with enormous potential financial consequences not in the direct self-interest of traditional schooling. Only recently, after all, has the opposite but analogous idea of "home schooling" acquired any respectability as a possible alternative to conventional day school arrangements.

Even among the affluent traditional prep market—the group Sargent expected to propel boarding enrollments upward in the future—the idea of boarding away from home waned in popularity. Elements of the boarding school idea have had important effects on private and public day schools, but most affluent youth have preferred the freedom of living at home. Americans—especially American mothers like Mrs. Carey—have been strongly resistant to giving up their children to institutional care. Sargent's most interesting public policy idea so far has had little impact.[6]

The School Home

More recently the idea of school as extended family has become more insistent and programmatic, expressing the larger role contemporary families wish independent schools to play in their lives. Schools are expected to provide support and protection to children and often to their parents as well, sometimes in ways (such as preschool programs) that might had stunned Mrs. Carey. Few things are more striking about contemporary prep schools than the sheer amount of students' time they deliberately consume. A mother happily exclaimed that one school almost "adopted" her children. "They have another family, an extended family that cares for them. All of our children have grown up here." Parents call another school "their second home."

Mrs. Carey hoped older students would arrive home at the end of the afternoon with homework done, ready for real family life in the evening, but her hope was never realized. A student who switched to an independent school in the 1990s reported that time allocation was one of the biggest changes he experienced. In public school he got home from eighth grade at 2 P.M., and would be alone until his parents returned from work at about 6 P.M. unless he hung out with other kids. "You basically have no structure. You won't sit yourself down and study." Now he got home at 6:30, after required school sports, and felt he had "no choice" after supper but to do homework. The new school had forced him into "time management" by organizing much of his day.

It is typical for secondary prep schools to end at 5:30 or 5:45, after athletics or extracurriculars. Interscholastic sports often start in sixth or seventh grade, so middle-schoolers might not be ready to go home before 5:00 on game days and not much earlier when they have practice. Many high-schoolers report that they never return home before 6:00 or 6:30.

Prep school tenth-graders nationally are significantly less likely than students in the most privileged public schools to go to their own house or somebody else's house when the official school day is over. They are more likely to be engaged in afternoon activities directed by the school. They are also less likely to have afterschool jobs. One mother especially appreciated that her two sons were able to play on the football team, which they would not have been in a larger school because they weren't talented enough. "I can't imagine what I would do with those boys if they didn't have training rules and weren't exhausted at the end of every day."

After supper, homework remains to be done even though many students spend time on it during study halls or open time between activities. Nationally, prep school eighth-graders report doing roughly eleven hours of homework per week, about four hours more than eighth-graders in privileged public schools. By tenth grade the gap between the two groups has shrunk to about two hours, but it is still significant. Corresponding significant differences exist in TV watching, although television is a pervasive influence on most youth. The prep school advantage is not that students rarely watch television—eighth-graders watch about 1.6 hours each school night—but that they watch less than students in other schools. Privileged public school students watch about 2.4 hours each school night, and public students more than three hours. A notable consequence of this schedule is that independent-school students do little outside reading on their own and no more than students in other schools. They read more than others, but it is school-assigned reading.

In light of this large time commitment to school, it is not surprising to hear prep students conclude, "You don't have a school life and then a home life, it's all the same. This is your home and this is your other home." School is where you "almost live." With resignation they say, "No matter how far away from school you get, school's always there." Or, "This is your life. From eight o'clock until six o'clock in most cases. This is where you are. And at home you have three hours [of homework]. So you have an hour to breathe and eat and talk on the phone, and then you start over again." At the end of the day "you don't really just sleep. You just kind of drift back to school again."

Close direction over how young people spend their time is one crucial way schools support and protect. It is a major attraction for parents who are aware that youth are most likely to get into trouble during the afterschool hours before supper. Many secondary schools even intervene in problem weekend parties held in private homes, events in one sense wholly outside their jurisdiction. They write letters home to parents expressing dismay at students' unseemly or dangerous off-premises conduct. Parents rarely criticize this outreach, although students often do. When one inebriated youngster "really clobbered" another at such an affair (both were from the same school), the school didn't feel it could suspend him. But it imposed a one-week "separation," which meant that he missed an important athletic event.

A teacher concluded, "It's almost like we're babysitters . . . The parents are delegating more of the responsibility to us to do a whole range of things with their children." And a headmaster was sure that support and protection would be major growth areas for independent schools in the coming years. "Schools themselves will be more like social institutions, social service providers, a model for extended services."

He knew that was a road down which public schools had steadily traveled for much of the twentieth century, and now it was a road prep school families found attractive as well. Busy with their own lives and jobs, and anxious about being good parents, they were less actively involved with their children "in a time sense." They did not seek remediation—their children were not "at risk" in the usual sense—but simply needed "a school which supports parents raising children." The headmaster recalled that parents once said to prep schools: "You teach European history and calculus and I'll take care of the values, interpersonal relations, weekends. Don't mistake your job for my job." That had changed. School was now a haven in a difficult world. An academic dean worried that market-driven prep schools would be pressed to be "everything to everybody." He lamented that his school always added, never subtracted. "Parents," he complained, wanted schools "where kids can learn about binge drinking, condoms, and everything else."

These parental priorities extend the family-school tradition. Boarding and country day schools have always been much involved in values and personal development, but a growing demand has pushed schools to mount more specific and visible programs. The emphasis now includes the needs of parents as well as students. Mrs. Carey and her allies never imagined prep schools giving families direct help. But by the 1990s one school offered a "Parents as Teachers" program where teachers helped parents with parenting skills, debated extending its preschool program down to age three, and maintained an expensive school bus operation when only a decade before its usefulness had been sharply questioned. "It's a school," said one father proudly, "not only for the children but for the parents as well."

Some parents even use the extended family school to connect with other parents. The school becomes their "neighborhood" community because they don't have a public neighborhood school, a functioning neighborhood, or any other structure that creates community for them. (Nor, of course, do many public school families, especially urban families and particularly when their children become teenagers.) One purpose of evening presentations on topics of parenting or youth problems is for parents to get together. Going to games or school events serves the same purpose. "Not only are you rooting for your kids, but you go to see the other parents because they've become your friends. It is a community thing."[7]

During the twentieth century, the essential elements of the independent family school—like-mindedness and school as extended family—became based more on general educational values than on specific, often social values. This transition reduced highly visible differences among schools and has made them less obviously homogeneous than they were earlier. But the power of student-body composition has never been questioned. The rise of meritocratic values and expensive advertising has caused prep schools to be judged far more on the academic quality of student bodies than ever before. The identification of good schools with smart students is far stronger than any previous identification of school quality with wealth or social prominence. Furthermore, the country seems a more dangerous place, especially for youth, than it used to be. Parents want safe and decent school environments, control over the peer influences that will be exerted on their children, and control over how children spend their time. They are, in part, paying schools for protection.

3

Governing Independent Communities

Whether "restructured" governance can help schools become more decent and effective communities has been a longstanding issue in educational reform. Many contemporary reformers seek virtual autonomy for individual public schools within the systems in which they are located. These bottom-up advocates believe that downward redistribution of educational power is a major source of school improvement. They sometimes disagree about whether school-site management should mean more power for officials such as principals, or more shared power with teachers and perhaps parents. But they do agree that more personnel decisions, curriculum and assessment decisions, and financial decisions should be made at the school site rather than at distant central offices or state education departments.

Other reformers are dubious that more school-site autonomy, however defined, is a good idea. They argue that performance mandates and other incentives from government or nongovernment organizations are necessary to prod schools and students to work harder. They contend that American schools are already among the most decentralized and autonomous in the industrialized world, with unsatisfactory academic results. Still others believe that bottom-up and top-down approaches can be creatively reconciled in one coherent and complementary approach.

The situation of independent schools is especially instructive in this debate. Their legal status as self-governing entities makes them, at least in some respects, rather pure examples of what many reformers advocate. They experience neither excessive external regulation nor the sense of being indistinguishable branches of centralized school chains. Their relative autonomy exemplifies much of what educators call school-based decision-making.

The Costs and Benefits of Jeopardy

The crises and dilemmas invariably brought forth by a commitment to independence can energize and deepen a school's sense of community. This is the constructive paradox of independence in independent schools. The struggle to sustain autonomy is both nerve-wracking and desirable.

On the one hand, almost all prep schools, even the few with large endowments, live in perpetual jeopardy. They are always at risk. Things can go wrong, failure has consequences, and there are no bailouts. Schools face potential ruin if faltering reputations or a flagging economy drain enrollments, if assets are managed ineptly, or if external regulation removes desirable qualities that distinguish them from other institutions.

On the other hand, the pressure to prosper and command public respect energizes their work. Jeopardy is also an asset. Schools must struggle to resist control from outside while demonstrating that freedom from it does not invite irresponsibility or license. Schools must also struggle to improve, stay ahead of the competition, and be accountable to students and their families. Schools not in such jeopardy would benefit from the moral equivalent of it. Independence without some risk—without the task of defending schools persuasively against outside regulation or finding resources to pay the bills—loses much of the community-generating drive that is jeopardy's ultimate gift to school quality.[1]

Regulatory Jeopardy

Independent schools have inevitably compromised some of their own independence. Almost all have missions affected by past history and the expectations of families. They are beholden to clients whose patronage allows them to exist and to benefactors whose munificence permits them to prosper. Further, as elaborated in Chapter 5, they are strongly influenced by an informal national system that helps regulate access to selective higher education. The schools are by no means free to tamper at will with many existing arrangements, ranging from class size to varsity football to AP.

This is why prep schools often look surprisingly alike despite their independence and admitted differences in personality or style. Independence does not guarantee educational differences if external constraints press toward similarities. Some schoolpeople once resisted calling their institutions "independent" rather than "private" because they thought the former term was seriously misleading.

In particular, government regulation has been a direct threat to the autonomy of independent schools. Few have seriously questioned the right of private schools to exist. The 1925 Supreme Court decision in *Pierce v. Society of Sisters* settled that question in the schools' favor. The Court also made clear, however, that states could regulate them on behalf of the public interest. The class-conscious atmosphere of the 1930s made many independent schools fearful that populist revenge against the rich would destroy by taxation those families whose assets had survived the Great Depression. The schools' clientele would simply wither away. Or, alternatively, government would attack prep schools directly by challenging their tax-exempt status or by regulating teacher certification, curriculum content, the length of the school year, or the length of class periods.[2]

The existence of a few corrupt schools increased the fear of state regulation. Many school leaders in the 1930s and 1940s changed their preferred nomenclature from "private" to "independent" to distinguish fiscally and educationally responsible nonpublic schools from fly-by-night or profit-making con games. A Pennsylvania private school, for example, was shut down in 1946 for its failure "to provide instruction savoring of academic content" and the arrest of its headmaster for "an inclusive range of statutory offenses, some involving the students."

To protect themselves against excess regulation, independent schools had to close ranks. They created national, regional, state, and local associations, especially in the 1940s and beyond. By such devices as accreditation procedures, principles of good practice (including financial-management practices), regional and national training workshops, and membership standards (even if minimal ones), membership associations enhanced the reputations of schools and dampened ardor for government intervention. The Pennsylvania scandal, for example, resulted in the formation of a Pennsylvania association to smother political demands for heavy-handed regulation of all private schools in that state. The NCIS, established in 1943, said of Pennsylvania that independent schools must "maintain a clean house or expect that government will undertake to do it for them."[3]

Sometimes associations or individual institutions successfully avoided regulation. NCIS lobbying reversed a discriminatory World War II federal ruling declaring all public high school teachers in certain states exempt from the draft because their work was essential. Private school teachers were not exempt unless 40 percent of a school's full-time faculty taught science or mathematics. And often regulations technically on the books have not been enforced. Informal agreements based on carefully cultivated personal relations between state education officials and private school associations have effectively moderated school-state relations for decades.

Success was not inevitable. Because the New Hampshire Supreme Court ruled that the dormitories of St. Paul's School were not educational premises and therefore not tax exempt, St. Paul's in 1947 was the third largest taxpayer in Concord, New Hampshire (just behind the Boston & Maine Railroad). Several states either require public school certification for private school teachers, or make official accreditation of schools contingent on certification.[4]

In the 1950s the federal government joined the states as an active regulator of private schools. Social Security forced schools to contribute dollars to Washington. Federal price and wage freezes during 1951 and 1971 limited schools' ability to set tuition and salaries. The Internal Revenue Service ruled in the 1970s that racial discrimination in admissions could lead to revocation of tax-exempt status. The Occupational Safety and Health Act (OSHA) required extensive record-keeping on employee injuries and the maintenance of safe working conditions. The Employee Retirement Income Security Act (ERISA) mandated additional paperwork on pension plans.

The 1974 "Buckley Amendment" on student privacy rights helped eliminate feedback to schools on students' college performance.

Other legislation prohibited compulsory retirement until age seventy, revised royalty payments for copyrighted musicals, changed school bus liability, and required schools to remove asbestos at their own expense. A survey of schools in 1976 concluded that "the most-voiced fear of the heads of even the strongest independent schools is the increasing encroachment of federal legislation and jurisprudence."

None of these federal regulations technically affected the educational independence of schools, but they clearly accelerated a pattern in which costly compliance obligations grew faster than academic innovations. At the same time, the rapid expansion of legal rights for students forced schools to spend more time and money developing due process policies and buying insurance. By the end of the 1960s, NAIS warned school administrators that they were no longer "fenced off from legal consequences in their relationships with students and teachers." Allocating time and money to such matters rather than to education was an indirect governmental erosion of independence.[5]

A veteran teacher remembered fondly how profoundly spontaneous innovation had marked his school before the 1970s. But then the fear of litigation crept into the school's life and began to smother risky ideas. Earlier, someone would suggest they try out river trips, but eventually "insurance cooled our ability to have river trips." The Outing Club used to rock-climb but couldn't any more because of insurance. The insurance company even required special permission to ski cross-country instead of downhill.

For years this teacher had taken students on trips to European museums, but had stopped because he hated the new constraints and endless paperwork absolving him and the school of responsibility for virtually anything that might go wrong. When in Spain and Italy, he had always made clear in advance that wine might sometimes be served at supper. "It's cheaper than water in many cases, and there will be no excess." Now wine was taboo; "one glass leads to a drunkard, the old litigious concept." Much that was educational was being lost because the school was afraid of lawsuits over rock-climbing, skiing, and foreign travel. He was sure independent schools had never been less independent.

Financial Jeopardy

The most serious danger independent schools face is not government regulation but financial collapse. The Great Depression of the 1930s suggests how vulnerable nearly all prep schools are to economic disaster. Between the fall of 1931 and the fall of 1932, national prep school enrollments declined 25 percent and school revenues declined 40 percent. Highly regarded, established schools such as the Country Day School of Boston, a pioneer of its type and a leading feeder to Harvard for decades, vanished without a trace. A knowing insider called these years the schools' "hardest and bitterest" hour.[6]

Schools mobilize far more forces to combat this threat than they do for all the threats of regulatory jeopardy combined. There is nothing deader than a dead school. No stones or monuments mark its grave. Yet financial jeopardy is as beneficial as it is fearsome. At a time when much educational reform emphasizes decentralizing resources from central offices to individual schools, it is useful to understand that a major source of community in independent schools is the necessity to generate income in the first place. In 1990 roughly 90 percent of day school income derived from tuition, fees, gifts, and other monies provided by parents, alumni, and friends. Few schools have endowments large enough to make them financially secure.

Raising money to keep a school alive and well probably builds community better than spending money that comes in without effort. This is the rarely discussed flip side of school-site management. If money flows automatically to a school, its allocation can easily become less scrutinized and more politicized. Resources can be taken for granted. Energy shifts to who gets what. It is difficult to imagine any competent school-site management plan that does not contain very clear provisions for financial probity, financial accountability, and some fund-raising.

Prep school families often say that paying at least some tuition motivates them to invest energy and commitment in the school. Further, they know that 100 percent of tuition goes directly to the institution itself, for salaries, plant, scholarships, and other expenditures. Not a dime goes to an unseen downtown. At the same time, teachers and administrators know that income is finite, and so spending must be finite as well.

Confronting financial jeopardy usually helps school community. The careful cultivation of regular annual giving above and beyond tuition among alumni and current or former parents aims to increase both financial stability and community. "Development" or "advancement" offices have sprung up in the past generation to work specifically on these issues. One battle-scarred veteran of telephone soliciting for the annual fund reflected on how hard it was but how educational also. She knew that some parents would avoid her in the supermarket because they knew she would be asking for dollars beyond the tuitions most were paying. But she called them up anyway because many didn't understand what membership in a prep school community entailed. They didn't know that the annual fund was an integral part of the budget, and that supporting it was part of their responsibility. Her calls were "bringing the community together."

Because alumni are crucial to fund-raising, prep schools maintain address lists and directories, plan reunions, and publish alumni bulletins to communicate news from the school and news about each other. A sense of community over time, a great chain linking the generations, is nurtured because graduates are not permitted to disappear. These activities and publications also help schools create and reinforce compelling myths of what is special about them.

The first reaction of one school head to questions about community was to cite the work of the alumni office and the programs it sponsors to keep the school's extended family together. The day before, sixty alumni had attended a lunch at which the speaker was a graduate whose theme was emerging careers in science for women. Current parents speak of community when they become involved in the nearly endless activities to raise money, activities that also bring them together: auctions, phonathons, fairs, selling cookies or wrapping paper, bringing sandwiches to games, preparing school calendars, newsletters, and student directories.[7]

Community and Internal Governance

How authority is distributed among administrators, trustees, parents, and teachers helps determine whether or not a school functions for adults as a quality community with high morale and pride.

If it does not function that way for adults, it is unlikely to be a decent and educational community for students. A publication for private school trustees wisely notes that "people make schools, but a school's procedures sustain its people."[8]

Although authority relations in prep schools have changed in important respects since World War II, key patterns remain largely intact. School principals or heads are unusually powerful figures, though somewhat less omnipotent than they used to be. Trustees are more heavily engaged in school affairs. Parents are surprisingly uninvolved in school governance but are crucial participants in other areas of school life. Teachers continue to have modest input into broad institutional policies but immense educational authority over curriculum and their classrooms. The ideal of school as a special community where everyone is part of a team or partnership has been strengthened. The reality of jeopardy exerts undeniable pressure on all adults to work together.

The School Head

The most important governance tradition within independent education is the powerful school head. The very identity of many prep schools until the 1960s was virtually indistinguishable from the persona of one or more heads of long tenure. He or she was the eccentric legend, the magnanimous despot, the educational visionary, the matriarchal or patriarchal head of the family.

When in 1925 a mother asked Miss Mira Hall of Miss Hall's School what she could do to be of help during the years her daughter would be in attendance, Miss Hall shot back, "Nothing." "If you wish me to put my mark on her," she sternly continued, "you will leave her in my hands." Veteran teachers tell stories about the authoritarianism of many a legendary headmaster: "He even went so far as to ask why your mailbox was empty, because if you didn't have anything in your mailbox, you must not be getting professional mailings." A veteran head believed that no independent school had ever grown to real eminence without the presence of one powerful and thoughtful head for a considerable period of time.

The traditional authority of school heads comes in part from the fact that many founded their schools and some owned them. In the 1920s the leading private school journal ran a regular column entitled "Is

Your School for Sale?" A representative advertisement stated, "A head-master with experience in one of the country's best-known schools wants to invest from $50,000 to $100,000 in a high class school for boys. He would buy a part interest and later take over the school."

Eventually it became clear that privately owned, for-profit (at least theoretically) schools were a dying breed. Even before Depression-era anxiety made many private school leaders scurry for the democratic cover of the "independent" label, practical financial realities pushed virtually all of them toward not-for-profit corporations governed by boards of trustees. Elderly founding heads or sometimes their descendants wanted to gain income for retirement, guarantee a school's continuation after they were gone, or create financial incentives for alumni to give money through charitable deductions available only to nonprofit institutions.

In the 1920s alone, well-known schools such as Hill, Browne & Nichols, Spence, Fessenden, Choate, Dwight, and Riverdale all abandoned private ownership. Schools such as Putney, which delayed the changeover, were placed at an enormous financial disadvantage. Hardly anyone made substantial gifts to institutions run by an individual or a family, regardless of the school's quality, integrity, or need. By World War II the standard governance structure was an incorporated nonprofit board of trustees whose broad functions were to appoint a head, make general policy, and raise money.

But the tradition of the strong head remained. Most trustees were businessmen. Familiar with corporate models of governance as well as governance models of private higher education, they were comfortable with hiring strong chief executive officers and giving them substantial power to run the show. Heads typically hired and fired faculty, admitted students and threw them out, and distributed available financial assistance. They often told students where to go to college and advised colleges on whom to admit.

A senior teacher recalled that in the 1950s the trustees met only once a year. There was always a reception for them. "We'd all troop in and have a little glass of sherry and then the headmaster and trustees would all have dinner. The chairman would get up and say, 'Would you like to make a report on the school?' The headmaster would get up and say in 15 minutes that everything is fine. They would say 'wonderful,' toast the headmaster, and that was it."[9]

Important aspects of the strong-head tradition remain intact and affect what kind of communities schools are. Many faculty and students credit headmistresses or headmasters with embodying community and "rallying" school members toward it. "The tone has to be set from the top," argued a typical teacher who credited the head with making his school more civil and relaxed because he modeled those qualities constantly. He greeted everyone by name each day, so there was no excuse for teachers or students not to treat others the same way.

Another teacher was certain that his school's sense of decent community came from the top because the head really believed the school was a community and was not bashful about making his feelings known. "He cares and he cares about everybody, and therefore we should all care about other people as well." The head insisted, for example, that all members of the community including the maintenance staff eat lunch together at the same time and place. It wasn't easy for everyone to care about everyone else, and no one claimed complete success, but at least the mandate to try was never absent from anyone's consciousness.

Further, although heads possess considerably less raw power than many had before the 1960s, they generally retain substantial power in areas that closely affect school as a community. Opinion surveys of independent and public school principals indicate that the former have considerably more authority over hiring, curriculum policy, and disciplinary policy. Prep school trustees, moreover, have far less influence over any of these three crucial policy domains than do public school committees or boards of education.

Many heads say their most important job is hiring faculty. Wise personnel selection is almost always regarded as the primary means to build an adult team committed to a community's values. "The faculty we have is more important than courses, requirements, or anything else." No teacher is ever assigned to an independent school, and certification usually does not constrain the search process. Almost all public school teachers are certified, but only about 45 percent of secondary and 67 percent of elementary prep school teachers are certified in their primary fields.

The actual process of finding candidates is frequently more chaotic than schools would like to admit. They are probably saved from disaster by the fact that there are not many independent-school teachers nationwide—fewer, for example, than New York City public school teachers. The task for most schools is filling a small number of vacancies annually. Despite this seemingly easy task—or perhaps because hiring is regarded as more complex than merely finding individuals with acceptable paper credentials—a much higher number of prep school heads (38 percent) report difficulty in finding sufficiently competent teachers in some fields than do principals in wealthy suburban public schools (18 percent).

A senior headmaster argues that the most important lesson of independent schools for public school governance is that all principals should be able to appoint their own faculties. It is certainly a time-consuming job. Teacher-placement agencies have long played a far greater role in independent-school hiring than in public education. Sometimes advertising is also used. Often candidates are sought and interviewed at national and regional independent-school conferences and job fairs. Many school heads attend such conferences primarily to search for potential staff. Most heads have their own personal networks and swap needs and résumés with colleagues. They do extra investigative work such as calling up individuals not listed as references. The heads use the placement offices of selective liberal arts colleges to find rookies, since graduates of these colleges often match what the schools themselves are attempting to produce in their own students.[10]

That prep school trustees expect school heads to be powerful and visible leaders is perhaps best illustrated by their policy of compensating heads extremely well. It is no secret that the salaries of prep school teachers have lagged behind those of urban and suburban public school teachers. For example, the national average cash salary for public school teachers in 1989–90 was $31,300, whereas the median cash salary for prep school teachers was $25,825. It is less well known that the reverse pattern is true for independent-school heads. Their compensation on average is not only higher than the highest paid public high school principals; it is also higher than that of public school superintendents.

Consider that the median salary for all independent-school heads in 1989–90 was $65,000. More than 46 percent of these heads were additionally given full housing by the schools, and 12 percent more received partial housing benefits. The median size of their schools was 320 students. Yet the mean salary for all public school superintendents in America that year was only $63,329, and few superintendents receive housing benefits. The mean salary of the highest-paid group of public high school principals was $56,934. Since virtually none of these principals receives housing benefits, the independent-head salary advantage is large.[11]

School head is a top job in an important sense besides compensation. Public school principalships and even superintendencies are often way stations to higher-status and higher-salary jobs above them. A principal can aspire to be a superintendent, a superintendent to be a state or federal official or a professor of education. In almost every school district except for small towns, there is a "central office" of varying size. Because of salaries, prestige, amenities, and perhaps the absence of children, ambitious adults are pulled away from schools toward the central administration. That is the way public school occupational mobility works; jobs in schools close to the educational process and children are not the top jobs in public education.

But jobs close to children are the top jobs in independent education, because there is no central office. There is no way to escape schools. When heads leave a school, they typically become head of another school, leave education, or retire to the woods or to consulting. Independent schools have the advantage of being able to retain their leadership corps in work close to teachers and students, instead of losing them to more remunerative but distant posts. Many heads and others playing administrative roles continue to teach. For the top leaders in independent education, the career action is not away from schools but within them. In these circumstances it should not be surprising that the selection of school heads is the single most important task for trustees.

At the same time, the days of despotic but benevolent heads are largely over. Since the 1960s considerable power has been dispersed upward from heads to boards of trustees and downward to middle-management administrators and faculty. Significantly, this process has not emasculated heads' authority. The diffusion of power in fact strengthened their position as leadership became regarded as a partnership between heads and other key adults. The process within prep schools has not been a zero-sum game, where gains by some mean losses by others. More people perceive themselves as "stakeholders," encouraging a broader loyalty to the school as a community. This benefits everyone, especially heads.

Trustees

A veteran teacher explained that more assertive trustee involvement in school decision-making (including a greater willingness to terminate heads) was inevitable given the increased role trustees assumed in fund-raising after World War II. "If you are going to tell the trustees, 'we want you to go out and raise money,' that means you are making them players. Players want to play." Trustees also had to confront, especially in the 1960s, a remarkable number of unprecedented policy questions simultaneously. Should schools expand in the wake of baby-boom applications? Should they contract in the wake of later enrollment declines? How should they handle new issues such as coeducation, racial integration, faculty unrest, and student rebellion?

If players wanted to play, they had to learn the rules. They had to learn how to function as good trustees and how trusteeship itself is the discharge of a solemn community obligation. Players needed to be taught. What is instructive in retrospect is that some trustees and heads saw the need to educate a new generation of trustees in ways that would support and not divide school community. They understood, as all schools must, that educating governing boards about their responsibilities is crucial.

In one sense the education of trustees might seem unnecessary. Prep trustees are almost always chosen by other trustees, not elected by a general public that might or might not care about schools. They are not outsiders. Even if a school's community of parents, alumni, or both technically elect some or all of the board, the elections usually ratify recommendations of nominating committees. Contested elections are infrequent. Service on prep school boards is not a springboard to further political office or an opportunity for financial gain. If a launching pad, it helps gain access only to other charitable boards. The incentive to be a trustee is mainly a strong feeling about a school. Nearly two-thirds of NAIS board chairs are parents of children who have attended the school.

So why worry about educating highly educated trustees who are already interested in the schools? In fact the effort was most astute. As trustee selection became increasingly determined by the ability to give money or by deference to new blood and diversity, it became clear that many "first-generation" trustees were ignorant of their role. They did not know the duties of nonprofit trusteeship. Some were not above bringing personal, narrow, and idiosyncratic issues to the trustee table. This is why initial selection and education afterwards became the most important mechanisms for trustees to help build positive school community.

The NAIS *Trustee Handbook* went through six quite different editions in the quarter century between 1964 and 1989. They chronicle the growing effort to instruct trustees about authority and community. When it first appeared in 1964, the *Handbook* assumed that trustees knew what their job was and how to do it, that their involvement with educational affairs would be relatively modest, and that actual or potential disputes would be settled informally. When conflict arose there would be "frank discussion, not in full board meeting [but] in a smaller group on a man-to-man basis." Troubles would be "amicably adjusted by men of good will."

By the third edition, which appeared a decade later at the height of the 1960s' questioning of authority, all such language was dropped. In place of private and informal talk, the *Handbook* advocated explicit and elaborate public communication about "roles, functions, and responsibilities." Like a train gathering speed, subsequent editions emphasized more forcefully that the way to avoid conflict and retain community was by the specification of nearly everything. The key to administrative tranquility and a broad sense of trust was to make sure that everything was written down, prepared for, communicated. The head of Lawrenceville proclaimed that "established procedure saves us from friends and foes alike—as well as from ourselves."

All this affected how trustees governed schools and how they governed themselves. For example, the number of heads with written contracts detailing matters such as terms of appointment and spouse responsibilities grew from about 19 percent in 1974 to 75 percent fifteen years later. Heads' job descriptions also became more explicit, and annual written procedures to set and review goals for the year were developed.

The biggest new responsibility for trustees was learning to manage themselves. Some of the instructions they received perhaps inadvertently revealed their less-experienced backgrounds. "Meetings should begin on time," they were earnestly counseled, and "must be discreet, for board meetings are absolutely confidential." Trustees became more explicit about their job descriptions, how to evaluate their collective performance, which training programs could improve their effectiveness, and how written "strategic plans" could guide the future of their institutions. Annual written goals with end-of-year evaluations of themselves grew, and the idea of board retreats or workshops became common.

Information about schools' futures was gradually moved from a traditional private domain to a more public and accessible arena. Long-range strategic plans being developed by trustees and heads were likely to be shared with faculty and affected by faculty input. It became routine for teachers to be included in planning processes. This dispersed a sense of broad "ownership" over where a school was going without dispersing much actual decision-making authority.

Finally, trustee identification and selection became much less casual. Selecting good trustees became as important as selecting good heads and teachers. In many schools the committee to find, orient, and evaluate trustees is the most important of all board committees. In all these ways schools deliberately attempt to increase the integrity and competence of their governing bodies.[12]

Parents

Prep schools urge parents to be involved in almost all aspects of school life except serious decision-making. Schools usually agree that the governance role of parents should be confined to their representation on boards of trustees. The kind of parent involvement routine in some public school districts and sought by others pressing for more school-based decision-making—representation on hiring committees, curriculum committees, and committees with power to spend money—is discouraged. Compared with public school enthusiasm for parent participation in school-site management, prep schools leave parents out in the cold.

Instead of partners in governance, the schools encourage parents to be partners in education. This means supporting the school's goals at home, participating in school events, especially those involving one's own children, and working for the school in voluntary capacities to raise money and deepen the ties that make institutions family schools. One school pushed these notions of involvement to the point of inviting parents to spend three full days a year in the school "shadowing" their children through their regular day. Encouraged to participate in all activities, many parents did so, most staggered out exhausted, and one was injured playing soccer in gym class. No one doubted they had been involved.

A generation earlier most parents accepted this ancillary role without much question. Ben Evans, a veteran teacher of nearly four decades, recalled a story that illustrates the point. In the 1950s, after he had been teaching for only three weeks, the headmaster walked into his classroom and politely asked for a few moments alone. "Ben," the head said as they strolled toward his office. "Mr. Charlie Wonder of the Wonder Bread Company is on the phone and he is concerned that the homework assignments you are giving his son are too hard. Do you think they are too hard?" Evans fidgeted a bit and replied, "If you think they are too hard, I'll make an adjustment." "No, you are misunderstanding me," said the headmaster. "Do *you* think they are too hard?" Evans steeled himself and confessed, "No sir, I don't think they are too hard."

By that time they had reached the headmaster's desk. He picked up the phone and said, "Charlie, Mr. Evans is right here and he assures me that Jeff's homework assignments are not too hard. As far as I am concerned, that settles the matter. Thank you for calling and give my best to your wife." Thirty-five years later Evans recalled the incident as if it had just happened. "One of the most powerful men in the area! Talk about standing behind your teachers! It has changed."

By the 1970s schools had become concerned that informal parental intrusiveness outside the board structure was increasing and posed a threat to teachers' authority. Some parents became or were perceived to have become pushy "killer bees." In the 1990s an administrator admitted to an "institutional paranoia about parents. There is a fear that they will dictate to us." Many teachers and administrators somewhat defensively attribute more aggressive parents to a consumer mentality where private education is regarded as a "purchase rather than as an investment or a gift."

Others complain that savvy parents have learned in public schools how to push and push hard, and those behaviors simply spill over when they enroll children in prep schools. Whatever the causes, virtually everyone believes that parents' attitudes about their authority have changed. Teachers speak of "ballistic parents" who want a conference when a daughter's quiz average slips from 100 to 99. When a boy did no science homework his parents asked the teacher what she was going to do about it. When a child got a C+ on a test, her parents wondered why the teacher did not immediately send a note home. "They want me to watch every blink in her eye." A student committed the terrible blunder of telling her mother that she had no math homework one night. "I'm paying $8,500 for you to go to school and get an education," the mother bellowed. "Why aren't they giving homework?" Then she called the headmaster to complain.

Thus changes in trustee and head relations that reinforced loyalty to school community were sometimes accompanied by contrary changes outside official channels. School could be less a community than a set of provider-consumer transactions. In the early 1990s this was not a pronounced threat to community, but it caused schools to think harder about what precisely they were accountable to parents for, and about how they could keep parents manageable when a rise in tuition was inevitably accompanied by a rise in expectations.[13]

Teachers

One of the longstanding puzzles in private schools has been the relative absence of rebellion or low morale among teachers despite the very sizable salary gap between themselves and public school teachers. The financial disparity between teachers and their heads is also far larger in prep schools than in public schools. Independent-school teachers are well aware of their situation, citing low salaries as the worst part of their job.

The gap is not diminished by additional family income provided by a working spouse or some other source. When total family income is considered, the prep-public gap actually widens. In 1988, roughly 58 percent of prep school teachers' family incomes were below $40,000, compared with 26 percent of teachers in wealthy suburban public schools and 43 percent of teachers in all public schools. At the other end of the family-income distribution, about 7 percent of independent-school teachers' families received more than $75,000, compared with 17 percent of those who taught in wealthy suburban public schools and 8 percent of all public teachers.

Some evidence also suggests that more independent-school teachers than public school teachers believe that teaching itself lacks prestige as a career. Aggressive and educated parents may know more about their fields than teachers and let them know it. Over-privileged and unmannerly students may subtly or not so subtly indicate their economic superiority. An additional problem may be that different teacher populations perceive "prestige" differently. Independent-school teachers who attended prep schools or selective colleges have grown up around peers bound for the most prestigious careers in society. It may be harder to make a commitment to schoolteaching when one's acquaintances routinely become doctors, lawyers, or business executives. It may be easier to view teaching as dignified, important work if one is a first-generation college graduate.[14]

Despite all this, surveys reveal that prep school teachers have higher morale than public school teachers. "God, they pay me to do this! I mean I love it here." They would make the same vocational choice over again in greater numbers and reject collective bargaining as a relevant strategy for improving work conditions. Although they teach far fewer students than instructors in almost any other school type, prep teachers work as many or more hours and complain about being tired out instead of burned out.

What nonmonetary compensation exists? The crucial role of student-body composition—having hard-working and reasonably well behaved students—was examined earlier. The important role of student load—how many students teachers are responsible for—is discussed in Chapter 9. Two other factors directly connect teachers' job satisfaction with professional autonomy: they have much control over their classroom life, and less but still relatively strong involvement in schoolwide policymaking. All these factors bring a sense of unusual dignity to independent-school teaching. They make it almost part of the same profession as college teaching.[15]

Independent-school teachers are unusually autonomous inside their classrooms. Teachers choose particular prep schools to work in for the same reasons families choose them—to achieve a good fit between the person and the environment. They feel freer to begin with because they have deliberately chosen where to work. Further, surveys of teachers indicate enormous differences between independent and public schools (whether wealthy suburban or public in general) in teacher control over choosing texts, content, teaching methods, and disciplinary styles, as well as in access to needed materials. For example, 58 percent of prep school teachers indicate "complete control" over text and materials selection compared with 24 percent of teachers in wealthy suburban public schools.

This autonomy is reinforced by the ordinary facts of prep school life. Students buy their books and own them, so it is easier for teachers to choose new, varied, and appropriate materials whenever they wish. Students are encouraged to take notes in their books just like college students. The area in which prep school teachers report less classroom discretion than their public colleagues is determining how much homework to assign. This is much less a decision for individual teachers, much more a matter of school policy.

A typical prep school teacher praised the "tremendous amount of latitude here . . . I've never had to turn in a lesson plan in my life . . . I'd feel tremendously hemmed in if someone was trying to say, 'What did you get accomplished this week?' or 'Did they meet the standards?'" Another teacher proudly announced, "I do whatever I want." His school was "teacher-centered. If you are good, you do what you want. Freedom without having to publish." The latter comment is interesting both for its qualifier ("if you are good") and for its association of schoolteaching with a larger teaching profession that includes college instructors.

In one school several teachers felt free enough to use an empty room near their classrooms as a tiny childcare center for their own toddlers. They simply hired a baby sitter while they worked a few feet away, and the school was happy to provide space. They were amazed when the state took a dim view of the enterprise. It violated numerous laws regarding day-care facilities and personnel. The head was amazed too—he gave the teachers 100 percent support until the authorities threatened to imprison him for five years and / or fine him $400,000. Then his enthusiasm waned. Teacher autonomy had some limits.

Indeed, the most important issue of teacher autonomy within independent education is probably whether there is too much of it. Prep school teachers speak often of colleagueship as a basis of community, and this usually means personal friendships, respect, and helping one another out. But good colleagueship and professional cooperation are not identical. Prep schools teachers report more of the first than wealthy public schools, but slightly less of the second. They know one another better outside their classrooms than within them.

Most American teachers have considerable in-class autonomy unless they are teaching a course with some external assessment such as AP examinations. But independent-school teachers appear to have more autonomy than anyone else. Most wish to "run their own business" within the classroom. This autonomy, paradoxically, can be a powerful source of community when the ideal vision of school community is the liberal arts college. There faculty are committed to "academic freedom" and unencumbered pursuit of the life of the mind. In this sense a good school community includes freedom not to cooperate or collaborate with one another.

This attitude helps explain why teachers in schools with apparently coherent academic missions sometimes speak as if their institutions are rife with dissent about basic goals. Teachers can be at odds with one another because the basic mission they share is one that encourages intellectual debate. Battles over issues such as the number of years of required science indicate the absence not of a shared academic mission but rather of a consensus on specific academic procedures. Teachers revel in such disputes, as do college faculty. They are an important dimension of community.

But extensive classroom autonomy correctly troubles schoolpeople who believe that some limits on independence are educationally desirable, financially necessary, and a better expression of purposeful community. A perceptive administrator, for example, notes that the very autonomy that gives teachers a sense of academic community can undermine community as defined by consistent procedures and expectations. "Kids," she observed about grading, "will tolerate anything as long as it is even. The worst system in the world is okay as long as it is fair and consistent to everybody."

What kids would not tolerate was one teacher's responding to a class cut by saying, "Don't do that again," while another responded to the same act by assigning eight hours of community service. The administrator was certain that in the future her school would support more aggressively a version of community that valued consistency as much as autonomy. It would be part of accountability to families paying more than $10,000 a year. The issue would be tough and she had little relish for its emergence. Many teachers would feel a serious loss if their autonomy was eroded, but she believed that prep schools that put their obligations to students first would eventually move somewhat in that direction.[16]

Teachers' authority also supports school community through their involvement in schoolwide decision-making outside the classroom. Surveys suggest that in virtually any decision about schoolwide educational policy—general participation in decision-making, discipline policy, in-service content, curriculum policy, ability-grouping policy—prep school teachers feel substantially more involved than teachers from any kind of public school. For example, the fraction of prep school teachers who believe they are involved in curriculum policy "a great deal" was 39 percent compared with 15 percent for teachers in wealthy suburban public schools. Prep school heads report that their teachers are much more involved in the process of appointing new teachers than public school principals report for their faculties.

Faculty involvement in independent-school governance grew substantially in the late 1960s. If the 1964 edition of the NAIS *Trustee Handbook* barely mentioned faculty at all, the 1970 edition argued that "the modern board of trustees needs the benefit of faculty opinion in many of its decisions." Four years later about 25 percent of boards had voting or nonvoting faculty representation. By 1990, teachers participated as full voting trustees in about 15 percent of prep schools, were regular observers of board meetings in 38 percent, and were regular members of certain board committees in two-thirds.

As a result, the tendency of many boards to replace informal decision-making with specific public procedures came to apply not only to relations among board members and between board members and heads, but to relations of boards and heads with faculties. An example from the 1970s is the "rapid, almost precipitous, movement from highly unstructured, traditional salary systems toward more highly structured, explicit salary systems that rely on one or more scales." The new emphasis on scales and deemphasis on performance or merit pay reflects faculty preferences as expressed through new faculty compensation committees. By 1990, 48 percent of prep schools used explicit salary scales.

Although the growth of specialized administrative roles in academic affairs (such as directors of studies, academic deans, and deans of faculty) struck some teachers as just more layers of bureaucracy between themselves and the school head, these roles give many teachers access to administrative power. Most people who hold such jobs continue to teach. They blur the boundaries between teachers and administrators, just as the power of faculties to make important curriculum and other decisions obscures where board authority ends and faculty authority begins. "Everyone has a stake in the place," an administrator explained, "so if you make a change, you sit down with a committee that has board members on it, parents, administrators, faculty and maybe even students."[17]

In very few independent schools does actual governing authority reside in the faculty to the extent that it does in most institutions of higher learning. Few prep schools are "faculty run." Most college presidents and public school principals would envy the power of prep school heads. But there is still extensive teacher involvement and participation, and the reasons are not hard to find. In the 1970s prep schools feared unionization as much as they feared financial instability and student unrest. Heads understood the advantage of a governance model that emulated that of liberal arts colleges. It treats teachers with respect. They also felt comfortable delegating some authority to teachers they had often hired personally, and who rarely had official tenure.

Perhaps more important, prep school heads need satisfied teachers. Heads lack tenure, and they know that the reputation of their school and hence their own job security depend in large part on the faculty. A school's reputation for having good teachers is among its most marketable features. Supporting the faculty in every possible way—through expressions of personal appreciation, gentle evaluations, involvement in school decisions, providing attractive facilities, professional development, progress on the compensation problem—is always near the top of most heads' priorities. In a society that generally does not regard teaching as attractive or honored work, prep schools try to remind their teachers—and their parent market—how important teachers are and how good they are. Involving teachers in decision-making is one of many ways to do this.

This is one reason prep schools often create named "chairs" the way colleges do, even if the chair carries little extra compensation. And it is one reason teachers have been included in the modern prep school emphasis on governance as a "partnership of mutual endeavor and trust" along with heads and boards in explicit challenge to "the traditional concept of hierarchical management." A partnership suggests respect and recognition. It strengthens a sense of community among all adults in a school, even when it is well understood that teachers are not equal partners in institutional governance. Much decision-making power resides with the head and the board, but teachers are more than equal partners in matters of curriculum and instruction. The impact of being respected should never be underestimated as a source of proof for teachers that their work has genuine dignity.[18]

In curious ways the traditions of school-based governance in independent schools seem often at variance with what is usually proposed as good practice in public schools experimenting with bottom-up approaches. Strong leadership from school heads or principals is crucial, for example, even extending into areas such as faculty appointments, where public school principals have been relatively impotent. Yet strengthening the principalship has rarely been a priority for advocates of school-based management.

The selection and education of the governing mechanism itself are equally crucial. Ignorant, single-issue, self-promoting individuals can ruin any governing body, whether it is located at the school site or at the district level, and whether it is public or private. The process of selection must generate individuals with integrity and dedication to shared educational purposes of some sort. The necessity to educate board or council members in the technical and ethical duties of stewardship cannot be overestimated.

Parents or guardians should understand that their first duty is parenting rather than power, and that involvement takes many forms besides governance. The idea of partnership clearly includes parents and the notion of the family school, but partners can work together in many ways. Teachers need more educational autonomy to work together, and perhaps somewhat less autonomy to do their own thing. Above all they must be assured that their work is regarded as important and dignified. Unless this occurs, the quality of those attracted to teaching will not motivate governing bodies or the educated public to press for greater teacher involvement in decision-making.

These prep school governance characteristics may exist because preconditions for purposeful community are already present. Greater shared objectives mobilize greater mutual trust. Institutional prosperity requires adult interdependence and cooperation. Without a distant central office, institutional loyalty is often easier to sustain and resource allocation easier to comprehend. There can be dispersion of authority among many players without compromising fairly strong leadership. Without centripetal forces pushing all the adult players together—financial jeopardy, accountability to clients, accountability to society to fend off regulation, and some shared idea of specialness—there is no assurance that decentralized governance produces any more purposeful community than rule from afar.

4

Diversity and Community

Until the 1930s, prep schools assumed that homogeneous communities were major assets. Public school problems, an independent-school leader explained, often arose because the "necessary presence of heterogenous groups interferes with the carrying out of a common academic purpose." But the Great Depression raised painful political, moral, and educational questions about homogeneity. Alongside celebrations of the family-school idea came several important critiques of it. By 1947 the rector of St. Paul's School longed for the day when his school might appear in the newspapers "without that abominable adjective 'exclusive' prefixed to it." It was as if schools such as his were regarded as a "curious survival from an aristocratic day, a kind of private preserve of the sons of the rich, bound gradually to disappear along with the rich."[1]

In those days independent schools were indeed exclusive by any sensible definition. But exclusivity was then and is now very different from elitism. Some schools embraced an unapologetic cultural elitism grounded in high standards and a decidedly negative evaluation of American popular culture. Andover's head in the 1930s and 1940s, for example, recalled that many parents expected schools like his to transport their children "out of the provincial and contaminating atmosphere" of their "sordid" communities into "something more gracious and stimulating." Independent schools offered protection "from the menace of the mediocre and the domination of the average." Claude Fuess's refreshing if perhaps shocking candor still contains truth about some parental motives, the cultural environments of some prep schools, and the educational priorities of most Americans.

But few prep school critics (and too few prep school families) cared much about grace or intellectual stimulation. Prep teachers or curricula were rarely condemned as snobbish or un-American—they were not controversial. Elitism defined as the pursuit of excellence and the rejection of mediocrity touched only a few raw nerves, especially before the 1970s. In contrast, the problem of exclusivity was not discriminating taste but discrimination against people. When critics called prep schools exclusive or snobbish, they were virtually always referring to their student bodies.

Alongside a cultural elitism irrelevant and uninteresting to most Americans lurked a social exclusivity very easy to dislike. Prep schools opened their doors to desirable student groups and closed their doors to the others. In the eyes of critics such as C. Wright Mills, who coined the famous phrase "power elite" in 1956, exclusive prep schools were agents in a conspiracy of the already privileged to perpetuate their privilege forever.[2]

Veteran teachers who had attended prep schools in the 1950s could recall decades later the tiny number of racial and religious minorities who were their schoolmates. Before the 1960s Jews were far more problematic than blacks; many more Jews wanted to attend, could afford to pay, and easily met admissions criteria. The problem was limiting their numbers. Unlike blacks, who after 1963 became the most sought-after and fought-over racial or ethnic group in the history of American education, Jews were never recruited by prep schools at all. The same Andover head who spoke eloquently about his school's gracious and stimulating environment also directed that it remain as "predominantly Aryan as possible." Nearly 5 percent of Andover students were Jews in the 1940s. The head wanted that number reduced, lest it frighten away his mainly Protestant constituency.

The story of racism is different because few blacks applied or were sought before the 1960s. In the early 1930s, for example, a Massachusetts boarding school accidentally accepted a Negro boy.

His father was a Richmond attorney, and the school literally did not know his race until he arrived on campus. The head patiently explained to father and son (presumably on the steps of the dorm) "that their dormitory system and their clientele would not permit their allowing such a student to remain." To the head's surprise and dismay, the boy became "haughty and indignant" and the father "more obstreperous still." A lawsuit was dropped only when the accidental Negro secured admission elsewhere. The tone of a contemporary newspaper account suggested that father and son should have understood immediately and gone straightaway back home.

With its proudly inclusive motto, "Youth from Every Quarter," Andover enrolled just two blacks in 1944. The head said more would cause trouble. Most schools had none—only about twenty independent schools enrolled any black students by 1948, and as late as 1960 only about one-third had ever enrolled a black student. The most integrated boarding schools before the 1960s—Northfield School for Girls and the adjacent Mount Hermon School in Massachusetts—enrolled twenty-one black boys and girls in 1949. But Northfield's headmistress admitted that at neither school had black boarders ever roomed with whites.[3]

The South was a special case. Once the 1954 *Brown* Supreme Court decision banning racial segregation began to be enforced in public schools, Southern prep schools became associated with the preservation of segregation in a way that their equally lily-white Northern counterparts had never been. Thirty-eight percent of the schools founded between 1954 and 1964 that eventually became members of NAIS were in the South. In the next decade, which saw much public school integration as a result of federal pressure, 56 percent of NAIS schools founded were Southern.

In these years, long-established Southern prep schools also found it easy to increase enrollments. The new or expanding independent schools were financially and academically stronger than the more numerous "seg" academies, and did not openly preach white supremacy. But the segregation motive or the fear of integration's consequences controlled the most respectable of them.

Weeks before Martin Luther King, Jr., began the Birmingham campaign that transformed the civil rights struggle in the spring of 1963, his young son and namesake was denied admission to a well-regarded Atlanta Episcopal prep school. When an Atlanta Presbyterian school accepted a black youngster a year later, 25 percent of the students were summarily withdrawn by their parents. In 1964 only two Southern prep schools enrolled blacks. In 1968 the NAIS board of directors balked at making nondiscrimination a membership requirement because it would undercut the efforts of school heads to persuade reluctant boards to integrate.[4]

This record of discrimination posed one set of moral and political problems, but other critiques of student-body composition were just as disturbing. Perhaps the century's most vigorous political attack on prep schools by a respected figure was mounted by Harvard president James B. Conant. A prep school graduate whose scientific career was initiated by an outstanding science teacher, Conant was also a social conservative who saw prep schools inflaming class conflict by clustering privileged students together. "The greater proportion of our youth who attends independent schools," Conant said in 1952 to wildly applauding public school superintendents, "the greater the threat to our democratic unity."

Conant had long believed that the way to encourage social unity was to educate everyone in a geographical community together. This was one reason for his endorsement of large, comprehensive high schools. The notion of school as democratic melting pot was unoriginal, but Conant recast it for the Depression era by stressing economic and class unity instead of cultural or ethnic assimilation. Class differences, in his view, became socially dangerous by their "visibility." Prep schools were a barrier to democratic unity because they made entrenched privilege more visible than was socially wise.

Further, independent schools made the job of public schools harder by removing from them numerically small but critical family constituencies supportive of academic learning. Conant wanted public schools to promote social mobility among the talented but impecunious—to create a Jeffersonian natural aristocracy—as much as he wanted them to build common bonds of citizenship. If prep school families were spread out among public high schools, they would press public schools for high-cost talent identification and development programs (such as advanced science labs and sophisticated college counseling) that otherwise might lack strong advocacy.

In 1944 Conant advised his own alma mater, Roxbury Latin School in Massachusetts, to transform itself into an experimental comprehensive high school. Its mission would be to investigate how the "selective" and "unifying" functions could best be carried on within one institution containing students bound both for college and for the workforce. Roxbury Latin declined. It continued to focus on boys of ability and ambition regardless of their economic circumstances. This strategy foreshadowed the way many independent schools would attempt, in the 1950s and afterwards, to refute Conant's charge that they were socially divisive. By emphasizing academic capacity in admissions, they could take much of the sting out of exclusivity and forge for themselves constructive new reputations.[5]

Conant's critique never disputed the prep schools' educational benefits, but gradually an argument emerged that homogeneous student bodies diminished the quality of education itself. Little Orphan Annie's assessment was one example. Millions of Americans learned from the comics in 1947 that Annie had rejected Big Brother's offer to send her to the best private school money could buy. She gave two reasons. "Public school is good enough for me. I've got all my buttons . . . I'm not specked or a little wacky or retarded." The prep school students she had in mind were abnormal and almost defective, not some cultural or social elite. She further explained that "when I grow up I'll be one o' th' 'public' . . . I don't want to have to start learnin' how to get along *after* I get through school." Prep schools did not prepare for citizenship.

Each criticism directly implicated student bodies. In one case the students were unsatisfactory. Who would want to be around such people? In the other case they were too different from the people with whom she would have to associate in later life. For what was private school preparation?

Annie's opinions were widely shared, and this was one reason many school heads angrily demanded (without success) that their national associations obtain a retraction from the cartoonist Harold Gray or his syndicator. Prep schools were frequently believed to be filled with troubled or untalented students who lacked the right stuff to succeed in public schools. This impression was especially strong in the Midwest, where good public schools and lack of family interest in preparing for Eastern colleges made building prep school reputations an uphill battle. Even the editor of the leading private school journal had conceded in 1926 that "perhaps rightly" most prep schools were popularly regarded as "asylums for the dullard and the morally shipwrecked" or "retreats for mental and moral perverts." Until the 1950s only a few were known to be regularly filled with academically able and psychologically intact youth.

Annie's other criticism gained momentum as the century progressed. Student-body homogeneity seemed poor preparation for modern American life. In 1941, a friendly critic argued that the "lad [who] has been taught from early days that he is to be a 'leader of tomorrow' . . . does not know how to cooperate." He needed exposure to the "boy . . . from the family of ten on the wrong side of the tracks," who could presumably teach the lesson of "sharing co-operatively." In a similar vein, another friendly critic warned soon after Annie's assault that prep school "social inbreeding" could only be avoided by enrolling a "cross section of the capable young people" of the country. The soon-to-be standard argument against student-body homogeneity was: "Strength and adaptability to meet whatever lies ahead derive from various experiences made possible by wide acquaintanceship and association with young people of background different from one's own." This was a long way from Virgil Prettyman's admissions advice to Columbia.

By the mid-1960s a liberal, friendly critic, Harold Howe II, the U.S. commissioner of education, argued that prep students would be "culturally deprived" unless their schools contained significant numbers of the urban disadvantaged. Later another liberal critic claimed that too much consensus around school purpose and values provided poor student preparation for "managing conflicts" in the "complex organizations" of a "culturally diverse society." She criticized private school environments that fell "below a threshold of social debate productive by public education standards." Here was perhaps the ultimate educational argument against homogeneity. Good communities required value dissonance more than value consensus.[6]

The various prep school responses to these criticisms of homogeneity became collectively known as "diversity." Although it was initially a practical economic and public relations strategy, many private schools claimed by the end of the 1960s to value diversity as a positive good. During the 1980s diversity became for some schools not the antithesis of a cohesive school community but an essential ingredient of it. When students and teachers in the early 1990s were asked what "community" meant in their schools, they often replied that it meant places that celebrated diversity.

The rise of diversity is best traced through three fairly distinct changes in student-body composition since World War II. Independent schools first attempted to diversify economically while also attracting more able students. Economic diversification proved useful as a meritocratic strategy, but it was financially difficult to attain and as a cause lacked moral urgency. Then in the 1960s schools confronted much more vigorously the genuinely urgent issue of race. At the same time they began to recognize that gender was another crucial diversity they could no longer ignore.

The overall results were somewhat more heterogeneous student bodies but not more divided ones. Independent schools attempted to become more inclusive without destroying their traditional commitment to community and the family school. They needed to strike a delicate balance between different values and valued differences. Near the century's end most were perhaps more apt to celebrate diversity than to attain it. But they also managed to reap many of diversity's benefits without yet becoming battlegrounds in the larger American multicultural wars.

Economic Diversity

The most obvious way to diversify affluent student bodies was to attract less affluent students. Initially diversity meant economic and social-class diversity. Economic diversity did not threaten the homogeneity the schools wished to preserve, since a large middle-class population shared the schools' values and would attend if they could afford to. The key was increasing scholarships.

Serious attention to financial aid began in most schools during the Depression, when they began to experiment on a large scale with tuition reductions or discounts. Their original intention was not to change the kinds of students enrolled but to preserve the financially embattled traditional market. Schools tried to assist familiar constituencies who had suffered severe reverses without adding to the tuition burden of other strapped families who could barely pay their own bills.

Depression-era statements of good practice thus advised that financial aid come only from funds specially obtained for that distinct purpose. Scholarships should not be funded from general school revenues. Financial aid was regarded as a benefit for those who received it, not as a benefit for those paying the full freight. The latter should not have to subsidize the former.

The virtue of economic diversity was linked to the equally democratic virtue of academically strong student bodies. The first often assured the second. Americans were more likely to forgive exclusivity, one shrewd independent-school leader observed, if it was associated with genuine merit. He wryly noted that "the fast section [of students] has never been considered undemocratic." In effect, many schools attempted to create a more diverse student body economically in order to create a more homogeneous student body academically. Attracting needy but able students was the central goal of financial aid policy from the 1940s until the mid-1960s. A veteran teacher summarized this version of diversity by pointing to his own career. "I was hired in 1958 to diversify the faculty and I am a white male!" He was Catholic and his social background was less advantaged than the faculty norm at the time, but he was very well educated. He was amused that when his school first used the word diversity, it meant people like himself.[7]

The idea soon grew that economically diverse student bodies benefited all students and not just aid recipients. Better students raised academic expectations as well as schools' reputations. Spreading this idea was especially useful since schools rarely could fund financial aid through special gifts or restricted endowments. They could more easily ask full-paying families to subsidize the education of scholarship-holders if the result was to improve the school as a whole.

The dependence on general revenues and annual gifts from parents exposed a major barrier to economic diversity: it was hard to fund. For one thing, the economic prosperity of the 1950s and early 1960s, the unexpected baby boom, and the sudden popularity of college all had the effect of erasing Depression-era enrollment anxiety. The fee-paying applicant pool rose rapidly, so schools could be more selective and even expand in size without worrying about financial aid. An important early motive for economic diversity—the fear of declining enrollments—was forgotten.

Further, the increase in public high school college preparation programs blurred the identification of prep schools with economic exclusivity. A large group of private-like "lighthouse" suburban public schools sprang up whose low buildings and green playing fields not only resembled country day schools but were often superior facilities. "Gee, sir," one prep school head remembered a student saying on viewing his renovated campus, "this is almost as good as a public school!" Prep schools were no longer the most notable educational symbols of a class-divided society.

Most affluent Americans have sent their children to public schools, not independent schools. In 1988 roughly 70 percent of all eighth-graders with family incomes above $75,000, for example, attended public schools, whereas 6 percent attended prep schools. The rise of suburbia helped rescue independent schools from the Conants and Orphan Annies without requiring them to increase financial aid, as private higher education was then busily doing. Suburbia was one of the best things ever to happen to independent education.

Reformers of educational inequality eventually found far more striking examples in urban-suburban public school differences than in public-private ones. Conant himself lost interest in the independent-school threat to social unity as the years passed. He discovered social dynamite instead in the growing disparities between slums and suburbs.

Thus little political or moral urgency remained to raise money to diversify prep schools economically, except for a few lucky institutions with wealthy and interested benefactors. Advocates of economic diversity tried to persuade foundations, corporations, and individuals to support national rather than school-specific aid programs. In 1954, for example, NCIS explored a possible national prep school scholarship program for the needy and able. But these efforts to raise money, often modeled on higher-education efforts such as "Give to the College of Your Choice" or the National Merit Scholars, had little success.

A major problem was public school opposition. NCIS realized that corporate or foundation support was unlikely without the tacit acquiescence of public schools. An exploratory meeting of Philadelphia private and public school officials was arranged in 1954 to test the cooperative waters. They proved ice-cold.

The public school authorities argued that Philadelphia's public schools already provided excellent college preparation. There would be "few if any instances where a child could be transferred to an independent school to his advantage." This remark nearly ended the meeting moments after it had begun. But surely, the prep school delegates retorted, some promising students did poorly in public school or resisted college preparation for reasons that did not reflect on the Philadelphia public schools. Philadelphia's officials disagreed. The able students sought by prep schools were students Philadelphia wanted to retain and then could retain.

In higher education, the political situation was very different. College was rarely free anywhere, college attendance was still atypical, and no national consensus existed that public colleges served the public interest better than private ones. Private higher education's national campaigns and programs did not offend public higher education and often benefited it. Within elementary-secondary education, in contrast, a large financial aid expansion for independent schools would have removed college-bound students from public schools at the very moment those schools were proudly adding to their college preparation capacity. The prep school national scholarship idea went nowhere.[8]

Nor did federal or state government help prep schools diversify economically, unlike their eventual intervention on behalf of both private and public higher education. In 1982, for example, more than 27 percent of undergraduates in the most prestigious private colleges received financial aid from federal and state sources. Stiffened eligibility requirements reduced this fraction to 14 percent in the early 1990s, but the contrast between government assistance to elite private higher education and elite private schooling was still dramatic. The latter received nothing.

Most prep schools never wanted the direct grants or guaranteed loans that helped make expensive colleges more affordable. The likely costs of any public assistance—government regulation, hostility from public education, entanglement in church-state issues, opposition from private higher education—always seemed to outweigh the small financial benefits that most aid mechanisms would provide even if held constitutional. Public aid to independent colleges was different from aid to independent schools because the former provided serious money without divisive controversy. When prep schools thought about government financial assistance, their concern was mainly what government could do for, or to, parents and alumni through tax policies such as the charitable deduction.[9]

Limited revenue sources for economic diversification produced limited but still visible results. The percentage of schools' expense budgets devoted to financial aid increased from roughly 6 to 7 percent in the 1950s and 1960s, to about 7 percent in the 1970s and 1980s, to about 8 percent in the early 1990s. The fraction of students receiving aid increased from around 12 percent in 1950 to around 18 percent in 1990. Given many other new expenses added to school budgets, such as fund-raising, admissions, and college counseling, these steady if unspectacular increases are fairly impressive. They are even more impressive considering that most of the money came directly from the schools rather than from foundations, corporations, or government.

Yet financial aid did not produce a major change in the income distribution of prep school families. Although the historical trend is toward somewhat greater income diversity, the stark fact is that independent education remains unaffordable to most Americans. Nearly 60 percent of prep school eighth-graders in 1988 came from families whose incomes that year (as reported by parents) were more than $75,000, compared with 30 percent of such families in very affluent public schools and 6 percent of families in all public eighth grades. Fifty-four percent of prep school seniors in 1990 lived in families with incomes of $70,000 or more (as reported by students), compared with 16 percent of college-bound seniors in public and all other private schools. If a $30,000 income then represented the bottom of the middle class, only 11 percent of these prep school seniors were below middle class, compared with one-third of college-bound seniors in all other schools.

Prep schools have become more economically diverse than in the days before any systematic financial aid, but few attained anything like the greater economic diversity of major liberal arts colleges. By the early 1990s the most selective undergraduate institutions supported with their own grants about 40 percent of their students. This excludes loans and all federal and state assistance. Their student bodies are by no means economically representative of the country, but they are much more so than those in independent schools.[10]

Nearly one-fourth of all prep school aid awarded since the late 1950s has gone to students from within the school family—faculty children—rather than to genuine newcomers. Schools used financial aid in the form of tuition remission to recruit and retain teachers. Giving priority to faculty children helped sweeten the package for poorly compensated teachers. In one sense, financial aid data overstate the schools' commitment to diversifying the student body, since an equal if not greater motive was improving faculty benefits. In another sense, the policy nicely exemplifies the earliest meaning of prep school diversity. Faculty children came mainly from nonaffluent, well-educated, academically committed, and middle-class white families.[11]

Racial Diversity

In sharp contrast to economic diversification, the prep schools' effort to integrate by race, begun in 1963, was a dramatic moral awakening to perhaps the most repulsive feature of their history. In that crucial year many events, etched in educators' consciousness and conscience by television, reshaped the meaning of diversity. Diversity became racial diversity because of the Birmingham demonstrations, the tense integration of the University of Alabama, President Kennedy's eloquent civil rights address followed by his legislative proposals, the summer March on Washington, and the November assassination with its aftermath of national rededication.

Only after a passionate White House briefing by Kennedy on the impending racial crisis did Cary Potter, an attendee and the soon-to-be president of NAIS, understand that most independent education ignored blacks. "Up to that point we had been relatively untouched by the *Brown* decision," he recalled. "There wasn't anybody who said you had to do anything." Two days before Kennedy's briefing, officials at the Fund for the Advancement of Education had expressed impatience with independent schools for seeking general foundation support without even acknowledging the "Great Negro Problem." But by the end of the year unprecedented prep school initiatives to alter their mainly white student bodies were actively under way.

The sudden response of organized independent education and many individual schools to the events of 1963 was remarkably different from their quarter-century modest engagement with economic diversification. For many, racial integration became a consuming passion, the moral chance of a lifetime. The intensity of the response is explained in part by the fortunate circumstances prep schools enjoyed despite years of shameful neglect. Two advantages in particular made their path toward racial diversification easier than that of most public schools.

Racial integration for independent schools was a voluntary act. Never in their history had such an opportunity been presented to make a visible contribution to a national problem. Never before had they been given the chance to be players in a truly significant national drama. Unlike many public schools that integrated because or in anticipation of court mandates, the prep schools were free to act on their own. Voluntarism gave integration a moral intensity easier to sustain than court-mandated change.

Further, their commitment to integration was only rarely accompanied by fears that their schools would be disrupted or changed fundamentally by the process. Some fear of white flight did exist, especially in the South, but after 1963 this proved mostly groundless. The reality was just the reverse. Prep schools could control integration, introduce it on their own terms, and focus on a few individuals since the schools were small to begin with. Small numbers of black students conferred large benefits on themselves and on the schools without creating large problems with traditional constituencies. Moral urgency and political savvy merged to create the largest recruitment effort in the history of independent education.

What enabled this sudden energy to be converted into concrete action was access to money that had never been available for mere economic diversification. Efforts that private philanthropy and public education had resisted only a few years before when aimed generally at able and needy youth became irresistible when aimed at black youth. Although important initiatives were taken by individual schools, the most interesting and best-funded programs were collaborative. With few exceptions these were dominated by consortia of metropolitan day schools that created summer and Saturday programs to improve skills and elevate aspirations. Early efforts such as Boston's Educational Enrichment Program, New York's Project Broad Jump, Detroit's Horizons-Upward Bound, and Hartford's Supplementary Program for Hartford in Education Reinforcement and Enrichment (SPHERE) were designed more to enrich public schools than to lure black students from them.

The best-known collaboration, A Better Chance, helped many boarding schools attract largely black and poor inner-city students for the first time. The idea had its origins in a 1963 "Independent School Talent Search" remarkably similar in outline to what had been unsuccessfully pushed as economic diversification a decade earlier in Philadelphia. But now foundation money was available for both boarding school scholarships and a summer-long orientation program (initially at Dartmouth College) to prepare city students for the rituals of rural residential life. As Porter Sargent had earlier suggested, boarding schools alone could make the compelling argument that they offered a total break from unsupportive environments.

In its first decade, A Better Chance served almost 4,000 students and spent nearly 40 million dollars. No collective effort of that magnitude had ever been mounted by independent education before, and none has been since. In those years $7.6 million came from foundations. Surprisingly, the federal government itself for a brief moment provided remarkable support—$7.9 million from the Office of Economic Opportunity and later from the Model Cities program. This was the most concentrated and significant federal aid ever received by independent education, albeit received indirectly through a nonprofit pass-through agency.

What linked all these programs was not only the unprecedented money and commitment they mustered, but the irony that they had to work hard to persuade students to attend. Many had the experience of Westminster Schools in Atlanta, which proudly announced in 1965 that it was open to all races only to find that no blacks wanted to enroll. Despite the competition among whites for admission to this well-known school, black interest at first was nonexistent.

This was not surprising, given that most of the students being sought knew nothing of prep schools (much less boarding schools) and were not especially enamored of the sudden chance to go to school with privileged whites. Privileged black parents, moreover, were long accustomed to working within all-black schools and all-black colleges. Few had family ties to any of the prep schools. Even in 1990 affluent and educated black families were somewhat less likely than white families in similar circumstances to send their college-bound children to independent rather than public schools.[12]

Still, the enormous recruiting effort produced substantial enrollment changes. The number of integrated prep schools jumped from 33 percent in 1960 to 84 percent in 1969. Black enrollments tripled to 4.3 percent of total enrollment in the decade ending in 1975 and approached 11,000 students. Although the growth rate then slowed, by 1990 blacks constituted 5.2 percent of independent-school students.

By the end of the 1960s, African Americans had caught up to faculty children in the percentage of total financial aid dollars each group received, although faculty children remained the largest identifiable group aided. In 1970 racial minorities (then virtually all black) and faculty children together composed only about 7 percent of independent students, but these two preferred groups received about 47 percent of all aid dollars. In the early 1990s they received 54 percent of all aid. A 1985 study concluded that racial minorities, and especially African Americans, received significantly larger grants than white students after controlling for financial need.

Although African Americans remained the most supported and most visible minority, racial diversification in the prep schools increased substantially during the 1980s because of the addition of new groups, especially Asian Americans. The latter surpassed African Americans numerically in the mid-1980s, and by 1990 they were (at 9 percent) the largest group of students of color in prep schools. Asian Americans were less likely than other minorities to need financial aid. In fact, by 1990 two-thirds of all students of color received no financial aid.

The total percentage of minorities in prep schools gradually approached that of the college-bound population in public schools. In 1990, 21 percent of prep seniors reported themselves as nonwhite, compared with 28 percent of college-bound public school seniors. This was a striking shift from the virtually all-white student bodies of only three decades earlier.[13]

Academic versus Social Integration

Perhaps the most striking aspect of racial diversity is that it has been moderated and muted by many shared educational characteristics. The ties that have bound racially diverse student bodies together—or at least together *enough*—are strong. Racial diversification in prep schools was accompanied by much more value convergence than dissonance. The experience of Asian Americans is the most obvious example, but that of African Americans is perhaps the most pertinent.

The most fundamental area of value convergence is commitment to academics. Prep schools attract a higher percentage of the pool of academically able college-bound black students than they do of similar white students. Among college-bound seniors enrolled in public and prep schools in 1990, 16.3 percent of blacks who did very well on the 1990 Scholastic Aptitude Test (SAT) attended prep schools. This compares with 9.5 percent of white seniors with similar scores.

The influx of African-American talent has produced a prep school black peer culture of greater academic capacity than the black college-bound public school cohort. The 1990 difference was a remarkable 236 SAT points—a mean score of 968 versus 732. Blacks in prep schools also outperformed black college-bound public school seniors from affluent and highly educated families by 87 points. They outperformed white college-bound public school seniors by 38 points.

In addition, this black prep cohort is majority-male in contrast to the majority-female college-bound public school black cohort. Most college-bound seniors in public schools are female, but in public schools the numerical gap between college-bound black females and college-bound black males is larger than for any other racial group. Sixty percent of college-bound black seniors in public schools are female (as measured by students taking the SAT). But in prep schools, black males constitute a slight majority. They are much less likely to be numerically overshadowed by black females.

On these dimensions of academic capacity and gender mix black students resemble the general makeup of prep school student bodies as a whole: academically capable students and a predominance of males over females. Racial differences in measured academic aptitude still exist in all schools, but the gap between white and black academic capacity in prep schools is far smaller than that between white and black college-bound students in public schools—90 SAT points instead of 198. These conditions may appeal to African-American families who seek a more academic and college-oriented male peer culture for their sons. They may also appeal to all families who understand that racial attitudes are conditioned by direct experience.[14]

Whether this movement toward common academic characteristics for black and white students is accompanied by movement toward genuine social integration, in the sense of lasting interracial friendships, is a completely different question. Providing better educational opportunities for blacks was a more urgent motive for desegregating prep student bodies than promoting social integration of the races or even removing white prejudice. When the psychiatrist Robert Coles was asked in 1963 what the role of independent schools should be regarding the moral crisis of race, he instantly replied that it was to offer blacks the opportunity for a "first-class education."

Only rarely did schoolpeople apply their traditional argument for the networking value of student personal relations to the new context of racial integration. When they did make the connection, it was more commonly in the earlier years of desegregation. "It is in our self interest, if we want to put it that way," a headmaster atypically noted, "to bring our children together. They will form a network of linkages that will become professional and social."

Gender integration, which happened in many schools at the same time as racial integration, was eagerly sought by most students. Boys wanted to be in school with girls, and vice versa. The point was to maximize daily contact between groups hitherto separated by school policy. The same motive did not accompany racial desegregation. Social integration between blacks and whites encountered formidable barriers besides the obvious ones of fear and inertia. The black identity movement was one, although it seems clear that black students would have sensibly and inevitably rallied to one another for support without it. Once some schools moved beyond tokenism in black admissions, it became obvious that "schools that have accepted a sizable number of black students have become less, rather than more, integrated."

The creation of a critical mass of black students helped produce a separate black peer culture. By the end of the 1960s, it was commonplace for black students to lunch together, form their own associations, characterize white preppies as cold and emotionless, and substitute the idea of "racism" as an inherent white trait for more limited and traditional notions of bigotry and prejudice. Typically, the black withdrawal from social integration was most common in liberal schools that had made the biggest investment in integration and enrolled both the greatest number of and the most able blacks.

Many cross-racial friendships were forged despite these barriers. But perhaps more important, the relative absence of significant social integration did not impede the academic progress of the newcomers. They used the schools as they had always been used by upwardly mobile whites. The authors of the most thorough study of the black prep school experience, based on early graduates of A Better Chance, were "surprised by the degree to which the graduates looked back on their prep school days with fondness." The study concluded that "the large majority of students who went through the program in its early years were well served and emerged not only well educated but psychologically intact." They not only endured but flourished. They became more independent and more aware of the possibilities open to them. They felt safe to work at academics without being ridiculed. And although blacks associated mainly with other blacks, this peer group was academically able and committed.

In these circumstances, few prep schools needed much social integration of the races beyond tolerance and courtesy to consider themselves educationally successful. "There is no real integration," one teacher observed in the early 1990s, but "they get along all right. There is probably less tension here than there is in any environment." There were no incentives for schools to push for closer interracial relationships that neither white nor black students themselves pushed for. The main goal was to avoid racial conflict, and the best way to do that was to praise and even canonize diversity as a community ideal. Ethnic food festivals and multicultural assemblies were not contrived efforts to promote integration but signals that too much of it was not really sought.[15]

Gender

Before World War II prep schools were dominated numerically by boys, by a male outlook, and by single-sex schools. By 1970 unprecedented changes were occurring in all three areas. One change, a steady increase of female students, went largely unnoticed. Another, the sudden increase in coeducational schools, is widely regarded by veteran schoolpeople as the single most important event in their entire careers. A third, the awareness that gender itself is a profound kind of diversity, invested the debate over coeducation with educational meaning that lasted decades after the actual mechanics of coeducation were completed.

In 1950 only 36 percent of prep school students were female. By 1990 that number had increased to 48 percent, almost the percentage of girls in the general population. This enormous change alone accounts for much of the increase of total prep school enrollment in the postwar decades. But it did not happen because prep schools discovered that female underrepresentation was a problem and resolved to solve it. There were no talent searches or recruiting efforts, nor any urgent financial aid appeals, as there had been when other diversity was sought. Girls quietly sought out prep schools on their own. They sought them out because girls in general were attending college in greater numbers, and more families were willing and able to pay for the private schooling of daughters as well as sons. In 1935, by contrast, only 31 percent of prep school students taking college entrance exams were females, compared with 40 percent of public school candidates.

The first edition of Porter Sargent's handbook (1915) relegated coed schools to a catchall "special schools" section that included music conservatories and kindergarten training institutes. Ninety-five percent of the "regular" schools in that edition were single sex. The prep tradition was overwhelmingly single sex, and schools wanting to be part of it usually started that way (Gilman) or switched to single sex (Collegiate). As late as 1931 a newspaper headline read, "Vermont Academy Becomes Boys School, Follows

Diversity and Community   103

Trend Away from Coeducation." In 1950 about three-quarters of prep school students were enrolled in single-sex institutions.

There was nothing mysterious about the predominance of single-sex schools. No elaborate educational defense was required. In 1950 one justification simply explained that single-sex environments gave adolescents "a more natural mental, physical, and emotional development." Since most of the colleges the schools prepared students for were single sex, a compelling model was already in place. And since many girls did not attend four-year college or any college, boys and girls schools usually offered quite distinct curricula. Different life destinations reinforced the logic of gender separation. In boarding schools, furthermore, the single-sex format was an easier and cheaper way to manage residential life. Finally, the women who established and sustained girls schools had opportunities for entrepreneurship available to few other women. They favored girls schools in part because they wanted to run their own show.[16]

The sudden decline of the single-sex tradition in the late 1960s was the result of many external forces that schools could not easily control. The 1960s provoked agonizing changes within independent education. Economic pressures unknown since the 1930s engulfed them: inflation, recession, federal price and wage controls, and the beginning of a decline in the number of schoolage children. To this was added the crisis of purpose and authority among the young (and not so young), often called with prep school understatement "student unrest."

In this climate students and many teachers sought less institutional rigidity, more sensitivity to student desires and alleged needs, and more rapid acceptance of the growing national tendency toward reduced adult direction over the lives of the young. One especially strong student desire was coeducation. When many other symbols of school traditionalism were giving way—dress codes, classroom formality, required religious observances, a narrow curriculum—the abandonment of single-sex environments was a major concession that schools (and colleges) could defend on educational and economic grounds. It could be portrayed positively instead of as abject surrender to the mob. A girls school administrator acidly suggested that coeducation was "perhaps related to an administrative hope that agreement to this step in the revolution of rising expectations of the young may stave off less manageable items."

There has been no larger single change in student-body composition in the history of independent schools. In 1968–69 a majority of students attended coeducational schools for the first time. Single-sex enrollments declined precipitously in the early 1970s as schools hurriedly went coed, merged with other single-sex schools, or sometimes closed. By 1975 only 29 percent of students were in single-sex schools, by 1990 only 19 percent. Between 1965 and 1975 more than one hundred of roughly seven hundred NAIS schools went coed, and an additional eighty merged to form thirty-eight coed institutions. About 77 percent of prep schools were single sex in 1950, but by 1990 the fraction had shrunk to 22 percent. Single-sex schools are by no means extinct and continue to provide families with one of the most dramatic available choices regarding student-body composition. Their qualities are widely noticed because they have become the exotic exception instead of the taken-for-granted rule.

It is hard to find written evidence of serious or principled opposition to economic or even racial diversity. In contrast, no student-body composition issue was ever debated more heatedly within prep schools than coeducation. The fact that so many schools made fundamental decisions on gender makeup—more than one-fourth of all prep schools went coed in one decade—made all of them aware of gender in a way they could not ignore and would not forget. Even longstanding coed or steadfastly single-sex schools removed from the fray could not escape arguments about where girls or boys best learned. The debate helped make gender a new diversity.

Boys schools faced more pressure to go coeducational, although each time one did pressure was increased on nearby girls schools. Boys schools were more adamantly pro-coeducation, and their officials more likely to be persuaded that segregating teenage boys from girls was unhealthy for the boys. In 1950, 79 percent of boys compared with 65 percent of girls were in single-sex schools. By 1990, only 17 percent of boys remained in boys schools. Coeducation also conferred benefits on some adult males. Between 1954 and 1979 the percentage of male school heads increased from 67 percent to 86 percent. Decisions by girls schools to take boys were often accompanied by decisions to appoint male rather than female heads.

A full-scale argument for coeducation at all-male Andover made three main points. First, "life was coeducational." It followed inexorably that boys and girls should go to school together "to grow continuously in mutual understanding and respect." This was the educational argument.

The second point dismissed single-sex education as "elitist." In an unmistakable allusion to the peculiar institution of slavery, it was called the prep schools' "one abiding peculiarity." Single-sex schools were bad because they helped maintain "a class of ladies and gentlemen, differentiated by tastes, accomplishments, manners and mores from the mass of the American people." Even the phrase "prep school" caused embarrassment, because it connoted "exclusiveness, special privilege, snobbery, and socially naive cultism." In the egalitarian spirit of the day, single-sex schools were "at odds with national priorities and trends." They were the moral equivalent of schools segregated by race.

Last but hardly least, maintaining single-sex student bodies could only accelerate the "current decline in applications to single-sex schools." This was the bottom-line argument. The tripartite appeal to healthy adolescent development (the idea of "natural" development was turned on its head), American populism, and the virtues of a doubled applicant pool proved unbeatable at Andover and elsewhere. Lauded as statesmanlike, the Andover report hastened the academy's merger in 1973 with a well-established nearby girls school, Abbot Academy. In a sentiment widely shared by schools similarly transformed, Andover's historian concluded that this was "far and away the most important change in the nearly two hundred years of Phillips Academy history."[17]

A Different Voice

The drop in commitment to single-sex education was less pronounced among girls and girls schools than among boys. One headmistress, Jean S. Harris, dryly observed that the Andover report seemed preoccupied with boosting Andover applications and making boys happy. If coeducation produced healthier relations between the sexes, why were graduates of traditionally coed public schools not notably superior as spouses or parents? She noted the lack of any evidence that coeducation was educationally superior, dismissed the claim that prep schools must mimic American popular taste, and suggested that no one really knew the best way to educate. Perhaps there was no one best way. Perhaps for some girls the best place to develop self-confidence and inner resources was a girls school. More than a few agreed. In 1990 a larger fraction of girls (22 percent) than boys attended single-sex schools.[18]

The independent-school rush toward coeducation took place exactly when the women's movement began in earnest. Just as the invigorated civil rights movement forced schools to address the "Negro Problem," the women's movement raised the stakes of the debate over single-sex or coed environments. For every argument that going to school together was healthy, American, and preparation for the real world, defenders of girls schools wondered whether such healthy American preparation was appropriate for a world where women's roles were rapidly changing. The historian of Abbot Academy noted ironically that the school's demise coincided with the appearance of provocative research from scholars such as Matina Horner on the decline of girls' academic and personal competence. Girls' "fear of success" was especially notable in coed institutions.

Any prep school enrolling girls—single sex or coed—found itself devouring a growing and perplexing scholarly and advocacy literature on female development. Carol Gilligan, for example, began arguing in the 1970s that girls' moral development was not the same as boys'—that girls differed from boys in heretofore unsuspected cognitive ways with considerable educational implications. It was not just that their bodies were different; girls thought about some things differently. Even before Gilligan achieved national attention in 1982 with the publication of *In a Different Voice,* many prep schools were discussing her ideas. Some actively participated in her research. The work of controversial advocates of a strong feminist perspective on schooling, such as Wellesley College's Peggy McIntosh, often found equally receptive audiences among independent-school educators long before they achieved wider prominence.

The new literature on female development and how male expectations for women could sometimes inhibit it was especially relevant to independent schools. They realized that cognitive development, academic achievement, and admission to selective colleges had become as important for privileged girls as they were for privileged boys. The schools gradually attracted a more academically capable and ambitious female student body. Between 1950 and 1990 the mean SAT score for all prep school girls increased 67 points (to 1,028), while that of boys increased 26 points (to 1,051). A long-standing SAT gender gap favoring males still existed, but it was reduced to 23 points within prep schools (compared with 54 for all SAT-takers). As was the case with racial differences, academic gender differences existed but were also diminishing. Shared educational purposes and converging academic capacity muted traditional gender stereotyping.

The prep school debates about gender were not overwhelmed by nonacademic gender problems such as sports equity or sexual harassment. A long private school tradition of valuing girls' sports prevented athletics from becoming a gender battleground. It was assumed that newly coed schools would continue to take girls' sports very seriously. In contrast, athletics became the central gender preoccupation of public education after Title IX of the 1972 Education Amendments effectively abolished single-sex public schools. Further, the behavioral attitudes that students and teachers brought to private schools somewhat reduced more blatant types of sexual harassment common in many other schools.

As a result, prep schools have had more freedom to address gender issues that are broadly curricular. These include opportunities and expectations in science and mathematics, the infusion of female perspectives into the humanities and social sciences, and whether girls learn differently from boys. The typical academic experience of prep school girls is more extensive than it once was and more comprehensive than that of college-bound public school girls. For example, more than twice as many prep school girls as college-bound public school girls study Precalculus (71 percent versus 35 percent). Although more boys than girls study Precalculus, the gap favoring males is smaller in prep schools (4 percent) than in public schools (9 percent).

The coed versus single-sex debate is not as central to prep schools as it once was. It has been kept alive mainly by girls schools that recognize that their survival and prosperity depend on vigorously countering the American adolescent preference for coeducation. But the evidence about whether one or another setting is fundamentally "better" is not conclusive, is not likely to be, and will probably not be settled by research findings in any event. Not surprisingly, many

factors besides gender affect school environments and the creation
of a good match between student and school. The differing gender
mixes of independent schools are perhaps most useful because they
ensure that gender will not be forgotten as an educational force and
a source of diversity.[19]

Shared Values

When students themselves reflect on school diversity, they first notice it as differences in personality, appearance, interests, and capacities among schoolmates. A student enthusiastically portrayed her
schoolmates as "such a diversity of people with so many different
upbringings, and so many goals in their lives, and so many different
priorities, and so many things that they're doing." When others
were asked if they agreed, they all said they did. "There is virtually
any type of person here that you'd want to hang around with."

But hearing their views expressed out loud often causes students
to backtrack in mild embarrassment. Just after the students had de-
clared how diverse they were, a young woman shouted, "Oh my
God! I'll take that back!" She explained that they were different in
only some respects. A boy then elaborated, "We almost all live in
the suburbs. And we almost all have . . .," at which point the young
woman jumped back in to conclude, "Basically, economically and
all that stuff there's not [diversity] at all." In similar discussions students offered comments such as "A lot of the majority are from
upper-class families," or "There is in fact no diversity of people at
all."

Yet once on the table, these generalizations about homogeneity
also seemed inadequate. A boy pointed out that "about 8 percent [of
the student body] is minority." A girl tried to reconcile all the previous positions: "I think once we all really know each other and who
we are as individuals, yeah, we have a lot of diverse thinking and
stuff. But as far as the outside we're not at all different." In the end
they believe that genuine diversity is on the inside. Yet they also
speak proudly of growing racial diversity, religious diversity, economic diversity, and the availability of financial aid. Group diversity
is regarded as modestly present, rarely problematic, and a valued
component of school community.

Diversity in independent schools does not conflict with community primarily because economic, racial, gender, and other differences are muted by what everyone has more predominantly in common: high family and school educational expectations and enough student capacity and willingness to do college preparatory academic work. The triumph of the contemporary generic or standard independent school is its capacity to attract enough families recognized as "diverse" in background but who nonetheless share general educational values. Diversity and community coexist peacefully in most independent schools that have abandoned specialized missions based on religion, pedagogy, or something else.

The typical prep school student of whatever background is likely to have little contact with the bottom half of the national academic population and substantial contact with the top tenth. Roughly 46 percent of prep school tenth-graders in 1990 scored in the top tenth nationally in academic capacity, compared with about 21 percent of students in the most privileged public schools. This academic homogeneity is not surprising given that the schools' central mission is academic preparation and that they accept about 63 percent of applicants.

Measured differences between independent and privileged public school students are most pronounced when they involve academic values or behavior and least pronounced when they do not. Sophomores enrolled in both school types, for example, are about equally likely to belong to gangs, to party, or to have steady boy- or girlfriends. But prep school tenth-graders are significantly less likely to cut classes, cheat on tests, or copy other students' homework. About 87 percent say they would never cheat on tests, compared with 64 percent of privileged public school students. When students describe the values of their own peer groups, the greatest single difference is the higher value prep students ascribe to studying.

Prep school parents have higher educational expectations for their children, who in turn have higher expectations for themselves. What is most revealing about academic expectations is that they pervade entire independent schools regardless of student academic capacity. They are a community value. The most able students—those in the top tenth nationally in academic capacity—have similarly high expectations regardless of whether they attend public or private school. But for average college-bound teenagers in the top half but not the top tenth an important change occurs. About 98 percent of prep school tenth-graders in this group believe they will finish college. The privileged public school percentage slips to about 86 percent, and to 74 percent for public school students as a whole.

These are large differences among students with similar academic aptitudes. "Average" college-bound students in prep schools have nearly as high educational expectations for themselves as do their "top" schoolmates. The advantage of independent schools for average college-bound students applies also to peer values such as studying. In these respects there is little diversity within prep schools. Robert Coles once observed that privileged children tend to "grow up with school on their minds." This seems clearly true for most prep school students and families.[20]

This shared commitment to a general academic mission helps keep potentially divisive national tendencies reasonably under control. Diversity need not factionalize. Prep schools so far have not had to confront the tensions and financial outlays that multiculturalism and politicized diversity have brought to higher education. The federal regulatory context, political visibility of institutions, and practical stakes for adults (that is, jobs) are very different. Only a very few prep schools have staff members or administrative units principally devoted to diversity advocacy. Academic departments devoted to gender, racial, or ethnic studies do not exist, although courses everywhere abound on subjects like "The African-American Experience" and "Women in American History." In the early 1990s, multiculturalism in prep schools could be safely embraced as desirable, democratic, and undivisive because the programmatic and financial effects of embracing it were minor.

A thoughtful educator sardonically observed years ago that prep schools' "occasional experimentation with underprivileged youngsters who show promise" obscured the basic fact that they contained little *serious* diversity in educational values. They had virtually none of the thousands upon thousands of youngsters with "no interest in education, no respect for education, [who] are threatened by the standards (both academically and non-academically) of a good school." Working with such youngsters was "frustrating, terribly

difficult, unrewarding, and considered by many persons to be socially demeaning."

   This is the one diversity prep schools work hardest to avoid. They
and their market tolerate and even celebrate most other diversities,
but not this one. What they require is not academic talent but a
minimal commitment to take the enterprise of education seriously.
Even when this commitment exists, building community still remains a complex struggle. But at least the struggle can be pursued
without student resistance or adult despair.[21]

II

STANDARDS

5

Student Incentives and the College Board System

Lord James Bryce once wisely observed that "to the vast majority of mankind nothing is more agreeable than to escape the need for mental exertion." Parents and teachers well know that hard mental work is not a natural preference of human kind, and especially not of American youth. Their options for undemanding pleasures are perhaps unrivaled in the history of the world. And their presence in school owes more to law, habit, peer relations, and the absence of anything better to do than to the active pursuit of knowledge. A significant educational task is thus creating incentives or motivation for most youth to work hard at serious learning.

Developing student incentives to learn has proven one of our toughest educational problems. Typically, physicians are sought when disease strikes and attorneys are consulted when legal problems need solving. If anything, our society suffers in these two fields from an excess of client and provider incentives. Fear and new technology together often result in unneeded medical procedures, and American litigiousness is world famous.

School is different. The incentives to learn are often far less insistent than those that drive us to lawyers and doctors. Further, unlike in many other provider-client relations, the educational "client" has to do most of the work. Teachers can't learn for students; they must learn themselves. This requires active and continuous student effort.

Swallowing an antibiotic does not. So it is crucial to examine why students should want to work hard to learn concepts and skills that are often difficult. Why exert serious effort in school at all? What desirable individual consequences flow from mental exertion and scholastic achievement? What undesirable consequences result from little work and consequent ignorance?

External Incentives

For most Americans in the twentieth century, desirable life consequences in an economic sense have not required superior educational achievement. How well one did in school did not much affect how well one did in life. Possessing a high school diploma did (and does) have real consequences, but the diploma could usually be obtained by persisting in school courses—attending regularly, behaving decently. Time served dutifully meant credits accumulated automatically. Persistence in many respects is nothing to scoff at. To most Americans it represents responsible behavior with clear workplace and civic implications. It was and is better to persist than to drop out—especially given that high school graduation opens doors to postsecondary education. A key incentive for Americans to finish high school is the economic impact of that choice.

Real school achievement, as distinct from persistence in winning a diploma, is supported by a much weaker foundation of incentives. Universal secondary education and near-universal postsecondary education have not mandated much in the way of achievement. At its best, American education provides genuine opportunities but usually little more. And why not? The idea of opportunity—of a chance, indeed of many chances—is quintessentially American. It is our national conception of the level playing field. That schools should do more than this, that they should aggressively press students to seize academic opportunities and master complex subjects and skills, has seemed unnecessary.

Policies that press students to achieve might even have perverse results. They might fail, and increase social inequality by increasing dropout rates. Or alternatively they might succeed, and reduce inequality by producing a large, educated population whose political leanings and clout would be uncertain. These potential scenarios doubtless contribute to our collective unwillingness to change the status quo very much.

Admittedly, the increasing desire to attend college after World War II became an important incentive for teenagers to undertake college preparatory programs. This was a form of academic press, especially in the twenty years or so after 1945, when the number of college-bound students outpaced the availability of college places. But higher education rapidly expanded to meet student demand, becoming postsecondary education in the process.

By the 1960s a more familiar situation was restored—the oversupply of postsecondary education. Driven in the nineteenth century by religious zeal and local boosterism, colleges had always been expansionist and entrepreneurial. College supply traditionally exceeded college demand. When supply once again exceeded demand by the late 1960s, as it has ever since, the historical reluctance of most postsecondary institutions to make serious academic demands on prospective students re-emerged. Live students were always preferable to dead colleges.

Why should admission requirements demand serious achievement when college survival depends on luring students in rather than on barriers that keep them out? In America there is a college for everyone somewhere—regardless of accomplishments, interests, or financial circumstances. For the last generation, postsecondary "enrollment management" has focused on recruitment and marketing, not selection and standards. Its success has been notable. In the early 1990s about 60 percent of high school graduates went on to some postsecondary education immediately after high school, and about two-thirds were so enrolled within two or three years of graduation. Nearly half of the entire nineteen-year-old age cohort were enrolled in postsecondary institutions. But this success does not support incentives for students to work hard in high school.

A few colleges and universities provide the exception to the no-incentives rule. Between one hundred and two hundred are somewhat selective in undergraduate admissions because of a surplus of qualified applicants. But this situation is new and atypical; it existed virtually nowhere in the country in 1940. The reality is that most high school graduates attend their first-choice college. For the vast majority not competing for admission to one of *US News & World*

Report's top-rated "national" institutions, what justifies grappling with four years of serious high school science?

If neither school policies nor college admissions requirements provide clear incentives for students to exert much mental effort in schools, what other external incentives exist? Employers of college graduates and graduate school admissions offices rarely look at high school performance—college attendance renders all high school work permanently invisible. More surprisingly, those who employ high school graduates rarely examine and evaluate what job applicants did in high school. Persistence to the diploma has been enough for them. Perhaps for most of the century persistence has served as a better predictor of workplace performance in the jobs that high school graduates filled than attainment in academic studies.

Our cultural incentives in support of mental exertion and learning itself are remarkably weak compared with many other industrialized countries. The historian Richard Hofstadter authoritatively described the pervasiveness of anti-intellectualism in American life a generation ago. He was not an unreasonable prig, and he has not been improved upon. This is the forgotten ism in our ism-obsessed society. It is not only that pop culture celebrates the fact that we "don't know much about his-tor-ree"; it is also that teachers seriously committed to academic learning— be they traditionalists or progressives—are often only one of many faculty interest groups. Serious learning is but one of the many agendas schools have, and it often loses out to more pressing social concerns.[1]

Many teachers instruct in fields that have little to do with the development of intelligence. Strong advocates for these fields—organized lobbies just like other political lobbies—argue for their continued inclusion in school budgets. At stake, as always, are jobs. Driver education is a classic but small-scale example. Think instead about the number of jobs generated by the need for "remediation" at all levels of the educational system, including college. If incentives supporting serious academic learning reduced the need for remediation, the chilling effect on employment of remedial teachers might rival that of the Cold War's end on military-related employment, and would be equally resisted.

Teachers and Students as Motivators

In this near vacuum of external incentives for scholastic exertion, almost unprecedented in the industrialized world, Americans have characteristically placed the greatest burden for generating incentives to learn on teachers and students. Perhaps the main task of the American teacher, a task that distinguishes her or him from teachers in many other countries, is the job not of teaching but of motivating students to want to learn—or at least motivating them to tolerate schooling without revolt. To be asked to motivate as well as to teach is daunting. It is equivalent to surgeons' having not only to operate but also to persuade patients not to walk out of the operating room. This responsibility is daunting also because good teaching is hard enough by itself, and society gives teachers so little support.

American pedagogy has traditionally emphasized the motivational function of teachers more than their instructional function. We hope teachers can motivate either by means of trained professional technique or by their charismatic personalities. But one way or the other, we expect them to do it. Without many external incentives to provoke mental exertion, the work of teaching is helped enormously if students try to learn because they want to learn.[2]

The central elements in the pedagogy of motivation have been a deep faith in the natural curiosity of children, especially younger children, and a deep faith in the strategy of building on existing student interests to develop new ones. Up to a point, it is hard to take issue with these propositions. Human beings clearly possess an abundance of curiosity and learn much of what they eventually know on their own without the need for any formal schooling. People of all ages also have plenty of interests derived from various sources that schoolpeople might tap for educational purposes.

Unfortunately, the endless efforts of teachers to build on existing interests and to presume endemic student curiosity have a long history of modest success and major disappointment. One problem is that serious academic work, at least at first, is often hard work and not always "interesting." This is especially true as students get older and are asked to remember and use what they have learned, to think about matters that have no sound-bite memorizable answers, and to confront material that is progressively more difficult. Students who excel in math or history rarely choose to do math problems or read history books in their spare time.

In addition, it is not easy to use existing interests to move students into new academic material because the new material is often unfamiliar and unconnected with the enthusiasms most of them have. Americans have long overrated the generative quality of children's "interests." Heroic efforts have tried to make academic learning entertaining, fun, and personally relevant in order to create interest. Sometimes this works. More often the unintended result is that complexity is removed, the material watered down, and the need for mental effort bypassed.

Another problem is that successful efforts to build on existing interests and natural curiosity tend to favor bright students from educated families who enter school with intellectual interests and skills that are already developed. Pedagogical intervention does not create new interests but accelerates existing ones. It is striking how disproportionately the interest-based "progressive education" movement has been supported by affluent and educated families.

A final problem is finding enough teachers with the skills to motivate youth to work and learn voluntarily. Some teachers can do this. Almost all schools have at least a few charismatic individuals with the ability to command the attention of students by the sheer force of their own unique personalities. Others induce students to put forth their best effort by showing their own commitment to working hard. The students don't want to let them down. "That motivates you back," one student explained. When a teacher asked his class to write an essay almost every night, "we were all willing to do it and try hard because we knew that the teacher was trying hard to get them all graded and back to us and to help us. But then if you have a teacher who's handing things back a month later, it's like, why should I try?" All schools covet great teachers, but unfortunately they are rare. We do not yet know how to produce them in large numbers, although the effort to learn how goes on and has happily attracted more imaginative researchers.

Just as American teachers are expected to motivate students, so students are expected to motivate themselves. This is the consequence of our choice-based educational system. We want schools to provide rich and varied opportunities for learning with minimal barriers to participation. But participation itself is voluntary. Voluntarism places an enormous burden on students and their families to seize opportunities through their own initiative.

Some groups routinely provide intrinsic educational incentives to most of their members because learning is a deep cultural tradition. Not many American schools, for example, have sustained a genuine intellectual community (as distinct from merely an academic one) without a critical mass of Jewish students. And everyone is aware of how Asian communities typically push their children to work hard.

Individual parents demonstrate to their children the pleasures of sustained academic work by the satisfactions they receive daily from vocations in which the active use of good education is regularly demanded. Parents also model the rewards of learning by personal reading, participating in the arts, or talking politics at the supper table. Some simply push their children to work hard at school as a normal part of the job of parenting—it is what they believe children need to do to get ahead or stay ahead.

Students from these groups or families are lucky. Intrinsic interest in learning, or at least motivation to work hard at learning, rubs off on them early. It is among the many tastes children acquire from family life in the course of growing up, tastes that are ordinary to them but unfamiliar and sometimes odd to students less fortunate.

Of course some students are naturally motivated to study and learn and others not motivated at all, regardless of family or group advantages or disadvantages. Teachers covet the self-starters who show genuine interest in the material, or who want to achieve, or who just enjoy meeting new challenges. But like superb teachers, these students are the exception rather than the rule. Not surprisingly, they often turn out to be quite proficient at the academic studies that hold their attention.

We greatly admire effective teachers and motivated students, but we should not be ashamed to admit that they are atypical. It seems foolish to place so many of our incentive eggs in these two baskets. Most American teachers have their hands full with problems of instruction without having to solve problems of basic motivation. Most American youth do not find demanding academic study either pleasurable or worth struggling with for the long-term benefits it conveys. It is not an activity they happily pursue on their own, nor an activity they work at because they believe serious learning will affect the quality of their future lives.

School reform must directly address how additional student incentives to learn can be added to America's modest current supply. Disconcertingly, incentives to work and learn appear only tangentially in many contemporary reform programs. Even so, most reform efforts have at least tacit positions on the issue.

Programs that advocate a larger governmental role in curriculum and assessment by the states or the federal government indirectly or directly aim to affect external student incentives. In different ways they try to transform no-stakes schooling into high-stakes schooling. Government mandates are by no means the only potential source of external student incentives. Colleges, even many of the selective ones, might explore how admissions requirements could be upgraded to encourage students to exert more mental effort while in school, without having devastating consequences for postsecondary enrollments. And those who employ high school graduates might examine how paying greater attention to high school achievement could make employees more productive in the long run.[3]

In contrast to these essentially top-down possibilities, other reform efforts contend that external carrot-and-stick approaches are less likely to build genuine, intrinsic incentives to learn than within-school efforts to improve teaching, curriculum, and student assessment. Granting individual schools and teachers more authority over curricular and budget decisions will, it is claimed, better engage students in learning because teachers will be freed from bureaucratic constraints and empowered to use individual and collective skills to motivate and instruct. In this view the best incentive to learn is a high-quality classroom experience. It may be the only way to make interest in learning lifelong and habitual instead of short-run grade-getting. Students have proven adept at sabotaging top-down mandates by doing just enough to satisfy the authorities and then promptly forgetting whatever they had "learned."

No one knows what effects these various ideas, combinations of them, or completely different notions might have on student incentives. But it seems reasonably clear that any successful effort to reshape student incentives must be powerful and many-faceted. Above all there must be more inducements from all corners for students to want to exert mental effort. The incentives are already many for most young Americans *not* to read, write, study, think, memorize, struggle, confront unfamiliar, complex problems, or converse about any of these matters outside class. Unless students long for admission to a selective college, no systemic incentives to exert themselves exist at all. The only positive incentives come from the accidents of birth, cultural traditions, or exposure to terrific teachers.

If all youth are to make an effort to learn to use their minds well, they must have clear reasons for changing familiar and pleasurable behavior to achieve that more difficult end. Equally important, changing their behavior must be seen to be in the immediate self-interest of agencies such as colleges or employers, whose opinions youth cannot afford to ignore. And schools themselves must have incentives to carry out with passion and focus the task of developing student intelligence. They too must win something for doing a good job.

The College Board System

A crucial asset of independent schools over the past century has been the looming omnipresence of college admission as a powerful student and parent incentive. In these schools student willingness to exert mental effort has not required eager youth engaged in academic study for the pleasures it gives; nor has it depended on superb teachers able to stimulate enthusiasm for the life of the mind. Prep schools have had their share of such students and teachers, of course, and always wish for more.

But they also have had many students willing to work, willing to give the material a fighting, grudging chance. One typical senior said that "the future" was the reason he worked hard at his studies. "You know that if you work hard in high school you can get into a good college and if you do well in college you can go on to a good career. You're just thinking about your future and you have to work for it. It just doesn't come." He never expressed real interest in his studies, only willingness to engage in them and try.

Although students often attribute their motivation to work to parents, peers, and teachers, lurking behind these close-by influences is the concern about college. A junior who thought the college incentive exerted "tons" of influence on him said his parents had been talking about college since freshman year. By sophomore year he was already visiting different schools. "You really start to worry about it."

The presence of this incentive in institutions defined as college preparatory should not be surprising. What was and is most significant is not the incentive itself, but how it began to be systematically mobilized to promote learning at the beginning of the twentieth century. What parents and students wanted for youth after school graduation—acceptance to certain colleges—became specifically contingent on how well they performed while in school. A desired goal for the future was directly linked to school academic performance. Incentives were utilized to create and sustain what were called academic standards.

It took an entirely new voluntary, nongovernmental organization, the College Entrance Examination Board, to organize student incentives as a lever to create and sustain school standards. From 1900, when it was founded, until 1942, the College Board administered a system of essay examinations that tightly linked the decision to admit a student to college with the standard of academic work done in school. A certain level of individual achievement virtually guaranteed admission to the college of one's choice. That tight linkage, rare in 1900 and rare today, was not easily achieved. Schools and colleges had to want it as much as families did—want it enough to cooperate and compromise with one another in ways they had not done before.

On the surface, the College Board was principally a treaty among colleges and between colleges and schools to solve logistical problems of college admission. When a market began to emerge for the modern independent school in the 1880s, many desirable colleges were simultaneously stiffening their entrance requirements. The pace and character of the changes differed according to what each institution aspired to become. But in most of the better-known private Northeastern colleges the trend was not only to demand more of students in traditional subjects, but to add requirements in "modern" subjects such as science and history, which began penetrating college curricula in the 1870s.

For tuition-dependent colleges the task was a difficult balancing act. They wished to attract more students just as their curricula began emphasizing the familiar modern subjects rather than religion and the classics. Professors of the newer subjects wished to teach students who had begun studying them while in school. They needed schools to offer those subjects and students to study them. How to get schools to supply both more freshmen and better-prepared freshmen was a vexing problem with several possible answers in the generation after the 1880s.

Most colleges needed live bodies to survive and consequently had virtually no admission requirements. For colleges with the luxury of entrance requirements, the most popular method was admission by certificate. This was a plan by which entire schools were approved or certified in advance by some external body—a state, a state university, a consortium of colleges. Cooperating colleges then agreed to admit any graduate recommended by the certified school.

Other colleges wanted greater control over the quality of entrants' preparation. A few actually established preparatory schools dedicated to meeting their own requirements—Hotchkiss for Yale, Lawrenceville for Princeton. An audacious proposal that Harvard absorb several existing prep schools, creating in effect an integrated K–16 program under one university authority, was seriously put forth.

But the more typical approach of these colleges was to have individual candidates take examinations, instead of certifying the schools they attended. This seemed a surer way to guarantee better-trained freshmen and force schools to teach what colleges wanted. The most vigorous defender of the examination system was Harvard's president Charles W. Eliot.

The emerging preparatory schools were strongly influenced both by the preferences of their well-off constituencies and by the colleges their graduates wished to attend. In curriculum matters they were clearly dominated by higher education—Eliot liked to say that "schools follow universities, and will be what universities make them." But college domination per se was not a major worry for prep schools. They really were, after all, college preparatory. Without that function a major reason for their existence would collapse. It did not occur to them that they would not be dominated in some academic way by higher education.[4]

Besides, most of the qualities that gave each school a distinct personality—its religious character, the ideals of its head, the role of sports, and so on—were not controlled by the colleges. The schools had enormous freedom to do their own thing in precisely the areas of greatest importance to them. "Learning from books is but one small part in the educational process," sniffed Riverdale's Frank Hackett. Most school heads agreed. Academic studies did not exert anywhere near the force they do today.[5]

The major strain on school-college relations at the turn of the century was not college domination but the chaos caused by the incredible diversity of college admission and entrance examination requirements. The head of Andover, a relatively large school that sent graduates to many colleges, complained in 1885 that "out of over forty boys preparing for college next year we have more than twenty Senior classes." Unreasonable diversity in admissions requirements inconvenienced not just universities wishing to increase enrollments and raise entrance standards, but also and especially the prep schools. So it was no surprise that a new agency, the College Entrance Examination Board, was created by the universities with representation from the schools. It prepared syllabi defining the content of major secondary subject areas and annual examinations based on the syllabi.

For four decades after 1900, the College Board did far more than just standardize admissions examinations among a small number of well-known colleges. It organized an intricate and coherent system of academic incentives to support serious academic standards. (The word "system" was used during the Board's heyday by its most astute observer to describe its many interconnected parts.) The system linked what students wanted—admission to the college of their choice—with what they had to do to get it, pass College Board examinations. The Board also organized school practice so students would perform well enough to demonstrate that their schools were effective and their standards sufficiently high. The Board pushed students to work hard and schools to do the same.[6]

Independent schools were an essential part of this system. Many relied on it for their very survival—it was perhaps their most important secret educational weapon. Their proclaimed identity as "independent" disguised their profound dependence on a larger voluntary system, a system few other Americans knew about because few used it.

The increasing complexity of college entrance examinations gave a tremendous boost to the few schools (including some public high schools) that specialized in preparing students to take them. Sixty percent of the small group of 973 candidates who sat for the first College Board examinations in 1901 were from private schools. By 1920, most of the important Eastern colleges used the Board's exams and had abolished their own separate admissions examinations. In 1925, when the number of candidates approached 19,000, the private school fraction was 70 percent.

Porter Sargent wrote in 1915 that "the private school is still almost essential . . . for the special training that has been necessary to enter the older universities . . . so that we find today at Princeton eighty percent, at Yale seventy percent, and at Harvard fifty percent of the students prepared at private schools." These fractions rose in the years before World War II. Fifty-seven percent of the Harvard class of 1944 came from prep schools, as did 85 percent of the Princeton class of 1934. Two schools—Lawrenceville and Hill—produced as many Princeton freshmen as all public high schools combined. The College Boards gave the prep schools a near monopoly over elite college preparation.

Years later a veteran schoolman summarized the system's workings. Parents sought out an independent preparatory school "to do a specific and limited job—the necessary intensive preparation of the student for the rigorous college board examinations." Prep schools occupied "a peculiar middle-man position in a process that was generally binding as long as the colleges and universities kept to their high academic standards and required for entrance success in these college boards." The "selling point" of independent education was a "virtual guarantee to place the young student in any college or university, however difficult the requirements."[7]

Four closely related characteristics account for the system's relative success in promoting hard academic work among often reluctant youth. All have close parallels with contemporary efforts to stimulate incentives and raise standards. First, the system developed and sustained a rough consensus about the content of academic standards—what college-bound students should know and be able to do. Second, it converted these standards into credible examinations with predictable consequences for individual students. Third, the standards and examinations directly influenced school curriculum, teaching, hiring practices, and professional development. Finally, the system fully understood its responsibility to deal with students of very diverse academic abilities. Its job was to prepare as many students as possible to undertake college work, not to select out the brightest among them.

Standards as Curricular Frameworks

Professor Carl Brigham of Princeton, a wise longtime observer of the College Board and principal creator of the SAT, admitted without apology in 1933 that the Board's major function was as an "institutional control." It controlled participating schools by the academic standards on which its yearly examinations were based. These standards were annually published descriptions of the essential concepts and themes in each of the fields where the Board examined. Called *Definition of the Requirements* for most of the 1900–41 period, they spelled out in greater or lesser detail, according to the subject or moment in time, what students should know and be able to do. Brigham described the *Definition* in 1934 as a "framework" in order to distinguish broad domains of knowledge from specific examination questions.[8]

Decades later one is struck by two aspects of the annual definitions of subject requirements. They were quite ambitious educationally considering the varied academic population they were intended to affect. They also embodied broad consensus among creators and users about the general nature, if not the particulars, of what academic standards should mean. The Board exerted a clear influence because it was a voluntary association run and used by people with roughly similar views and interests. Both aspects of the annual *Definition*—ambition and consensus—had similar sources.

There was general consensus behind what high standards meant because the individuals who established them shared many values about the primacy of academic education organized by the disciplines. These individuals were drawn primarily from higher education and particularly from various commissions of national scholarly associations. They included many of the most famous scholars of their day. In spite of disagreements about what was most important to learn within their fields, they shared a general ideal that high educational standards and high academic standards were one and the same. The College Board did not have to debate whether the disciplines should be the centerpiece of middle school and secondary education. Independent-school people generally assented. A headmaster believed it was self-evident that the quality of a person's mind was determined by the kind of material he or she directed toward it. "If he confines his reading to trash, he will be a trivial person."[9]

The standards of knowledge and skill embodied in each *Definition* were regarded outside Eastern private schools and a few public schools as out of tune with the needs, and certainly the preferences, of most students. Most colleges and schools had nothing to do with the Board's program. They had no use for an array of college admissions examinations based on academic school courses. The famous 1918 "Cardinal Principles" of secondary education, the leading public school manifesto of educational purpose in the first half of the century, allowed the academic or cognitive domain only one of seven school goals ("command of fundamental processes"). The College Board would have liked more schools and colleges to have accepted its examination program because student registration fees provided most of its income.

But prep schools were not evangelists promoting the cause of serious academic work for all American youth. They were not (nor are they now) reformers seeking converts. If anything they tended to promote themselves as the last refuge against educational barbarism. "We hold that every idea must be made as interesting as possible," one prep school advocate submitted, "but we refuse to water down its essence for the pseudo-democracy of leveling and mediocrity." Self-congratulatory arrogance was hardly an effective counterattack against the rampant anti-intellectualism that in fact plagued much of American education.[10]

The idea of high academic standards took on an exclusionary and old-fashioned tinge when the truth was almost the opposite. In fact, the College Board exams held a varied academic population accountable to serious and similar demands. The academic standards represented by each *Definition* were a triumphant victory of modern subjects—history, English, science, modern languages—over the traditional domination of the classics and formal mathematics. They were a victory for progressive and democratic forces, not for forces of reaction and exclusivity.

Curricular wars were fought within virtually all the disciplines. They ranged from the importance to be given this or that topic to the balance between mandated coverage and teacher freedom. In English, for example, the *Definition* gradually moved toward less prescription of content. The early English *Definition* specified one list of books about which students were to know "the most important parts" (for example, *The Merchant of Venice* and *The Last of the Mohicans*). It also specified another list they had to know in much greater detail (for example, *Macbeth* and Burke's speech *Conciliation with America*). But by the end of the 1920s a Board Commission on English won a less restrictive conception. The English *Definition* for 1934 had no required books and a simplified overview: "The requirement in English is designed to develop in the student (1) the ability to read with understanding, (2) knowledge and judgment of literature, and (3) accurate thinking and power in oral and written expression."

Those involved furiously debated whether or not the changes lowered or raised standards, but the debate occurred within a context of basic agreement. The new "suggested" six-page reading list included fourteen Shakespeare, eight Shaw, and two O'Neill plays, four Conrad novels, and contemporary poets such as Frost and Yeats. Teachers were advised that the composition tasks would "assume continuous and thorough training in mechanics." The *Definition* specified that this training implied "mastery" of such matters as grammar, punctuation, spelling, and vocabulary and "a command of varied and flexible sentence forms." The instruction required to produce such mastery, teachers were told, "necessitates constant and painstaking practice by the candidate in criticism and revision of his own written work." In such ways as this, subject by subject, the Board defined and refined what it meant by academic standards.[11]

The College Boards

The College Board examinations were created by committees of "examiners" with substantial private school representation. They were largely of the essay variety and usually three hours in length. The College Boards converted *Definition* standards into concrete tasks that defined how student performance would be demonstrated. They also extended the notion of standards to define what levels of performance were considered outstanding and minimally acceptable. The exams were administered nationwide in test centers during one hectic week each June. By 1940 more than 37,000 June examinations were taken in 36 subjects at 318 test centers.

The examinations were not only created outside individual schools; they were scored outside schools by teachers and professors who did not know the students whose work they evaluated. External assessment was done by hundreds of "readers" assembled at Columbia University during a week soon after the tests were given. Nicholas Murray Butler, the Board's first secretary, was pleased that "the one criticism that the board could not afford to face, namely, that the questions set were too easy, has not been made." Only 59 percent of the exams received passing scores in the program's first year.

But this did not mean that the examinations were unusually demanding. Initially, the traditional 0–100 grading scale was adopted, with 60 defined as the minimal passing grade. This made it possible for all candidates to do equally well or equally poorly. They were graded against a single standard or criterion determined by the readers rather than compared against each other. A later, test-savvy generation would call the Board's assessment method "criterion-referenced."[12]

Annual academic essay examinations produced and assessed outside schools were common in Europe but almost unique in America. They profoundly affected participating schools, mostly for the better. Frank Ashburn of Brooks School called the Board's exams the prep schools' "staunchest ally" in standard-setting. He believed that they "probably did more than any other single factor to emphasize the value of good teaching." Wilson Farrand, a College Board leader since 1900 and headmaster of Newark Academy in New Jersey, thought the Boards were strongest where most American high schools were weakest. They provided standards of "thoroughness and genuine mastery of the subjects taught" instead of "sloppiness and superficiality."

The exams promoted thoroughness and mastery in part because they created incentives and standards for teachers. Their external creation and assessment introduced an outside judgment about teachers' performance as well as students' performance. The chairman of the Secondary Education Board (SEB) praised the College Board in 1936 for its "guiding and standardizing and controlling effect on school curricula and teaching." He did not fear a loss of teacher or school autonomy, but welcomed the stimulation of external accountability.[13]

The headmaster of Gilman School regarded the College Boards as a "measuring stick" against which he could raise the educational standards of his school. They made it possible to "use continuing poor averages in any particular subject as a whip on masters who taught the subject." Teachers predictably responded by developing extensive practice or coaching sessions in which examinations from previous years were carefully reviewed. The "almost airtight system" developed to make Gilman boys study served its purpose well in the judgment of the school's historian. It raised educational standards from the level of "average good schools to the level of the highest in the country."[14]

The thoroughness and mastery produced by the College Boards also exposed a classic tension about standards. On the one hand, the examinations often encouraged memorization and cramming. Topics and sometimes questions were repeated from year to year. They could to some extent be studied for in advance. Sometimes knowledge alone could get students through without the need to demonstrate much analytical capacity of the sort a later generation would call "higher-order thinking." To some this was a weakness.

On the other hand, the examinations improved academic achievement. Many students needed a practical incentive to work hard. The link between the Boards and college admission provided that incentive. In 1932 the headmaster of St. Paul Academy in Minnesota believed that the exams made lazy privileged boys work hard for the first time because they had to. The mental exertion required was regarded as a good thing in itself—an outcome schools valued as a worthy lifetime habit quite aside from whatever momentary academic achievement it produced. In particular, the examinations could be attempted by students with limited academic skills for whom "uphill thinking is the best way to think." They enabled "hard and specific work" to pay off.

Furthermore, prep school proponents emphasized that the examinations, like the *Definition*, were constantly improving in quality. Standards were becoming more ambitious. Gilman's founding headmaster vigorously denied in 1932 that they could be passed by candidates who had "only facts in their possession and no knowledge of their meaning nor power to think." On the contrary, the Boards were "tests of power which require a knowledge of facts." Power to think required knowledge. The head of Detroit Country Day School believed that the English examination had become "a test of creativeness and appreciation."

The last three-hour English essay examination ever given by the Board, based on the revised English *Definition,* lends backing to this assertion. In June 1941 one of four questions asked students to read W. B. Yeats's poem "An Irish Airman Foresees His Death." They had to respond to eight different assertions about the poem, and would be graded on understanding the poem, accuracy in writing, and clarity in writing. Forty minutes. The question combined a concern for standards, for differences among the students, and for sensitivity to the real-world times in which they lived.[15]

Teachers and Professional Development

The examinations pressed teachers to perform to an outside common standard. The system clearly opposed the idea that teachers could or should define their fields as they wished. Instead, they taught to their predictions and hopes about how the next examinations might resemble those of prior years. A historian of the College Board believed that "individualism in American schools in the 1900's had so far run riot that the establishment of a uniform standard of excellence had become not only desirable but even obligatory." At the same time a teacher bitterly complained that "slight chance for continued professional service has that teacher who fails to 'get results' in the 'College Boards,' valuable and inspiring as his instruction may otherwise be."[16]

But there were compensations for teachers who saw their classroom freedom somewhat eroded. One was that externally set and scored examinations tended to make students and teachers allies rather than adversaries. Instead of grading final exams, teachers crossed their fingers and rooted for everyone. The objective was to move all students forward, not to stress differences in attainment. Gilman's historian concluded, "If everyone passed . . . the master was considered to have done a fine job."[17]

Another compensation was that thousands of the small cohort of private school teachers were not just passive recipients of College Board commands but active participants in the grand enterprise of creating and grading the examinations. This was surely one of the most powerful professional-development experiences in American educational history. It was task oriented, deadly serious, and enormous fun. Teachers and heads welcomed the close ties that entrance examinations promoted with well-known colleges. They enjoyed the sense that in some respects they were all part of the same cause, profession, system—that the boundaries between good secondary schools and good colleges were permeable and not divided by high walls of differing status. This gave them a feeling of membership in a large and respected professional community—a feeling of dignity denied many American teachers.

Most of the "examiners" constituting the crucial committees that created the examinations were always drawn from colleges. Yet in 1941, the final year of the program, private schools provided more than a quarter of them—19 examiners, compared with 42 drawn from higher education and 13 from public schools. Even more impressive was the prep school domination of June readers. These were the teachers who descended on Columbia dorms and Barnard dining halls to confront thousands of blue books. In 1932, 313 private school teachers were readers along with 112 public school teachers and 216 college professors.

The huge June gathering resembled an "educational congress." Between 1900 and 1941, it was perhaps the largest regular occasion at which high school and college teachers struggled together at a common task and from which teachers brought back to their schools helpful criticisms and broader points of view. The College Board believed that the annual reading session "helped immeasurably in upholding standards," but perhaps more important was the colleagueship, stimulation, and prestige it gave to participating teachers.

Readership was a professional plum, readers hated to rotate off, and public school teachers resented private school dominance. (A practical problem was that many public schools were still in session when the examinations were read.) Their protests led to a 1934 College Board decision to change the reader ratio toward a goal of 4:3:2 among colleges, private schools, and public schools. Yet in 1941 more than 42 percent of readers were still drawn from independent schools. To the end, readership remained largely a private school privilege.

The fact that a large fraction of private school students took the exams and many private school teachers served as readers solidified the loyalty of many independent schools to the College Board system. The system seemed to work for the schools. Their students decisively outperformed public school students on the examinations during the 1901–1941 period, and most graduates went on to attend the colleges of their choice.[18]

Some private schools even hoped to incorporate the College Board system of coherent instruction into K–12 education itself. They wanted clear-cut performance standards operating in the middle of precollegiate schooling, not just at the end of it. They believed that high standards required student incentives and formal accountability. Even for sixth grade they did not shy away from these ideas. Their dream was to regulate the transition from elementary to secondary school just as the College Board regulated the transition from high school to college.

In 1924 a group of schools founded the Secondary School Entrance Examination Board (soon to be renamed the Secondary Education Board). It created examinations in middle school academic subjects—English, mathematics, French, and Latin—designed to be taken by students seeking to enter secondary schools in grades seven, eight, and nine. The SEB chairman emphasized that "uniformity in the essentials of certain subjects universally taught" in no way contradicted the proud traditions of freedom and diversity among independent schools. Although "standardization imposed from without" could be deadening, it was a completely different matter for a group of schools to arrive at a "mutual understanding regarding the fundamentals of courses common to all." By 1928 more than one hundred independent schools were members, although the SEB never acquired the financial stability and educational influence of its progenitor.[19]

Student Variety

Before the 1950s few students gained admission to prep schools on the grounds of special academic promise or aptitude. Committed to preparing most of their students for colleges such as Harvard, Yale, and Princeton, the schools contained a mix of the academically gifted, the average, and the truly slow. They enrolled far more scholastic diversity in the first part of the century than they do today. Some students were enrolled literally at birth, when gender was the only selective factor. (The story was that St. Paul's fathers enrolled their male newborns by regular letter, whereas Groton fathers sent telegrams. Without amniocentesis, it was impractical to enroll candidates for single-sex schools while in utero.) Years later McGeorge Bundy recalled his schooldays at Groton in the 1930s. "If you weren't a notorious and incorrigibly stupid or lazy person you could go to any college you wanted. You really could."

All this was accepted at the time as simply the way things were. Prep schools catered to an economic class, not to an academic class. They routinely assumed that public high school graduates who attended prestigious colleges were, on the whole, more able and motivated than their own students. Frederick Winsor, Gilman's founding head and later the founding head of Middlesex School near Boston, told a Harvard alumni meeting in 1930 that the job of private schools was to "give an education to all the sons of such men as you if you want to send them to us, not to a selected few of your sons." It was not the "bright boy who specially needs the best and wisest of handling," Winsor went on, "but the boys below the average in intelligence." He assured the sympathetic crowd that true leadership in later life depended less on brainpower than on "determination and fight and character."[20]

Most independent-school commentators followed Winsor's reasoning. Their institutions should be broadly accessible to those who could pay. Being bright conveyed no special cachet. Some independent-school leaders trumpeted the "true talent of the slow, cautious, and searching mind" or unfavorably compared the "facile, lazy student as against the hard-working slower student." Slower students might not excel at their studies or care much about them, but they would often exert considerable leadership in extracurricular and social activities in school and college. The prep schools were undefensive about the academic quality of their student bodies. Their students could usually enter any college they wished if they worked hard.[21]

This was one of the most significant assets of the College Board system. Its essay examinations were not designed to be impossibly difficult. The examination game could be played for genuinely "high stakes" without seeming to be beyond the power of diligent students to control. The idea was not to keep students out of college but to ensure that they knew enough to stay in.

The College Board essay examinations, though regarded as more rigorous than the written examinations of individual colleges that had preceded them, were constructed with a broad student-ability range in mind. They attempted to pull everyone up to a minimum standard in the possession of knowledge and the capacity to use it. Until the late 1930s, few influential educators—and extremely few schoolpeople—cared about winnowing the brightest students from the merely proficient ones. Harvard's President Conant defended the essay exams as "particularly necessary" for students "of somewhat less than the highest" academic ability.

Of course there were limits to what could be accomplished when academic raw material was extremely weak. The secretary of the College Board lamented in 1919 that some students with abominable Board scores aspired to college only for social advantages and should not be encouraged to advance beyond high school. The most thorough survey of boarding schools of its time found large differences in the average age of graduating seniors in 1921 at certain boarding schools compared with the Cleveland, Ohio, public high schools. Cleveland's average graduating age of 17.1 years contrasted with Lawrenceville School's average of 18.7. The reason for so many "overage" private school seniors was parental desire that children with limited academic capacity attempt the Boards just one more time. Older students got better scores. If they passed, tutoring schools in towns like Cambridge and New Haven were ready to assist them with the greater rigors of college work.

A private school research group sardonically concluded in 1933 that the "non-academic pupil" had been an issue for years, but that research had been deferred because "just now many schools are engaged in laboratory experience with that very problem, after which a thorough study will have a better point of departure." Despite these concerns about the limits of educability, what was most significant about the relation between the College Board system and student aptitude was the expectation that a wide variety of aptitudes could succeed on a serious academic examination if the stakes were high and the preparation specific.[22]

In 1942 important elements of the College Board system were dropped as college priorities changed. The old system ceased to exist. Some aspects were restored in altered form during the 1950s as the Advanced Placement Program. AP courses survive as the best systemic example of incentive-driven, externally assessed standard-setting in American education.

But the earlier, more elaborate system has been largely forgotten or stereotyped. This is unfortunate even though many of its procedures were primitive first steps. We should not remember the old system to repeat it or to make excessive claims for its effectiveness. Nonetheless, it contained several provocative features of great interest to anyone concerned with student incentives, academic standards, and assessment.

The old College Board system was voluntary and nongovernmental. Certain schools and colleges had particular problems that could be solved by inventing a new collaborative regulatory body. The new system was remarkably broad-based and democratic regarding student aptitude. The presumption was that varied student abilities could rise to meet the same standard, although it would be easier for some and harder for others. The system rested on a consensus that valued high academic standards and assumed that this consensus existed within an educational culture broader than that of individual schools. It was legitimate, given this consensus, to use external assessment to press both teachers and students to work harder than they otherwise would have done.

These features gave prep schools considerable educational advantages. They indicated systemic support for student incentives to learn. Privileged students became doubly privileged. Even if they were lazy and average, they were part of a system that forced them to work. This is a bitter irony. American schooling gave educational incentives to students who already were its most privileged, but few similar incentives to anyone else.

6

The Collision of Standards and Meritocracy

On Sunday, December 7, 1941, the "Three Musketeers"—as the admissions directors of Harvard, Yale, and Princeton were affectionately called—were meeting informally at the New Jersey home of the Princeton director. When the news from Pearl Harbor arrived after lunch, the men decided that the sudden war emergency might permit them to achieve instantaneously what one admitted would otherwise have been "a long hard fight": the complete abandonment of the College Board's program of three-hour June essay examinations. They conspired to destroy the central element in the coherent system that had prevailed for forty years.

Days later the three universities announced that, instead of the June essays, all candidates would be required to take a series of short-answer, multiple-choice tests, including the SAT, given on a single Saturday in April. Later, after other colleges announced their intention to follow the lead of the Big Three, the College Board decided to cancel the June 1942 essay examinations altogether. They were never given again. The decision marked an era. The system that had governed college admissions, student incentives, and academic standards in many prep schools since 1900 was suddenly no more.

Like many dramatic events that occur without apparent warning, the abolition of the old College Boards was actually no surprise. For years the perspective of many colleges on the purpose of college admissions procedures had diverged from that of the older generation that first organized the Board. The latter saw the Board's mission as bringing order out of the chaos of varied admission requirements. Equally important, the *Definition of the Requirements,* school courses based on them, essay examinations, and external assessment methods were all designed to sustain a minimum of academic standards in participating schools.

In contrast, college admissions officers increasingly regarded the Board's job as enlarging the pool of applicants who could do college work and especially the pool of applicants who were likely to perform well in college. They cared much less about school instruction or standards. Indeed, they gradually realized that traditional Board concerns in this area were now contrary to their own interests. Eventually their perspective—"the role of the test as an accurate index of pupil ability rather than as a means of controlling the curriculum"—won out.

The older perspective meshed nicely with the goals of most independent schools. The new one did not. Curriculum-driven college entrance examinations gave prep schools and some public schools a near monopoly over access to the best-known Eastern colleges. But tests that did not depend on prior specific study could end the monopoly, and thereby threaten the incentives independent schools used to mobilize mental exertion among the young. When the old essay examinations were abolished, Millicent McIntosh of New York's Brearley School observed, "At one stroke the special privileges of the private school student disappeared."[1]

Breaking the College Admissions Monopoly

Powerful converging forces, especially the psychological testing movement and the awareness of educational inequality, pushed prestigious colleges in the 1930s to rethink their use of entrance examinations. The essay exams were intended to demonstrate levels of previous school achievement and training. They were indicators of past performance, of what individuals had learned and how hard they had worked. The exams also assessed how well schools taught a curriculum and how hard they pressed students. Success on these indicators was what schools meant by high academic standards. If this was what colleges wanted examinations to measure, then the tests were fairly satisfactory instruments.

But if they wanted tests to predict how students would actually perform in college, they were notoriously unreliable. And prediction was increasingly what colleges wanted. Fortuitously, new measurement instruments were suddenly available from psychologists and test developers—not from scholars in academic disciplines—that justifiably claimed much greater predictive power than the essay exams. By the 1920s, the rapidly expanding psychological testing movement had convinced most psychologists and many admissions officers that intelligence was mainly innate and conveniently measurable.

Statistical studies from the Big Three and similar institutions revealed that private school students with higher Board scores than public school students were soon surpassed academically in college by public school graduates. Other studies used the new aptitude tests to demonstrate that public school graduates in prestigious colleges, on average, were brighter than their private school counterparts. Analyses of the Harvard classes of 1932 and 1933 showed that 40 percent of public school alumni graduated from Harvard with honors, compared with 20 percent of private school alumni. The latter were twice as likely to fail to graduate for academic or disciplinary reasons. The College Boards clearly gave an admissions advantage to students who could afford the schooling needed to prepare for them, but were a barrier to college for many able students who could not.[2]

At last colleges realized that things did not have to be this way forever. They could be changed. Well before 1941 many small cracks had appeared in the old system, and they were widening rapidly. In 1916, for example, the Board introduced "comprehensive" essay examinations as an alternative to the regular kind. These were not linked to particular courses but covered entire fields of knowledge assessed at the end of high school. The Board hoped the new exams would appeal to more students because they were not tied to exact topics specified in the *Definition of the Requirements*. They were also designed to be more challenging for able students.

The central question asked by the Board's regular examinations was how much a student had learned in the past. Yet the answer to that question, the Board's secretary pointed out, might be wholly unrelated to a student's "originality, imagination, or ability to meet a new situation." Dull candidates who worked long and hard might do better on a Board examination than bright candidates who did not. A more interesting question was how much a candidate was capable of learning. Capacity to learn depended on "mental gifts," which the Board's regular examinations were not designed to reveal. Comprehensive examinations might do a better job.

An even superior method was just around the corner. In 1926 the Board introduced the short-answer, multiple-choice SAT. One of the most famous products of professional testmakers, the SAT promised to identify talented students regardless of the education they had previously received. The SAT was perceived as a democratic mechanism to rescue able students who had attended poor schools and to assist colleges in differentiating mentally superior students from the merely well trained. The SAT proved so popular among public schools and colleges that it was given in April as well as June for scholarship candidates, and was joined in the late 1930s by one-hour, short-answer "Achievement" tests in various subject fields.

Another enormous crack in the old essay system appeared in 1936, when its familiar 0–100 scoring scale was abandoned in favor of the 200–800 scale of the SAT. The new method no longer ranked students against a common standard. College admissions purposes would best be served by "a score which indicates how a candidate stands with respect to the total number of candidates taking Board examinations." No longer could everyone do well by exhibiting proficiency above a certain level. The fear of admissions and financial aid officers was that students might score about the same. The new "norm-referenced" scoring would create a student pecking order. Informed admission and financial aid decisions required test results that separated students from one another.[3]

Arguments favoring objective tests were overwhelming. They promoted fairness and democratic access, since they required no special courses or demanding standards in schools. Their very nonintrusiveness into school affairs was touted as a major advantage, especially when the large, untapped public school market was considered. Why should colleges "control" schools anyway? By 1948 the director of the College Board concluded that the new policy of "minimum interference with curricula" represented a "complete abandonment of the position which defined requirements in each subject as a frame of reference." The Board was out of the business of standard-setting.

The new tests were also inexpensive to administer—a serious financial consideration, given the large cost of bringing hundreds of readers to Columbia each June. They could be scored rapidly, making quick decisions possible. They seemed to predict college performance better than essay exams and contained no element of human subjectivity in scoring. The head of the College Board claimed in 1943 that the best way to assess writing was not to have students write but to have them answer multiple-choice questions.

By the time the College Board dropped the essay examinations altogether, they were being taken by only a minority of College Board registrants. Yet 65 percent of those who took the essay exams in 1941 were from independent schools. In 1944 the number of College Board candidates from public schools surpassed the number of prep school candidates for the first time. By 1949 the College Board's annual reports stopped breaking out independent schools as a separate statistical category. The old monopoly was decisively broken. In 1990 only about 5 percent of those who took the SAT were from independent schools.[4]

No university combined all these different tendencies more fully than Harvard—a desire for more students from public schools and especially more able students, an infatuation with the SAT as a scientific and democratic predictor of collegiate performance, a deep suspicion of the social impact of the private school admissions monopoly, and a disinterest in school standards verging on boredom. No important university's actions better clarified how these attitudes would affect the future college admissions fate of private school students.

Under President Conant, Harvard vigorously used the SAT and other methods to find the natural aristocracy of talent that Conant hoped to rescue from poor schools. In addition, the Harvard administration almost single-handedly provided much of the leadership for the postwar growth of the testing industry, including the impetus for the creation of Educational Testing Service. Harvard was breathtakingly candid about where its priorities lay. Richard M.

Gummere, its admissions "Musketeer" and a former private school headmaster, perfectly summarized the long-term meaning of the shift from essays to the SAT and Achievements. "Learning in itself has ceased to be the main factor [in college admissions]," he told a private school audience in 1943. "The aptitude of the pupil is now the leading consideration."

After the war, the reliance upon promise rather than training had the desired effect. Applications everywhere shot up as Americans surged unexpectedly toward college. About 28,000 high school students participated in the various College Board examinations in 1941. By 1952 the numbers surpassed 100,000 and tripled in the next four years. Of the 1,181 final applicants to Harvard for the fall of 1941, 1,092 candidates were accepted and 1,004 enrolled. This was not exactly selective admissions. But by 1952, the new admissions dean, W. J. Bender, reported a genuine revolution. For the first time in its history Harvard could "consciously shape the make-up of our student body" because it had a real surplus of qualified applicants over places. Echoing Gummere, Bender said, "In effect we now admit students on the basis of ability and promise and a secondary school diploma. Little attention is paid to the content of their secondary school programs."

As prep school enrollment percentages plummeted at Harvard— from 57 percent of freshmen in 1941 to 32 percent in 1980—Bender reported that the number of freshmen who fully met official entrance requirements at the time of matriculation was also dropping. But admissions authorities believed that any reemphasis on the content of secondary education would only "reverse the general trend of recent years towards an abler and more nationally representative student body." McGeorge Bundy, the dean of the faculty of arts and sciences at Harvard after his Groton schooldays, fittingly proclaimed meritocracy triumphant in 1956. "The really bright boy is desirable in the college, even if the schools have hopelessly mismanaged his educational training up to the age of seventeen or eighteen. The untrained boy of real brilliance is more valuable to us than the dull boy who has been intensely trained. Therefore, we are committed to the notion of a talent search."

At first the decline in private school percentages at Harvard and similar colleges did not affect the prep schools very much, for colleges were also expanding in size. But in the mid-1950s the actual number of prep school freshmen at Harvard began to decline—from 537 males in the Class of 1957 to a low of 292 males in the Class of 1985. Since these changes were not accompanied by a drop in prep school applications, the impact of the new policies was obvious. The old incentives were not applicable. No longer were there subjects to study that, if mastered to specified levels as evinced through examinations, would lead almost automatically to Harvard and similar colleges. The issue of incentives became problematic, as did the issue of what special advantages modern prep schools conveyed on their graduates.[5]

Prep Schools on Their Own: The Standards Dilemma

Prep schools were not serious political actors in the College Board drama that affected them so deeply. They had never been official members of the Board, which was controlled by a few universities. But the problem facing defenders of the status quo was not only their lack of clout but also the fact that their arguments seemed quaint and amusingly out of touch with the times. The most important issue in the minds of the protesting prep schools, for example, was their responsibility for maintaining educational standards. From the standpoint of elite colleges, the school standards issue was anachronistic and silly. Dean Bundy cared about who students were, not about what schools did. It was easy to laugh at the idea of standards; for many, they meant nothing more than the habits of a privileged class—educational manners analogous to table manners.

But many prep schools believed that standards were their central justification. It was standards that kept them linked tightly to serious higher education, giving their work meaning and dignity that were rarely associated with schoolkeeping in the United States. Frank Ashburn argued solemnly that a new burden of responsibility had been placed on independent education as a result of the College Board's abdication of responsibility. "Almost by definition," he proclaimed, "we *are* interested in standards. By inheritance we are custodians of the idea that if native ability is important, so is good teaching and so are all the overtones and undertones implied in the disciplinary values of liberal education."

Such prep school leaders lamented the collapse of the old system mainly because they regarded maintaining standards as a cultural problem requiring more than just committed individual schools. They believed all schools needed external, societal supports to get students to exert mental effort. It was tough to do this in a vacuum, especially in America and even in the protected world of independent education. To the extent that the College Board constructively influenced teaching, curriculum, and student incentives in the schools, defenders of the old system welcomed outside interference. Whereas some educators proclaimed that prep schools were free at last from college domination and could maintain standards "without benefit of a shot in the arm each June from the College Board," others regarded such optimism as misguided and the freedom as bittersweet.

The danger was precisely that all responsibility for standards would rest on what schools did in isolation. A thoughtful veteran English teacher, Louis Zahner, concluded that the reduction of specific college entrance requirements ironically created a more ominous form of college domination than had occurred under the earlier system. By not telling schools what to do, colleges influenced school behavior—largely to legitimize their making fewer demands on students—much more deeply than they ever had before. The older exams, argued Hart Fessenden of Fessenden School near Boston, had been a "rallying point" for schools. He feared a decline in the quality of teaching if there were no formal examinations to point toward, and if courses were not kept "vigorous" by the standards and prestige of the College Board and the SEB.[6]

The chairman of the SEB, Arthur S. Roberts of St. George's School in Rhode Island, freely acknowledged that aptitude tests surpassed traditional achievement exams "as prophesy." But they had a vicious effect on school curricula and student incentives. They fostered the idea that "solid work done is of little value and that a high grade of aptitude may erase the need to cover ground in the traditional subjects." Ashburn rose to new metaphorical heights to warn colleges— and not a silly warning it was—that their focus on aptitude rather than training would one day come back to haunt them. "Unless the schools build their own dikes, the colleges will, in a space of years, be inundated by a flood of sparkling, white-capped brilliance which will form marshland on the campuses: unharnessed, unlinked to power and purpose." Colleges would rue the day when they had to provide training in basic skills and cultural background that earlier they had expected from schools.[7]

Such arguments had little persuasive power. The dynamic operating in selective college admissions—a talent search rather than a search for the well trained—was beginning to operate within prep schools as well, especially at the point of transition between elementary and secondary education. Applications to many independent schools were booming. They could pick and choose more than ever before, but they rarely utilized the written examinations of the SEB— examinations modeled on the old College Boards. In 1947 fewer than half of the SEB member schools took any part in its examination program. Prep schools seemed to be allowing their own standards to slip at exactly the moment when they could have raised them.[8]

Meritocracy in the Schools

The reason was that many independent secondary schools wanted more students and more able students, just like colleges. The largest source of these students was public elementary schools, but these had rarely heard of SEB examinations, much less prepared for them in sixth, seventh, or eighth grade. *Huckleberry Finn* and *Gulliver's Travels* were suggested sixth-grade English reading, and examinations in first-year Latin and French (two hours each) were offered based on seventh-grade study of those subjects. Such texts and subjects were not curriculum staples in typical public middle schools.

Most independent secondary schools admitted students on the basis of aptitude tests or no tests at all, thereby undercutting the few elementary schools that took the SEBs seriously. At a meeting of elementary and secondary admissions officers in 1946, a representative from Choate School in Connecticut admitted that a middle school curriculum that prepared for the SEBs acted to "hold up the standards for both sides." Such a curriculum kept elementary schools on task and created a performance floor for secondary schools. He further admitted, "If the SEBs were dropped, the standards would drop." But rigidly demanding them of all candidates was impractical. No public school and few private school boys outside the East would ever come to Choate if it had such a policy.

Someone in the audience asked how the two groups "amalgamated" at Choate—those who had prepared through SEB syllabi and those who had not. The school's representative replied that the realistic difference was "between able boys and slow boys, rather than between boys prepared in one way or another." One shocked listener retorted that the issue should not be how Choate tried to attract able students; the issue was "mediocrity" in elementary curriculum and instruction, as against "the setting of a higher standard which public schools might follow." In this view Choate abandoned the standards cause in the same way and for the same reasons as Harvard.[9]

The head of the SEB worried about decreasing revenues caused by declining exam sales, but was more concerned about the head-on collision between standards and meritocracy. Arthur Roberts admitted that it was natural for schools to accept "bright unprepared boys" instead of "rather dull trained boys, who can pass our exams because the elementary school teachers have been able and required hard work." But the basic issue was: "Shall secondary schools and the colleges follow their own interest and educate only the bright?" Or had they an obligation to "stiffen education by insisting on achievement before advancement?"

Roberts believed the entire system of education would be sabotaged if Americans were content to say, "Oh, forget the years gone by. We will take a chance on you even if you have done no specific work up to now." He feared that the country and the prep schools would settle for an easy-going sloppiness that steadily reduced the need for youth to engage in mental exertion. "Americans still love labels and hate to face facts," he concluded. "They don't really believe in education. Colleges hand out B.A.'s and M.A.'s without insisting on real achievement, for they don't think the matter important." His gloomy if not original judgment seems still on target.[10]

Many other independent-school leaders were similarly troubled by higher education's infatuation with mental ability. Much of their worry, to be sure, derived from self-interest. Often their students were not brilliant scholars, but they were still the prep schools' bread and butter. The tuition payments of their parents were no less than (and often more than) those of more proficient classmates. Why should Daddy continue to shell out all that tuition if Harvard and Yale were beyond reach?

The concern for average youth went far beyond financial self-interest. Prep schools had the unique historical experience of preparing a varied student population for serious entrance examinations to notable colleges. They understood the work. Their heads and teachers further understood that academic ability was not the only important ability in life. "Citizenship, leadership, and high grades do not necessarily correlate." Many schools felt a special, almost primary responsibility for educating average college-bound students—students who needed prep schools more than did bright self-starters. The old requirements, examinations, and standards were designed mainly for average students. Their abandonment, so it was thought, hurt average students most.

Even Harvard's Dean Bender, the symbol of meritocracy, became at the end of his tenure an even more prominent symbol of its limits. As the 1960s began, he warned of disaster if academic promise became the only criterion for admission to Harvard. One practical reason was that "the scholars, the *summas,* and the Phi Beta Kappas" could never give Harvard the money it required to remain preeminent. Another was that "the top high school student is often, frankly, a pretty dull and bloodless, or peculiar fellow." Bender did not want "character and personality" banished from the admissions process, nor diversity for its own sake, nor families long loyal to Harvard.[11]

Roberts had no solution to problems whose roots were as much in the prep schools as they were in the colleges. In the end he could only advocate honesty and resolve. "It never ceases to be our duty to exact hard and earnest mental work and to face our results without equivocation." But by the 1960s the SEB exams were no longer used anywhere for admissions purposes, and only rarely as course placement exams or as school finals. In 1965 NAIS changed the name of its Academic Standards Committee to the Academic Services Committee, on the grounds that the word "standards" implied an unpleasant "rigidity." In 1968 the *Definition of the Requirements,* which had the same negative connotation, was replaced by various booklets entitled "Curricular Suggestions." By 1970 NAIS decided to phase out the examinations altogether. They met the same fate as the old College Boards and for similar reasons.[12]

Although some schoolpeople believed that the end of external examinations foreshadowed lower academic standards, many other school leaders hailed the post–1941 changes as liberating. They believed prep schools had been "emancipated from the tyranny" of the College Boards and had finally come of age. One important group, progressive educators in the tradition of John Dewey, had been especially opposed to the College Boards and the SEBs. They welcomed the comprehensive examination alternative to course-driven regular exams, and endorsed more variety and student choice in the prep school curriculum. Ultimately, they wished to set their own terms for students to gain admission to college—to reinvent the old certificate system. Prep schools participated disproportionately in the famous Eight-Year Study evaluating the effects of progressive high schools on later college performance.

The main link between these prewar ideas and postwar changes in independent education was a concern for the superior student. It was on behalf of such students that the progressive appeal to student interests was mainly made. Prep school progressives thought bright students should be able to specialize in subjects like Chemistry far earlier in schools than the dominant liberal arts tradition permitted. They also thought the range of subjects taught should be expanded to include more music and art. The scientific and democratic spirit of aptitude testing perfectly fit the progressive temperament. Here was a tool that could simultaneously identify talent and rid the country of the need for prescriptive curricula with little student appeal.[13]

Schoolpeople did not need to be educational progressives to welcome the new world of aptitude tests. Many understood that the future reputations of independent schools depended upon their becoming just as meritocratic as colleges. Meritocratic admissions were the ticket to a kind of public acceptance that, though not eliminating the scent of social exclusivity, would make it less obviously a school's central feature. The American public was more accepting of privilege when it was based on merit rather than money. High standards for some schools gradually came to mean enrolling bright students who would gain entrance to prestigious secondary schools or colleges.

When the headmaster of Lawrenceville sought to justify independent schools to a wide public in 1951, he was painfully caught between past and future defenses. The traditional independent-school strength had been working hard with "middle-of-the-road students" who were "kept up to snuff" by teachers' devoted efforts. But the result was that the most neglected students were the most able ones. Watching the meritocratic revolution unfold before him, the headmaster concluded that the future of prep schools was the "carefully selected superior student."

Luckily for many schools, a new and unexpected student market arose in the 1950s as a result of the baby boom, postwar economic prosperity, and the anxiety of many parents about college admissions. The country itself supported a greater emphasis on academics, especially in the face of Soviet advances in science and technology. Independent schools found themselves without warning "in the forefront of academic fashion." Everywhere there was talk of "educating the gifted, of accelerated and enriched programs, of special small classes, of emphasis on writing and mastery of fundamental bodies of knowledge."[14]

As applications grew beyond anything previously experienced, many private schools successfully converted themselves into meritocratic institutions. The socially exclusive Hill School, for example, had 743 applicants for 130 places in 1960. It and others redefined exclusivity as brainpower. They emulated numerous college practices to support that mission, creating admissions offices, increasing financial aid, and developing a School Scholarship Service to advance the idea of need-based financial aid.[15]

In 1957 they also created their own version of the SAT to identify young talent, the Secondary School Admission Test (SSAT). The idea of replacing the SEB essay exams with an aptitude test, just as the College Board essays had been replaced by the SAT, was not new. The SEB itself had long recognized a potential market, and had developed a Junior Scholastic Aptitude Test in the late 1930s. But the JSAT never took off, largely because the SEB lacked the money and resolve to make the test convenient to take and score. When the major Eastern boarding schools decided that a secondary school aptitude test was needed to cope with increased applications, they bypassed the SEB and enlisted SAT experts to construct it.[16]

All that was missing in this new program to recruit bright students was an attractive curricular justification for them to come. Only a few schools were known for courses and teaching aimed distinctly at superior or "gifted" students. But during the 1950s a few ambitious prep schools joined with ambitious colleges to create AP, the grandest expression of school meritocracy.

Back to the Future: The Rise of Advanced Placement

In important respects the AP program is eerily reminiscent of the old College Board system that the Board itself decisively rejected in 1942. The voluntary, nongovernmental AP program consists of three-hour "college-level" examinations in many high school subjects. They are closely linked by published syllabi to courses taken in school, are externally assessed by human beings as well as by machines, use essay as well as short-answer questions, and provide college credits to those who pass. Unlike the College Board's short-answer "Achievement" tests in the same subjects, AP is curriculum driven.

Thus it is not surprising that the 1950s College Board had nothing to do with the AP idea or its early development, and agreed to administer the program (with Educational Testing Service providing all technical and administrative services) only after lengthy soul-searching. The decision proved wise. About 1,200 high school students took AP examinations in 1956, the first year of College Board sponsorship. By the early 1990s, more than 400,000 participated annually. AP is probably the most important and successful examining program developed for American schools in the second half of the twentieth century.

AP arose from two separate projects in 1951 funded by the same foundation. One was initiated by John Kemper of Andover, and soon involved Exeter and Lawrenceville as well as Harvard, Yale, and Princeton. The other was the brainchild of the president of Kenyon College—in the years before 1956, AP was commonly known as the "Kenyon Plan." Both initiatives dealt with problems concerning the transition of able students from high school to college. These included better articulation of coursework, avoiding repetition of material, generating student motivation through academic challenge, and confronting the financial tensions that resulted from allowing able students to enter college early or allowing them to receive college credit for work done in school.

These problems were of great concern to prep schools confronted with many bright students and wanting to attract more. The schools were overrepresented in discussing, developing, and piloting the practical program of courses and examinations that emerged when the two projects informally joined forces. Independent education alone did not invent AP, but helped shape it and gave it strong support throughout its history. In 1958, 53 percent of independent schools already offered AP courses. In 1993, a majority of the country's secondary schools did not, although increases in public school and racial minority participation have happily occurred in the last decade. Roughly 62 percent of prep school sophomores in 1990 said they planned to take AP courses, compared with 35 percent of sophomores enrolled in privileged suburban public schools.[17]

The incentives mobilized by AP are somewhat different from those generated by the old College Boards. At first, the major reasons to participate were straightforward. Superior students would not have to repeat routine introductory courses in college. They could specialize earlier and might save some tuition dollars in the process. Today these incentives are weaker than they once were. College course requirements are less restrictive than in the 1950s, and frequently nonexistent. It is much less likely for colleges to force students to repeat material they already know. AP research also suggests that relatively few students who could have graduated from college early because of AP credits chose to do so.[18]

A more lasting incentive is that college-level work challenges and excites bright high school students. Sometimes the attraction is the material itself and the effort required. There is abundant research that AP courses are typically more demanding than the college courses they are designed to duplicate. One senior remembered AP as "a lot of work, and it wasn't easy. But I sort of liked it. I mean, it was fun almost." Another "read a lot of things and I did a lot of things that I wouldn't have been able to do if I hadn't been in the AP course." AP English required much more research and writing than regular English. The teacher graded papers, journals, and essays "as if you're on the college level." "You have to actually do things on your own without the assistance of the teacher."[19]

Sometimes the attraction is more subtle. Students say AP courses are appealing because the other students enrolled are able and motivated and the teachers are a select group, too. "The people who are in the classes are the people who want to be there. That's the way you want it. You don't want people in there who are forced to take the APs." For good students who want to learn, AP courses often filter out important barriers to learning—uncommitted students and inept teachers. The same process operates with teachers. Serious courses with students who are eager or at least willing to work are an enormous incentive for serious teachers to remain in teaching.

Prep schools must attract and hold teachers who are competent enough in their subjects to meet the demands of AP instruction. This is one reason they have always tried to find teachers familiar with and committed to the liberal arts tradition, who experienced it in their own educations, and who performed reasonably well when students themselves in school and college. Just as it is helpful for schools to contain students and families who value academic learning, it is also helpful to have teachers who value it, too. That a teacher has experienced a good academic education and has been a successful student does not guarantee good teaching, but it is a reasonable place to start in the hiring process.

Compared with privileged suburban public schools, independent schools appear to have been quite successful in hiring such teachers. Consider three groups of colleges and universities characterized by a commitment to the liberal arts and by some admissions selectivity: twenty very selective private institutions (including Stanford, Yale, and Amherst), ninety-six private, selective liberal arts colleges (including Dickinson, Grinnell, and Earlham), and finally major state university central campuses (including Madison, Chapel Hill, and Austin).

Very roughly, about 10 percent of independent-school faculties are drawn from the first group of highly selective institutions, compared with 1 percent of the faculties of privileged suburban public schools. When the selective colleges are included, roughly 27 percent of independent-school faculties are drawn from the combined group of private colleges, compared with 5 percent of the faculties in the other schools. And when central campus state universities are also included, the total prep school faculty jumps to roughly 46 percent, compared with 21 percent of teachers in privileged suburban schools. In short, there is a substantial educational fit between the college origins of prep school faculties and prep school academic missions. The fit does not guarantee good teaching, but it is hard to see how very good academic teaching can consistently occur in its absence.[20]

External Assessment

External assessment helps legitimize AP courses as representing high standards. Students are judged anonymously against a national standard; they are not judged by their own teachers who have personal standards and sometimes personal favorites. AP adds student incentives because it makes exam results and the courses on which they are based more credible. Students say they care less about the form of external assessment—"authentic" projects instead of old-fashioned multiple-choice items—than they do about the fact of external assessment.

One junior explained, "It's a way of standardizing things so you can tell how difficult the course is and how well you've learned the material." As an example, he described how friends in another school were taking an Honors Chemistry course that was less demanding in every respect than the regular Chemistry course at his own school. The designation "honors" meant grades were weighted to give an edge in the state university admissions process. But if "Honors" Chemistry everywhere meant AP Chemistry, students in all schools would be held to one clear and fair standard.

In the movie *Stand and Deliver,* a true-story depiction of how AP Calculus meets the inner city, the external examiners and test security personnel seem at first the bad guys. They cannot believe that so many students at the impoverished Garfield High School in East Los Angeles passed the examination without cheating. They made twelve of eighteen students from the school retake the test, and all passed again. But it is exactly the testmakers' preoccupation with the integrity of the examination, along with the fact of external assessment against a national standard, that eventually makes the students more proud than angry. The AP system legitimized their efforts as work of genuine quality.

The power of external judgment is well known in higher education—undergraduate colleges such as Swarthmore and Haverford still import strangers from the outside to examine honors seniors orally. The exhibition is always taken very seriously. It is an incentive to work hard, and the process itself emphasizes that students are accountable to a public standard independent of the habits and traditions of their own institution.

External assessment creates nearly as many incentives for teachers to work hard as it does for students. They too are judged by their own performance. Garfield High's Jaime Escalante achieved celebrity status because of his success as a teacher of AP math. A further incentive is that teachers and students are on the same team—each has an incentive for students to do well. And since the examination scoring is criterion referenced, students are not competing against one another but against the standard used to assess everyone. Mr. Escalante could create a team approach because students were not graded on a curve. All were potential winners in the examination game.

Student success on exams made credible by the quality of content and assessment gives teachers dignity and respect they get in few other ways. They can point to curriculum-driven, teacher-driven results. A teacher of both AP Spanish Language and AP Spanish Literature considered the examinations an "external criterion for standards." She was proud that "four out of six kids got two fives. That's the highest score." She was also pleased that they had received straight A's in her class. "That made me feel that what I was doing— and I've been teaching Advanced Placement for sixteen years now— was right." Almost the entire faculty returned to the school on the mid-July day when AP scores were released just to learn the results. Many teachers establish reputations on the basis of how well their students do.

AP also gives schools useful feedback about what their standards actually are. An upper-school head knew that "we've got a lot of kids around here who have B+ grade point averages," but didn't know if that meant a common pattern of high-quality work or simply grade inflation. Some external validation seemed essential for the school to know which was which. "Your aptitude testing may be all over the place, but it's not a bad rule of thumb that how kids do on the Advanced Placement exams really does reflect something about the quality of the environment and the kind of teaching and the sort of material that's been covered."

But external assessment can easily become synonymous with external control, and few schools today are as comfortable with outside direction as most prep schools were before the war. Yet a majority of prep school teachers do not feel that their freedom is compromised significantly by AP curricular frameworks, although there is some variation from subject to subject.

AP is voluntary in a way that the old College Boards were not. The latter were required for entrance to many colleges, but AP growth depends in large part upon its acceptance by teachers and students. Nobody has to teach AP if she or he doesn't want to, and nobody has to take AP courses. AP curriculum frameworks cannot be excessively rigid or teachers would refuse to participate and the program would shrivel. The teacher's guide to the U.S. history course, for example, includes five quite different year-long syllabi as examples of the notion that there are many ways to skin the same history cat.[21]

Many teachers simply combine their own conception of a good course with the AP version. They make students and themselves work a bit harder, but believe the practical compromise is worth it. An AP Chemistry teacher, for example, scheduled an additional weekly one-hour evening class three months before the examination to make sure the students would be prepared for AP Chemistry and not just his own. That was increased to two evenings a week two months before the test and three evenings a week in the two weeks preceding it. "I usually didn't get home until 9:00 at night," a student explained, but the extra classes were helpful because "we didn't go over the old stuff covered during the day."

Typically, most criticisms of AP as unreasonably intrusive come from teachers who respect the concept but dislike how their field is treated or what the program in its entirety implies about the capacity of individual schools to set credible standards on their own. A Spanish teacher, for example, fumed that most teachers were shut out of AP decision-making in Spanish Literature. He would only teach the Spanish Language course because he thought the literature syllabus was too narrowly focused on a few authors. They were outstanding authors, to be sure, but he opposed the excessive specialization they represented. He was sure a small cabal controlled the exam's content and would not let go.

An experienced mathematics and English teacher made a larger point. Mr. Posner deeply believed in "rigorous academic standards" and in public "accountability" for the upholding of those standards. The contrast between school English and math, for example, amazed and perplexed him. In math there was a corpus of knowledge and competencies. In English he was "astonished at the kinds of sixties' stuff" you could get away with and how much "license" was allowed. It was so easy to say, "Oh, the kid will develop," give a B, and be done with it.

Yet he was uneasy with the AP solution. AP was too invested in the needs of colleges and of his own students' college applications. "Creating external standards," he argued, "in the end takes away one's integrity as a school." By integrity Mr. Posner meant a sense of special purposefulness that individual independent schools once had but rarely, in his judgment, had anymore. To his chagrin, his school had never been able to merge the idea of credible performance standards with the idea of institutional uniqueness.

He recalled, for example, faculty conversations about whether every student in the school should be able to read music by graduation. This was a fresh and exciting goal, and a measurable one. It was not mush, but it went nowhere with the faculty. Less discipline-specific goals might, he supposed, command more faculty support if anyone pushed hard for them. The school might have said that all graduates should be "articulate." This was another worthy objective. Students might demonstrate being articulate by playing a complex piece of music, drawing a serious picture, working out a serious equation, or writing a decent poem. "Not just a portfolio," he emphasized firmly, "but a portfolio with standards." Such projects required "definition" and should be able to withstand scrutiny by those who knew what real standards in different fields were.

In spite of his earlier remarks, he admitted that this goal probably necessitated outside involvement by examiners who would look directly at students' work. Some external, expert verification was essential, but it didn't have to take the form of an AP-like national examination. External assessment could be responsive to what individual schools wanted to do. Mr. Posner struggled for a way to attain AP's admirable credibility while still being true to a particular independent school's special vision.

He was not optimistic. Among the obvious obstacles was whether many schools could ever articulate serious and lasting academic visions. Would they have the quality of personnel, the stability of personnel, and the stability and commitment of students and families to do that over extended periods of time? High quality, stability, and commitment were all indispensable. So was the money needed to support qualified external examiners. Mr. Posner cared deeply about public education, but despaired that even a free-standing advantaged institution like his own had not been able to combine any special vision (beyond AP) with responsible outside assessment. Perhaps AP was after all the best solution a large country with many different schools could muster.

Marketing Students, Marketing Schools

Perhaps the most important contemporary incentive to take and to offer AP courses, one virtually unmentioned in the early AP literature, is to help sell individual students to the colleges of their choice and to help sell schools as going concerns. This is why AP participation varies greatly from state to state. The variation depends on whether state universities are considered desirable postsecondary destinations and whether they "weight" AP enrollments in calculating the grade-point averages that help determine admissibility. In states like California it is not uncommon for students to have taken five AP examinations upon graduation, and not unusual for some to have taken more.

Selective colleges and universities increasingly analyze the "degree of difficulty" of applicants' programs of study because high schools typically offer significant curricular variety and choice and demand very little of students beyond what students demand of themselves. In this respect high schools behave like colleges, and both behave very differently from the prewar years. Enrollment in AP becomes a convenient indicator of strength of program, of whether students are willing to enroll in demanding versions of courses that outwardly may have the same name. A student explained, "In college they look at transcripts to make sure that you have taken advantage of the courses offered at your school. If you push yourself, you are trying harder and colleges notice that." AP literature itself points out that enrollment is highly advantageous in the college admissions process.[22]

It is therefore no accident that the number of AP courses taken prior to senior year in all schools and in prep schools especially has steadily increased over the years. At first AP was regarded almost by definition as work done by high school seniors. But by 1984, 38 percent of prep students who took the examinations did so as ninth-, tenth-, or eleventh-graders. That fraction increased to 43 percent in 1993. Taking AP exams before senior year guarantees that scores will be available to colleges as part of the admissions process.

AP has become so recognized as a college admissions plus that one school which rejected AP science classes provoked a "war" with angry parents who felt shortchanged. Science has always been among the more controversial AP subjects, because many schools have felt that science exams are excessively narrow and many college scientists have had little faith in any high school study of their subject. In this particular school, a creative science teacher helped engineer an unusual curriculum reform in which physics became a sophomore requirement and biology a senior requirement. The scheme was justifiable but its organization precluded most AP science.

The school administration understood that angry parents cared far less about science or science sequencing than they did about gaining an advantage in the college admissions race. They couldn't have cared less about AP itself. So the school created a biology option (Biological Anthropology) that was as exotic as they could make it. It was different, was offered with serious collaboration and credit from a local university, and cost extra. But it satisfied parents who, as a senior administrator put it, were "panting for the transcript thing."

AP markets schools as well as students. Many prep schools have attempted to upgrade institutional reputations and attract more able students through AP. This continues a long tradition of using extensive AP offerings to compete with public schools for bright students. One upper-school head could recall without notes the number of AP examinations taken the year before, the passing rate, and how that compared with the state and county rates. He knew these figures cold because everyone important to him wanted to know them— colleges and prospective parents. Results were crucial. The school was concerned with the "public relations aspect of our pass rate."

Almost anyone could take AP courses, but the school carefully monitored who could take the examinations. Since the school would be judged by prospective families on its pass rate, it had to control it.

AP has survived as long as the old College Board essay exams, but it is far healthier after forty years than its conceptual predecessor. One important reason is that it has retained a tradition of examinations based in large part on meaningful student work—writing essays, or listening to and making audiotapes in foreign language exams— while at the same time avoiding the testmaker's criticisms of subjectivity, unreliability, and unscientific softness. AP has more credibility than the old Board essays ever had because AP never neglected the technical aspects of test preparation and assessment.

In 1933 Carl Brigham wisely chastised the College Board for being an organization of readers instead of true examiners. The Board placed all its bets on the expensive annual process of reading examinations, and ignored how examinations might assess individual potential. Little technical psychometric knowledge about reliability and validity existed for curriculum-driven essay examinations. Creating the SAT and other aptitude tests required serious research and development, but the Board had no interest in comparable research and development on essay examinations.

Brigham believed that examinations should improve school standards and not just assist college admissions. He argued for a major financial commitment by the Board to experimental research on essays to save them from the clutches of professional testmakers. But the Board did nothing. The gap between defenders of the old system who cared not at all for research, and psychologists who had little interest in the quality of schools, was then too wide to bridge.[23]

One of AP's achievements has been to close that gap while retaining many of the better assessment characteristics of the old system. Course syllabi and examinations are created by "Development Committee" teams of professors, teachers, and test specialists. The examinations, strongly biased toward essay or "free-response" questions, are read externally in June by more than two thousand teachers and professors who gather together for a week just as their predecessors did. The professional development experience for involved teachers is just as powerful as it was in the 1930s. In 1992, the readers scored

nearly three million free-response or essay answers. Scoring is criterion referenced, based on a simple 1–5 scale with 3 being the *de
facto* passing grade. The result is that scores have credibility and the
scoring process is reasonably efficient despite the enormous numbers of participants.[24]

This largely happy story is marred mainly by two correctable
problems. The most obvious is that AP is not accessible to enough
able young Americans. It costs students money to participate, it requires teachers who know their fields and are willing to put in extra
effort, and it usually requires smaller classes because students do
more work that must be assessed regularly. Its history as an admittedly elite academic reform makes many schoolpeople and parents
believe that it has little to offer children who are neither brilliant nor
privileged. In 1991 the *Baltimore Sun* reported that only 140 AP examinations were taken that year by all public high school students
in Baltimore, a circumstance one school official attributed to the
system's "priorities." This is less participation than that of a typical
independent school with a high school population of fewer than
400.[25]

Another problem concerns opportunity of a somewhat different
kind. Unlike the old College Boards, AP was not designed as an incentive for the large majority of college aspirants; it was designed for
gifted and talented students. AP was perhaps the central symbol of
prep schools' relentless emphasis on academic excellence, smart students, and college admissions in the 1950s. It responded to a national preoccupation and to the immediate self-interests of many
schools.

As an effective incentive and instructional system, AP appealed to
those who probably needed it least. The average college-bound student—the primary target of the old College Boards—was in the
main unaffected by AP. Neither the College Board nor the colleges
created any comparable incentive system to promote mental exertion by the vast majority of young Americans. "We are being
spoiled," admitted a headmaster in 1965 who understood that the
SSAT enabled many prep schools to eliminate average students altogether. "I miss in our schools the stimulus that came from having to
fight for the academic life of each pupil."[26]

It is disgraceful that the powerful incentives contained in AP have been unavailable to most students. There is no reason a voluntary, incentive-based, externally assessed, curriculum-driven, and teacher-produced system of syllabi and examinations cannot exist for most young Americans. Then a fundamental advantage of the old system—that it served a wide variety of talents—could be restored. Lacking such a system, prep schools that could not easily reshape their student bodies to contain only the gifted would have to find different ways to uphold and define academic standards.

7

The Challenge of Average College-Bound Students

After World War II, greater access to higher education made going to college an expected part of growing up American. No longer a privileged minority, college-bound students are now the norm. Some 2,100 four-year institutions grant at least a bachelor's degree, and 1,400 two-year institutions grant associate degrees. They are supplemented by 6,500 postsecondary vocational and technical institutes. Although the expectation of universality is not fully realized, two-thirds of high school graduates and a majority of late adolescents attend college. The 10,000 institutions devoted to the cause have advanced it more successfully in America than anywhere else.

Despite this social triumph, mass schooling has often not resulted in mass education. Once higher education expanded to serve the 1960s baby-boom generation, it had few incentives to make educational demands on schools. When the adolescent cohort inevitably declined and colleges faced a student shortage (called "excess capacity"), their response was to devise marketing techniques to attract students rather than ways for students to learn more. When mental exertion in schools is neither demanded by many colleges nor valued much by students, schools are not likely to make it a first priority.

Here lies a great irony. Public schools naturally concentrate their limited resources on students who lend them the most prestige, give them the most trouble, bring them the most money, appear the most needy, or are backed by the most powerful pressure groups. But the great increase in the number of college-bound students made that large population the least problematic of all school constituencies. The biggest group became the least important because they were the least troublesome and had the fewest important lobbies behind them.

College-bound students brought few special-purpose dollars into schools. Government money for them was substantial, but was largely siphoned away from schools as grants and loans to fund college attendance. Most of the money went to higher education. Government's priority was college access, not school programs to educate the college bound. Yet these students are one of history's great experiments—the extension of advanced educational opportunity to an entire population.

Pressure to prevent schools from attending seriously to this great democratic experiment comes from both ends of the total student population. At one end are savvy parent advocates of talented or ambitious children. In some communities school reputations depend on the success of top students in the college admissions race almost as much as they depend on the success of athletic teams. If a school has resources, it is likely to create honors tracks to insulate the most able from the merely college bound. This is one way schools take for granted the education of average college-bound students.

Even greater pressure comes from the other end of the student distribution, where targeted public funding often substitutes for pushy parents. Federal and state legislation enacted during the 1960s and 1970s mandates special programs for individual handicaps such as attention disorders or social handicaps such as poverty. For every possible handicap, a lobby advocates special funding and school attention. Relatively few students served are college bound.

Individual public schools are thus internally unequal in funding and commitment. The extremes of the student body tend to get more attention and money. Youth in the middle—usually the middle class—get less. Most students who go through the motions without incident are taken for granted; they graduate and continue on to postsecondary education. Schools are grateful for their dutiful passivity. They are the forgotten if indispensable majority.

Schools accommodate them by expanding curriculum variety, emphasizing student choice over how or whether to participate in the curriculum, and negotiating treaties inside classrooms to balance academic demand against keeping the peace. Learning is profoundly voluntary for the forgotten majority. They mainly attract attention when a notorious event—murder, suicide, sexual molestation, or hate crime—brings brief puzzlement about why apparently typical students act angrily. Sometimes anonymity is too much to bear.[1]

These conditions, more than the urge to give sons and daughters an extra boost in the selective college admissions game, explain much of the attraction of independent education. Many private school parents believe their children were taken for granted in public schools. They believe they were ignored because they were not sufficiently gifted, troubled, or "at risk." They were not special enough to galvanize schools to work hard on their behalf.

Average Students in Independent Schools

No schools have had more experience with average or below-average college-bound youth than privileged private schools. Affluent families for a century have wanted their children (especially boys) to attend college regardless of capacity or interest. Many schools proudly regard the services they provide to average students as their best, most distinctive, and most satisfying work. "The greatness of the private school," claimed Louis Auchincloss's fictionalized version of Groton's founding headmaster, is that "it can sometimes turn a third-rate student into a second-rate one. We can't boast publicly of such triumphs, but they are still our glory."

Few prep schools had sufficient applicants or financial aid to push postwar meritocracy to its extremes, and few wanted student bodies filled only with the academically talented. One teacher urged colleagues, at the peak of the meritocratic movement in 1965, to attend faithfully to "the typical student, who will be a typical adult, the vital nucleus of a democratic community." In the 1990s a school believed that students "in the middle and at the bottom" got the most for their parents' money. The superstars would do as well almost anywhere. Many schools accept preschoolers of unknown aptitude along with their siblings. After eighth grade the few who cannot handle their high schools are counseled out. But that still leaves K–12 schools with many "average, middle-average" students who have never been screened.[2]

If SAT scores are a reasonably credible indicator of academic aptitude, large numbers of prep school students today are average college-bound youngsters. The SAT score range is between 400 and 1,600. Only the most selective colleges regard scores above 1,000 as merely "average," since only one-third of all SAT-takers achieve them. But scores below 1,000 are clearly average or below average. Sixty percent of public school seniors score in the 600–999 range, but so do 39 percent of prep school seniors. The distribution of prep school SAT scores is almost identical to that in high-income, well-educated public school families.

Many prep students, of course, do well on the SATs. In 1990, 25 percent of seniors scored between 1,200 and 1,600, compared with 9 percent of public school seniors who took the test. But prep schools are not skimming the cream off the American student population. During the 1950s John F. Gummere, the head of Philadelphia's William Penn Charter School, even made the reverse argument. He protested publication of College Board statistics showing a public school SAT advantage. They were misleading because "the cream of public school students were being compared with the run of the mill of independent school students." Only top public school students took the test whereas everyone in academically diverse prep schools took it.[3]

This large number of average students posed special educational challenges in the postwar years because most sought admission to well-regarded colleges and universities. The prep schools were expected to make their wishes come true. But the old College Board system that had permitted prep schools to achieve that goal for average students was in shambles by the late 1940s. Average students lacked high SAT scores, high rank in class, and high grades. The prep school culture itself, in which all students were college bound and tough grading was traditional, now seemed to work against average students. It was harder for them to be ranked near the top of their class or to have high grades than it would have been had they attended most other schools.

An ambitious early effort to "peddle the bottom half of the class" to colleges suggests how crucial this issue has been for independent schools. In the early 1940s, Headmaster Herbert Smith of Chicago's Francis W. Parker School proposed a deceptively simple way for prep schools to prove that their average graduates would usually do better in college than grades, scores, or rank in class would indicate. Each year collect student grades in secondary school, subject by subject, and then collect for the same students comparable grades during freshman year in college. Convert these school and college grades to a common scale and display them side by side in an annual publication. A college admissions official could then compare student grades from a given school with the freshman grades those same students subsequently made at his college. He could roughly predict how an applicant was likely to do without any knowledge of scholastic aptitude or rank in class.

To produce these elaborate annual reports, the NCIS established a National Registration Office for Independent Schools (NRO) in 1944. For years it put forth the message that demanding schooling could compensate for average academic aptitude and that class rank, school grades, and aptitude scores could be misleading predictors if used without knowledge of particular schools. The training received by prep students would enable them to "outperform" expectations based on conventional indicators of scholastic aptitude. The University of Minnesota admissions office, for example, could see from the 1949 NRO *Annual Report* that its previous enrollees from Minneapolis's Blake School had been C and D students there but became on average B students once enrolled in the university. Blake alumni at the bottom of their school class outperformed undergraduates from most other schools with higher school grades.[4]

Despite this evidence, logistics and history were not on NRO's side. The costs of data collection were mind-boggling in the years before computers. College grade inflation eventually challenged the notion that grades were reliable indicators of achievement. The growth of pass-fail grading and of privacy rights surrounding transcript releases further eroded the quality of NRO data. Its methodology had always been controversial, especially the arbitrary coding of school and college grades on a common scale without regard to the standards of various institutions. Many of the better colleges developed their own techniques to predict student performance. Moribund by the 1960s, the NRO was finally abolished by NAIS in 1971.[5]

Nevertheless, the notion of outperformance became a recognized prep school virtue, although school reputations were sometimes so dependent on high academic ability that average students were mentioned rarely if at all. An admissions director explained that he could never publicly admit that it was "the more average student who just clicks and blossoms and eats this place up," even though he was sure that was true. He could not admit that "our bread and butter is not the top student who can take Physics AP" because the school wanted to attract as many talented AP-type students as possible. Even schools that actively seek average students use code words like "underachievers," or "near or slightly below the national average," or "as able as most of their peers but not working to their potential." American children are expected to be above average.

The learning disabilities movement and especially the reading disorder dyslexia have given prep schools a way to avoid being typecast as places for slow learners. They can enroll students who do not perform well on conventional measures without loss of status because of the imprimatur of medical science. Learning disabilities suggest not the absence of cognitive ability but the presence of a neurological disorder that prevents students from reaching their academic potential. Such students can be comfortably labeled as smart kids with school problems.

Reflecting on the dramatic rise of specialized diagnostic testing for disabilities, a headmaster observed that parents want "a label to get rid of the thought that maybe the kid is just average as far as horsepower. Horsepower and words like that are very much out of fashion." It is more comforting for parents to regard their children as special and talented. "If they are not getting A's there is almost some sort of medical problem." Even so, some schools worry about the tipping point at which a school gets defined by the public as an "LD" (learning disabilities) school rather than as a regular school with an LD program.[6]

Yet the main challenge that average college-bound youth have posed to independent education goes far beyond demonstrating success in good colleges or redefining students as neurologically special. Without the old College Board system but with strong family incentives to gain entrance to selective colleges, the main challenge has been to show how the independent-school educational process can maximize learning. Two broad and contrasting approaches to maintaining standards for average college-bound youth have dominated prep schools in the second half of the twentieth century.

One approach continues the old tradition of pressing all students, regardless of aptitude, toward a relatively common academic standard and school experience. Since the competition for places in selective colleges is more intense than the older process of gaining admission by passing examinations, external exams are not as essential as they once were to mobilize students to work. A more forceful internal press of expectations substitutes for the old external press.

The second approach regards standards, at least in part, as unique to each individual. There is no universal bar that all must clear at the same predetermined height. Individuals have distinct strengths and weaknesses, and schools should concentrate on developing the potentials of each student. Reaching high academic standards means achieving one's personal best after exerting one's best effort.

Although these two approaches at first seem very different, they coexist surprisingly comfortably in most prep schools today. The pragmatic embrace of both is perhaps the most striking quality of the schools' educational strategy. They have discovered that they can address many practical problems posed by their commitment to standards for average youth by pursuing both approaches simultaneously and ignoring the contradictions.

The Full-Court Academic Press

The most sustained prep school strategy to educate average students well is to use every means at the schools' command to push them to learn more than they would ordinarily prefer. Although some students say their drive to work is self-generated and others emphasize the pressure of parents, most prep school students feel directly the push and challenge of school. "A place like this is needed for people who may need some extra pressure," reflected one student in the bottom half of his class. Another admitted, "They push me more. I think they push the bottom third or so more than anybody else because they need it. The top, they're doing okay." If you slack off, "they're just not going to let you do it. Someone is always on your back."

Schools carry out the job of pushing average (and indeed all) students in two broad ways. First, they attempt to provide challenging learning opportunities and to maximize access for all students to those opportunities. Second, they actively attempt to induce students to participate in learning opportunities and to cut off avenues of escape from them. Encouraging or requiring students to engage in learning is expressed in explicit school policies and deeply ingrained school expectations.

In practice, challenge and participation occur simultaneously to maximize academic press. A lower school, for example, had traditionally offered a choice of French or Spanish beginning in third grade. Twenty minutes of instruction twice a week. But then a new headmaster concluded that so minimal a program was accomplishing nothing; it was an empty catalog boast, not a challenging opportunity to learn. So he summarily dropped French, began Spanish in kindergarten for every student on a daily basis, and increased the time commitment to forty minutes every day. By fifth grade all students had experienced Spanish daily (and in Spanish) for six years. Most were comfortable with and modestly functional in the language. Only in sixth grade were additional language options introduced. A serious learning opportunity had been created, with participation mandatory for everyone.

Challenging Opportunities

If we wish subjects such as foreign language and Algebra to be started by most students in eighth grade, eighth grades must offer them and eighth-graders must study them. There is nothing preventing students from learning them later, as numerous accelerated and adult programs attest, but if our goal is the broad one of affecting most youth, it is important to reach them at an early and appropriate time. It is discouraging that virtually all prep school eighth grades offered Algebra and a foreign language in 1988, whereas only about 78 percent of public school children were offered Algebra and only 63 percent a foreign language.

The existence of an opportunity does not guarantee that students will seize it. About 70 percent of independent-school eighth-graders report that they studied Algebra in 1988 and about 85 percent say they studied a foreign language. Still, prep schools exert a greater press to participate than other schools. Only 32 percent of public school eighth-graders took Algebra, and only 24 percent studied a foreign language. When privileged public schools in which these subjects are usually offered are compared with prep schools, student participation in Algebra (45 percent) and foreign language (51 percent) still lags far behind.[7]

The comparatively strong academic press exerted on most students by independent middle schools is the product of a focused curriculum that most students experience together. Algebra is commonly studied in eighth grade because that is what eighth grade mathematics is. Students with math difficulties may be in special sections with a remedial tone. But if they are, there is usually no parental opposition because the objective is to prepare them for Algebra I as soon as possible.

Students are there not to avoid Algebra but to hasten their way to it. A tacit understanding is that years of serious secondary mathematics lie ahead for all of them, even those to whom math does not come easily. Similarly, the basic choice concerning foreign language is not whether to take a language but which one. Early exposure to a foreign language is a longstanding independent-school tradition. The very notion of mandated exposure has a positive connotation. It is what educational opportunity is presumed to be about.[8]

Challenge is similarly sustained at the high school level by a serious but limited curriculum and by requirements that substantially restrict student choice. Fewer courses and fewer options create a relatively egalitarian student experience. The curriculum does not function to widen the aptitudinal and motivational differences students inevitably bring to their studies; its function is just the reverse. Schools can show parents who are paying the same price that their different children are receiving the same service. One benefit of economic privilege is greater equity in access to a challenging curriculum.

Because a limited curriculum provides a common academic experience it supports purposeful educational communities. To the extent that educational content is more shared than individualized, students have a common intellectual experience to talk to one another about in addition to the common experience of being adolescents. The same applies to their teachers. If more teachers are teaching the same courses, they too may talk more with one another about intellectual substance, perhaps work together, create common topics, methods, and exam questions, and in general become less isolated and more collegial.

A related advantage of a limited curriculum is the ease in making intellectual connections among subjects. If, for example, most students study American History the same year they study American literature, the possibilities of imaginative crossover work are affected less by the schedule than by the will of the teachers. They can collaborate individually if they want to, or on a larger scale involving an entire grade.

The secondary curricula of ten typical independent schools are all divided into six areas: the Arts, English, Foreign Languages, History or Social Studies, Mathematics, and Science. Each curriculum requires all students to complete years or credits in each area. What is most striking is not the number of years required but the specificity of the requirements.

Nearly 100 percent of one school's program from the ninth through the eleventh grades is prescribed. All freshmen study World Literature and Mythology, Geography, Geometry (or Algebra I if they did not complete it in eighth grade), the first year of an integrated Biology-Chemistry two-year sequence, a year of either French or Spanish, an arts course for part of the year, and sports for most of the year. Sophomores go on to American Literature, American History, Algebra II (or geometry), the second year of Biology-Chemistry, a second year of whichever language they studied as freshmen, and more arts and sports.

Juniors encounter British Literature, European History, Precalculus (or Algebra II), a lab science of their choice, a third year in the same language, and arts and sports as before. Seniors take a full year of English electives, an arts course, and sports. This school takes the core curriculum concept farther than most, but resembles the rest more than it diverges from them.

Sometimes schools seek to push students to undertake challenging programs not by making many classes mandatory but by the clever, "sleight-of-hand maneuvering" of a few requirements. A school with a science requirement of only two years, for example, was proud that it succeeded in persuading 90 percent of its students to study science during all four high school years. The goal was to accomplish on a voluntary basis participation and persistence in demanding work for the entirety of high school. The issue is instructive because science has traditionally been the most neglected prep school field. In contrast to foreign languages, science has not been associated with privilege. Prep school graduates have been less likely than college-bound public school students to respect it, study it in college, or make careers in it. This school knew it had to approach science more imaginatively than French.

The school took the courageous step of moving its eighth-grade Physical Science course, used in many prep schools, to the ninth grade and making it mandatory. The course seemed lost on most younger students, and reinforced beliefs that science was only accessible to brilliant nerds. Students were memorizing right answers instead of struggling to understand concepts.

Another tactic was to make Physics a sophomore course—before students and especially girls had fully internalized the belief that Physics was too hard and unfeminine. The most dramatic move was to make Biology a required senior course. The academic reasoning was that modern Biology presupposed knowledge in the other sciences; the educational reasoning was that this would eliminate the common decline in senior science enrollments and give seniors a common experience when their programs were most likely to diverge.[9]

The effect of these various curricular policies is to make the academic experience of independent-school students different in important ways from that of other college-bound students. The differences do not lie in the number of courses, credits, or units amassed in the academic fields; these are largely the same regardless of school governance. The singular exception is the arts, where prep school students spend substantially more time than students in other schools.

One important difference is that in mathematics and foreign languages, the subjects most often organized sequentially, a larger fraction of prep school students take more demanding courses and course sequences than college-bound public school students. In many cases this is the direct result of beginning subjects prior to ninth grade, of fewer course options, and of the influence of selective college admissions requirements.

More than 73 percent of prep school seniors in 1990, for example, reported taking Precalculus, compared with 60 percent of privileged college-bound seniors in public schools and 39 percent of all college-bound public school seniors. More than 40 percent of independent-school students studied one foreign language for more than three years, compared with 31 percent of privileged college-bound seniors in public schools and 17 percent of all college-bound public school seniors.[10]

The general direction of prep school academic push is clearly upward. "They said to me you're doing too well in regular algebra, so we're going to put you in honors." "When good seniors try to take low-level science courses, they won't let them." One student contrasted his independent school with other schools that offered tough courses but "actually try to keep people out of them." A parent praised a school for keeping her son in Honors Biology despite his C's instead of allowing him to take regular Biology, where his grades would go up.

Perhaps the best example of prep school upward academic push is the gradual expansion of AP courses and enrollments. As AP has become a more important factor in the college admissions competition, more students have been drawn to courses originally designed only for the gifted and talented. In most prep schools AP is no longer just for top students. Many schools have eliminated separate AP courses in fields such as English or American History. The assumption is that these subjects can be usefully taught at an AP level to almost all college-bound students. A school that reorganized English in this way moved in one year from fifteen juniors taking the English Literature and Composition exam to ninety-nine, virtually the entire junior class. A high percentage received at least passing grades. "If we can give kids the confidence of that outside affirmation of their abilities, and let that go on their college transcripts," the English department chair explained, "we're doing what we should do."

Another school deliberately built its reputation by carefully adding AP courses and encouraging able students to take them.

Once the desired reputation for securing high scores had been achieved, the school relaxed and encouraged average students to take the classes and the examinations. If all AP students were getting high scores, a teacher reasoned, that meant access to them was too restrictive and should be eased. Even if some failed the examination at the end, the experience of a challenging course disciplined by external assessment made the effort worthwhile. Besides, the failing score would not be entered on the college transcript. "I had a student get a 2," explained a teacher (a 2 is considered a failure on the 1–5 grading scale). "But was it a worthwhile experience? Yes. I think we serve the middle kid very well."

Given that so many average prep school students take AP examinations, it is not surprising that they often have lower SAT scores and lower class rank than public school participants. There is also some evidence that a higher fraction of prep school students fail the AP exam than public school students (31 percent versus 23 percent, in one 1986 study). All this makes perfect sense, considering that in prep schools AP is no longer exclusively for the gifted. If more average prep school students experience AP courses than students elsewhere, the prep students may have lower scores but a higher percentage of student participation in serious academic work.[11]

Participation

The acid test of whether prep schools really push average college-bound students is the school experience of such students. No one would be surprised if schools filled with able students from ambitious families showed far higher enrollments in challenging courses than schools containing students with lower aptitudes and family ambitions. Consider the study of Algebra I by students in the top tenth of the national ability distribution. Independent-school students in this top tenth study Algebra I about as frequently as similar students in the most privileged public school eighth grades—89 percent versus 84 percent. The most able students in privileged eighth grades study Algebra regardless of whether their schools are public or private.

This pattern continues in high school. High-aptitude students take demanding academic courses wherever they go to school. When SAT scores rise above 1,200 there is no difference between prep school and privileged public school participation in challenging academic courses.

But the story is very different for the average college-bound student. Average prep school eighth-graders, defined as students in the top half but not the top tenth of all eighth-graders in academic aptitude, study Algebra much more frequently than similar students in privileged public schools. The difference is 60 percent participation versus 40 percent. (This very large difference will appall many prep school teachers who realize how small 60 percent is.) The same pattern exists for foreign languages. Average college-bound prep school eighth-graders are pushed more than similar students in privileged public schools.

This fact is nontrivial because these are sequential subjects where important high school decisions depend on what students do in eighth grade. Although virtually all prep schools offer Algebra I as a ninth-grade option—reflecting their ninth-grade intake from a variety of schools—most prefer that ninth-graders have studied Algebra already so they can begin high school with Algebra II or geometry. Students who have not completed the bulk of Algebra I by the end of eighth grade have nearly lost the chance to study Calculus as seniors unless they are unusually talented, study in the summer, or enroll in two math courses at once.[12]

The same pattern of participation persists among average students in high school. Average or below-average students in prep schools are more likely to experience a challenging high school curriculum than average but privileged college-bound students in public schools. They are much more likely to do so than all average college-bound public school students.

Consider the 27 percent of prep school seniors and 27 percent of privileged public school seniors whose 1990 SAT scores were between 800 and 999. Students with such scores are often in the bottom half of the SAT population in their own prep or public schools because they attend schools with above-average SAT scores. Yet they constitute the middle third of the entire national population of SAT-takers. With respect to scholastic aptitude they are the most average of American college-bound seniors.

Sixty-seven percent of these prep school seniors studied one foreign language for at least three years, compared with 51 percent of privileged public college-bound seniors and 42 percent of all college-bound public school seniors. Fifty-eight percent of them studied Precalculus, compared with 38 percent of the privileged public group and 36 percent of the all-public group. Sixty-two percent of the prep seniors studied Physics, compared with 57 percent of the privileged group and 52 percent of the all-public group.[13]

A further indicator of whether average students are pushed academically is homework. If prep schools have one clear academic expectation for all students it is that work will be done outside classrooms. Homework is the common denominator of standards—the minimum everyone is responsible for, the basic academic obligation everyone has. Parents assume as a matter of course that students will perform differently in their studies because students are different. But they assume that they should "all be performing the same" when it comes to working hard. "The standard to which all kids should be held accountable is work effort."

The course-taking patterns described above apply to homework as well. Eighth-graders in the top tenth of the national ability distribution spend about the same time on homework wherever they go to school. They spend more time than their average schoolmates. But average independent-school students do more than four hours of homework per week more than similar students in public schools. In privileged public and all public schools, this pattern continues unchanged in tenth grade. The top tenth of sophomores do more homework than the average college-bound population. And the gap between the homework done by average prep school sophomores and privileged public school sophomores remains as substantial as it was in eighth grade.

But by tenth grade one important element in the pattern changes within prep schools. Average independent-school sophomores report doing roughly three more hours of homework per week— roughly 12.5 hours total—than their top-tenth schoolmates. In fact, average prep school sophomores do more homework than *any* other group of American sophomores. This is surely because curriculum expectations for them have not been lowered, dumbed down, or made voluntary.

The average prep school sophomore does more homework than the top prep school sophomore because she or he needs to. The curricula both prep school groups encounter are still largely the same. An able senior who completed eight AP examinations calmly explained that "school work doesn't take that much time. I'm able to do everything during the day with minimal homework, an hour or two of homework, and I don't think an hour or two of homework is that bad. I still fit in soccer practice." When another top-track senior asserted that very little homework produced for him automatic B's, a schoolmate quietly retorted, "For some people it's hard to get a B." Mixed-ability student discussions about time spent on homework are among the most awkward conversations one can have in independent schools.[14]

These examples suggest benefits from school policies that push average students, but they also raise questions about a tradition that relies so much on a limited curriculum, modest student choice, much homework, and the expectation to enroll in ever more difficult courses. Is there a point at which the full-court press breaks down or is broken? When will the average student break or decide the rewards are not worth the effort?

An exhausted senior admitted that "a lot of things don't come very easy for me. So I have to work that much harder. It's like I've worked so hard that I can't do it anymore." For a one-hour test in AP European History on a Monday, he did the reading, paid attention in class, and studied three hours on Saturday, "which is a great length of time, three hours looking at a book, a history book much less." On Sunday he studied five hours more.

The outcome was a grade of C+. Perhaps this was a "reality check" on his own capacity. He regarded a B as an honors grade; it was his uppermost goal. The possibility of an A never crossed his mind. Maybe he just wasn't B material. But still, "it turns you off when you try that hard." And what about the next test? "What do I have to look forward to? Another eight hours of torture and study, cramming, and coming up with another grade like that one?"

Stronger students were not immune from the pressure of academic press. "If I mess up in Calculus now," worried one, "what am I going to do in the future? If you don't do well in something you're cutting out a whole piece of your life." His not wholly satisfactory solution was "to do well in everything so I always have options when I get older."

The Achilles heel of the academic-press strategy is that students can break the press themselves by stopping the game. "They can say we're going to push you, we're going to work you until you're bloody." But the adults really don't have complete power. "If they have mandatory study halls you could sit there and read the same page over and over and over again and not really care." Ultimate power resides with students. The senior concluded that "the student either cares or he doesn't care. The school cannot determine whether the student cares about learning or not." Academic press has advantages but can make no guarantees. In schools that take a clear stand about purpose and expectations, reluctant or discouraged students must exert much energy to subvert prevailing community norms. They must work hard not to work hard, but it can be done.

Individualizing Standards and "Personal Best"

The Assault of the 1960s

The full-court academic press was broken briefly but on a large scale at the end of the 1960s, when societal changes intruded upon even conservative institutions like independent schools. At virtually the same moment, schools and students faced disaffection with adult authority, adult competence, and tradition itself. They confronted coeducation and racial integration, the new morality of permissiveness toward drugs and sex, anger and anxiety over an unpopular war, and financial reverses owing to enrollment difficulties and the national economy. College admissions seemed an "intellectual rat race in which victory is possible only for the rats." The race ceased being rational when colleges accepted only one applicant out of nine. Then "the seniors start to withdraw from it and cower, like laboratory rats, over their guitars."[15]

One effect of the 1960s was to erode the authority of academic standards. Heated adult disagreement over the particulars of standards had always characterized prep schools, but now some teachers rejected the broad intellectual framework within which previous debates had been fought and others questioned whether the struggle to find standards had itself any value.

In 1949 the response had been quick when a boarding school teacher dared publicly to praise comic books and declare so-called great books obsolete. Comics understood "the pace and content of modern life," and Buck Rogers's "sensible realism and intelligent forward look" had genuine educational value. His outraged headmaster immediately reassured parents that comic books were banned at the school. "Buck Rogers, even though he rides a rocket, will enter here over my dead body." Another, traditional teacher asked why education should ape Buck Rogers and put students in tune with the modern world. What was so great about modern times? "Isn't it equally important to try to modify a tune that strikes many of us as monotonous, vulgar, and harsh?"[16]

By the late 1960s the idea that some standards were superior to others had lost much credibility in privileged educational circles. At that time a prep school teacher could attack the entire liberal arts curriculum for "nonpertinence and overabstraction." Liberal arts was nothing more than one historical tradition ("Western humanism"), and at that an "aristocratic" tradition designed only for a "cultural elite." It had little relevance for the liberationist needs of American youth. The word "elite" acquired a pejorative connotation from which it has never recovered. The word "vulgar" merely disappeared.

Psychology joined with politics to provide additional ammunition against academic learning. A professor prominent in prep school circles argued in 1969 that the schools' emphasis on "rational, abstract, critical reason" prevented students from expressing "suppressed" needs. He asserted that cognitive development came at the expense of more important things—"sharing emotionally" and "interpersonal relationships." Campus riots were valuable therapy. "A riot makes one feel alive, primitively and vitally whole again." These attacks did not represent the prep school majority, but they put defenders of standards, always swimming against the American current anyway, at their greatest disadvantage of the century.[17]

Within schools, academic press was diminished and daily life became somewhat more relaxed. There were reductions in academic requirements, including less emphasis on skills and reading, a rise in pass-fail grading, and a dramatic increase in curriculum electives, especially in the arts. Instruction was organized in new ways—

minicourses, independent study, experiential education outside schools, the open classroom, more film and fewer words, more discussions and fewer lectures, more informality in relations among teachers and students. Many nonacademic requirements were also eliminated or reduced—attendance at religious services, dress codes, weekend residence at boarding schools. A school head concluded that students in all respects were less in "quarantine" than ever before.[18]

The nasty confrontations of the 1960s were mainly confined to a few privileged schools and had largely run their course by the end of 1972. Eventually, student unrest was held in check by teachers, students, and parents who longed for stability. Drug abuse was the most sobering consequence of fewer constraints on freedom, and an urgent practical reason for restoring some of those constraints. The advent of AIDS a decade later reinforced the reaction. A further conservative force was the most publicized indicator of American educational weakness since the 1957 Soviet launching of Sputnik: the decade-long decline in SAT scores, announced with much publicity near the end of 1973.

Gradually it again became acceptable to talk favorably of academic standards. In 1974 a teacher cogently argued that prep schools should be academic institutions rather than "reflections of life" because privileged children already possessed an abundance of rich life experiences outside school, including travel, athletic and arts camps, and psychotherapy. The only thing they did not learn outside school were "how to read and write and figure." A veteran headmaster who withdrew from the 1960s by teaching in Botswana praised his African students for understanding their responsibility to acquire rigorous knowledge and skills. They did not study folk dancing, ethnic cuisine, or themselves. He lambasted privileged America's infatuation with "self-fulfillment, 'finding oneself,' and developing individual interests."

A teacher with similar values incisively described how what he called the "good-bad" class of the 1960s involved a tacit treaty between teachers and students to "replace a program that promised sustained mental toil peppered with teacher-student confrontations about individual progress with a program that promised minimal anxiety." Instead of this relaxed and undemanding kind of class, he proposed a future where "mastery" was a goal, participants were held accountable for "specific tasks and material," and manageable levels of anxiety were included without apology. When Senator Edward M. Kennedy spoke in 1981 to independent schools, he praised their traditional strength of providing "essential, basic education." And he wondered aloud if public schools were up to that vital task.[19]

The Standard of Doing One's Best

Independent education's legacy from the 1960s is neither liberation from academic tradition nor a restored full-court academic press. All prep schools have struggled with the same contemporary dilemma: can they be faithful to individual differences and to academic standards at the same time? The one thing they know with certainty is that the struggle becomes harder as the students become more average.

The prep school definition of academic standards has shifted somewhat from emphasizing common knowledge or skills to emphasizing different individual potentials. One school, for example, constantly celebrates for external consumption its devotion to excellence and high standards. But the inside reality, according to the academic dean, is that "excellence is only excellence if it isn't some arbitrary standard, particularly in a school like this where we really work well with kids in the middle range of ability. The reason we do so well with these kids is that we don't have arbitrary standards." The school's job is to get everyone to "succeed in some way at his or her level. By high academic standards we always want their reach to exceed their grasp, but we don't want it to be so far beyond their grasp that they become frustrated."

Although some prep school parents think of academic standards as concrete skills, the overwhelming number believe standards must be "tailored to the individual student." They retain the idea of common standards in the face of uncommon students by defining standards as working to potential. "Excellence for one youngster isn't necessarily going to be excellence for the next," a mother pointed out. Another added, "That's right. But the expectation is the same for each youngster." She meant that "they will achieve excellence whatever that might be for them." Implementing high expectations means, not pushing students to the "same level as someone else's talents God gave them," but helping them be "the best student that they can be." Teachers are expected to "get the most out of a kid" and students to become "the best they possibly can." The standard remains the same for everyone. "The norm here," explained a head-master, "is do your best."

Behind this conception of individualized standards, so different from that of the old College Board exams with their passing grades, lies parents' belief that academic abilities are relatively fixed. By and large abilities are regarded as God-given, rather like good looks or superior running speed. Practice can help, but once children are be-yond the elementary basics parents are usually most interested in discovering and developing what they are particularly good at. They are less interested in dwelling on what they cannot do well or prefer not to do. Their children generally share this view, or at least em-brace happily its educational consequences. It also has deep cultural support. The American media endlessly praise specialized excel-lence in almost any endeavor.

Like most American parents, prep school parents seem more in-clined to attribute academic attainment to innate factors than to per-severance. They deeply believe in the work ethic, but minimize the value of hard work as a compensatory strategy. They tend to see diligence as an abstract end in itself—a mark of character—or else as a method to become more excellent in areas where proficiency al-ready exists. The belief in clear academic limits for individuals seems somewhat of a contradiction in a country traditionally known for optimism about the potential to better oneself through self-help, discipline, and pluck. Perhaps our tendency to emphasize academic limits is related to our deep cultural acceptance of modern IQ and aptitude tests.[20]

Prep school teachers generally accept parents' reasoning. Of course they believe that all children can learn, but they place this empty generality in a practical context. Large student differences are their daily reality. "The standard here is pretty individual," one teacher concluded. "There's a pretty broad range of kids, so you have to get everyone to do what they can do." Another recalled a ninth-grader who could not read five pages in a history book and pull out the key ideas no matter how many study skills or how much time and teaching were devoted to the effort. Another student in the class could spot the ideas after a few seconds spent skimming the text late at night in bed with his stereo blasting away. A classics teacher described a student who had studied Latin for five long years. "He has hung in there. He has tried." But he knew virtually nothing. The puzzled teacher wondered, "Is this an embarrassment for me or should I boast?" Colleagues assured him he should be proud. The student had produced his personal best.

Teachers often make up their own minds about different student potentials and assess them against those criteria instead of against an external standard. This allows grading to be partially influenced by effort or potential and not just by performance—a helpful incentive for both stronger and weaker students and a godsend for teachers. Students can improve grades by "extra-credit" work or lower them by not producing what teachers believe they can.

On what basis do they make these estimates? Teachers say they must know students well and apply professional judgment acquired over time. "It's only after years of teaching that you get a fair sense of how far a particular student can go in a subject before getting in over his or her head or cracking or just becoming non-productive." An English teacher explained that experience with the same assignments over the years gave her a sense of the range of possibilities for students within a class. By careful attention to how well students wrote and read on their own (such as examining the comments they made in the margins of their books), she formed a view of individual capacities.

"In English the range of abilities is so diverse that you can't simply point to one student and say, 'that's the best English student in the class.' Somebody may be wonderful at discussing ideas out loud and a minimal writer, while the student who writes a wonderful personal experience essay may be a very limited literary critic." Few teachers arrive at these personal judgments by consulting standardized test scores or other diagnostic data regarding learning "styles." Most teachers seem to make their own judgments of potential on the basis of direct experience.

This illustrates one way teachers soften the potentially harsh determinism of the fixed-abilities position. They identify many abilities within a subject and reward students for those they are good at. They also explain differences as "developmental." It isn't just that abilities are fixed; students have their own timetables for learning, so teachers can never be certain when a student's personal best has been achieved. But the most common way to soften the fixed-abilities position, while still maintaining the idea of standards, is to search diligently for student strengths across the entire curriculum. Teachers work hard to discover talents and develop them.

Especially for average children, prep schools seek strengths "so kids can have success at their level." Like parents, they often appear more concerned with identifying and building on strengths than with lingering over defects. Schools are proud of the many opportunities provided for students to "shine at what they are beginning to excel at." Students value excellence in one area, whatever it is, as much as well-roundedness. "If you're a good athlete," one student explained, "you're accorded the same kind of honors as if you're a good mathematician or writer. They try to make what you do best stand out. So if you're great in foreign languages they'll get you involved in foreign languages."

It is as if one strategy for supporting the average student is to deny the idea of average students. "All the kids here," asserted a hopeful student, "have some sort of talent that really stands out." By finding and developing such talents, prep schools retain the 1960s commitment to building self-confidence while also taking pride in the high standards individuals achieve in particular areas. The search for an area of special excellence is wholly consistent with the assumption that basic abilities are relatively fixed. The challenge becomes to discover the strongest ability. It is also consistent with the postwar college admissions habit of downgrading well-roundedness in favor of exceptional skill in desired areas.

But individualizing standards is a perilous strategy. If teachers consciously or unconsciously have too low (or too high) expectations for groups or types of students, or if they are simply mistaken about particular individuals, too little or too much academic press may be applied. Everyone is familiar with the self-fulfilling prophesy of tracking groups of students into undemanding programs because of assumptions about their lesser mental capacity. And if a school is mesmerized by a student's special talent, it too may relax its efforts to develop additional skills or interests. Individualizing standards can become a justification for dumbing them down.

Varied Opportunities for Growth

Another problem is that individualizing standards is extremely expensive for schools that are worried about offering sufficient opportunities to attract students but also about keeping costs reasonable so as not to drive them away. The logic of the approach requires a much more varied—and hence far more costly—program than that of the more traditional conception of academic push. Parents often demand that high tuitions provide their children with more than just access to challenging opportunities and institutional push; they also insist on opportunities no less broad in scope, and sometimes broader, than far larger public schools offer.

This is especially true when parents of average children hope the school will offer some opportunity to spark a special talent—so that ordinariness suddenly becomes specialness. A headmaster discussed a "very average" student who suddenly discovered that he had real artistic talent. "He's not in the most demanding program, but he'll go to a very good arts-oriented college." The point is that parents want as many opportunities to discover hidden talents as possible. Ten years before, when this same school lacked serious opportunities in the arts, it would at best have hoped for the student's academic survival. Now the attitude was different. "If we don't have something that matches his talents, then we have a problem."

School administrators and teachers thus emphasize "providing as many opportunities for growth as possible." They routinely say, "We have so many activities that are good for some students that we hate to drop anything." Or, "We put more and more in and rarely take anything out." Or, "Our students need various outlets to express their interests. They learn more if a course grabs them. Telling them to take a particular course is like putting a round peg in a square hole." Even schools with many core requirements agree that the more curriculum variety, the better. Less in this sense is definitely not preferable to more.

Four kinds of program expansion stand out in the upper grades of most prep schools. First, all aspects of the traditional extracurriculum—especially arts and sports—have grown in size, professionalization of adult direction and facilities, and formal requirements mandating student participation. A veteran teacher and coach explained that the sophistication of the athletic and drama programs now required so much time that students were giving less time to academics than a generation before. They were more engaged with school than when he first taught, but less engaged with academics. "We've become much, much better at valuing the things that are not strictly academic," observed another teacher. "I see the largest change in the honor and due we pay to our musicians and our actresses and our art students and our athletes."

These opportunities are often justified as enabling students to "catch fire and feel proud and become accomplished and move on to other things." Although valuable for themselves, they are a means to intellectual engagement. An administrator didn't think most of the privileged adolescents she had known over the years were responsive to straight book learning; the way to hook students was to get them to make "a beautiful pin in metal smoothing class. That gets put on display and the adults go by and say what a gorgeous pin. And all of a sudden they start writing better English papers."

The activity itself is often of primary interest to students. Several students in one school saw the swim team as the main thing in their lives. "If we closed that pool," an administrator admitted, "those kids might well leave." Just the chance to participate is a tremendous lure for students with average skills. This is a virtue of smaller schools. "It's much harder at a big public school to be in a play," a student explained, "or to have a lead role, or just to be in it at all." You didn't need to be a superstar to "have a chance to shine."

The second program expansion, which has occurred during the past decade, involves student services, mainly academic services but sometimes psychological counseling services. Prep schools' most significant investment remains college counseling, which became a specialized professional function in the 1950s. But during the 1980s more schools hired learning-skills coordinators on a full- or part-time basis. Most formal psychological counseling still is conducted by private therapists with only a tangential relation to the school. But in-house counselors increasingly coordinate program packages from outside that bring into schools speakers and resources on every imaginable social or emotional issue.

A third program expansion is nonsequential electives, especially in English and Social Studies. The 1960s emphasis on a multiplicity of courses expressing faculty as well as student interests has abated only partly. All schools have representation in some non-Western area studies (Russia, China, Japan, Latin America, the Middle East, Africa South of the Sahara); in areas of contemporary political or social significance (Black Faces, Black Voices; Women in American History; Racism; Coming of Age in America; The Holocaust); and in areas of idiosyncratic teacher interest (Children's Literature; Nature Writing; Conducting a Trial).

Although in some sense an academic smorgasbord, this menu is strongly defended by schools on educational grounds. A wide variety of electives helps match student strengths with curriculum content. "If we have a slow reader," a teacher explained, "we don't really want her to take Russian Lit because she can learn to read and write as well in a short story class." To this teacher high academic standards meant "working with material that allows kids to maximize their potential." Such schools are not shopping mall high schools, but specialty shops with carefully chosen differentiated product lines. Their electives resemble on a smaller scale the curriculum content of important liberal arts colleges. Unlike most of the latter, they complement but do not replace a core curriculum.[21]

A fourth important curricular expansion is the different ways schools offer and organize somewhat similar material. The fields in question are most likely to be sequential ones such as foreign languages, math, and science. In these areas the curriculum has deepened to better match content and pace with perceived differences in student abilities. This expansion represents perhaps the ultimate practical test of individualizing academic standards. Is it a positive contribution or just a canny accommodation to customer preferences?

Most schools have a common if sometimes tacit objective in math, science, and foreign languages, a common standard they strive for in addition to encouraging personal best. That standard is to keep students engaged with these subjects for as long as possible without resorting to off-putting, rigid requirements. Just as inner-city schools try to prevent students from dropping out of school, prep schools try to prevent students from dropping out of serious subjects.

The typical consequence of dropping out, especially for average students, is that the subjects will not be pursued in college. Once

dropped, they are likely dropped forever. Continued school participation, even at different levels of demand, reinforces content and
impedes forgetting. It reinforces the fact that the subjects are central
to liberal education, and supports contact with material different
from American pop culture. Participation keeps options open for
students to pursue these subjects after high school.

Some schools spread a regular year of foreign language instruction over two years for less proficient students. A school that once
routinely waived its foreign language requirement for the learning
disabled finally concluded that bilingualism was an obvious life skill
for all Americans. It designed a special, slower-paced Spanish course
just for LD students. The Art of French Cinema, a conversational
French course whose "text" is classic French movies, attempts to
lure less proficient French students to a fourth year by bypassing
conventional French IV or AP French. Schools offer "conceptual"
versions of Physics, Chemistry, or Biology that minimize mathematics but retain laboratory work. Some spread Biology over two years.
Many offer science electives to entice the science-shy to stay connected (for example, Science and Humanity, Human Physiology,
Ecology).

Perhaps no subject has more circuitous paths than mathematics.
In a school in which virtually all students study math for four years,
the superstars begin Algebra I in seventh grade, the average students
in the middle of eighth grade (completing it by the end of ninth
grade), and the weakest in ninth grade. This pattern permits many
possibilities for tenth grade—all of which are available to students
regardless of when they start or finish beginning Algebra. They are
regular Geometry, Honors Geometry, or Geometry with Algebra.
The last reinforces Algebra I and addresses fewer topics in Geometry. The strongest students study regular or Honors Geometry in
ninth grade.

Even more possibilities exist for junior year—Precalculus for
strong students who will study Calculus as seniors, Algebra II for
average students comfortable with math, and a course called Problem Solving that ranges back over Algebra and Geometry to reinforce basic math. Students in this course normally study Algebra II
as seniors. Juniors who study Algebra II but are nervous about

Precalculus can find senior options in Probability and Statistics or "College Algebra," which keep them in math and reinforce Algebra II.

Multiple pathways permit all students either to move upward at any time, or simply to consolidate where they are. No humiliation exists over being tracked, though everyone has, in fact, been individually tracked. Where one stands in math isn't obvious. Students believe everyone is engaged with real math but at different paces and levels. In the end, almost everyone meets the standard of completing four years of serious mathematics.

When asked whether the standard of holding students in real math for four years was accompanied by a minimum standard of math attainment (such as measured proficiency in Algebra II), an administrator admitted that the school was "a little wishy-washy." Some teachers thought that everyone should complete Algebra II, whereas others believed the key issue was not to lose students from math. The tension between mastery and participation was not resolved but fuzzed over.

Fuzzing over the problem for this school was a way of resolving it. Like most independent schools, it believed in both mastery and participation and addressed them on a case-by-case basis. Each position converged on the other. Everyone expected students to engage mathematics seriously and continually. That in itself was a standard. The math curriculum did not separate students unfairly or dumb-down mathematics to accommodate teacher or student wishes to avoid effort. It was a practical attempt to fuse commitments to individual differences and academic standards.

Academic push in prep schools has two simultaneous dimensions. One emphasizes limited variety and choice to get all students to participate in a challenging curriculum. The other emphasizes considerable variety and choice aimed at getting all students to achieve their personal best. Despite the tension between these approaches, schools and families prefer that they exist together. They regard the tension as fruitful, inevitable, and characteristically American.

III

PERSONALIZATION

8

The Power of Personal Attention

The case against factory-like schools that process masses of students is apparently settled. Almost everyone wants schools to provide significant individual or personal attention, and to be places where students are known and cared for as unique people and learners. Who could possibly object? Americans regard personal attention as an end in itself. Modern psychology, affluence, consumerism, and education have all strengthened our traditional commitment to the pursuit of individual happiness. Attention to self need not conflict with concern for society, but Americans are unlikely to favor social visions that are not perceived to be in their self-interest.

Personal attention is an objective of education, but it is also a means to other important ends. It is widely recognized as a powerful if deceptively simple educational force in an age where impersonalism and anonymity are pervasive conditions of life. It bears directly on several contemporary tasks: reducing the isolation of the young from caring adults; increasing their incentives to engage in serious learning; and making mass schooling more responsive to the realities of individual differences.

Personal attention helps bring structure, purpose, and positive adult influence to young lives. It reduces isolation and anonymity by showing students that adults know and care about them. This function is one reason educators increasingly use the word "personalization" instead of the more traditional term "individualizing instruction." The task is broader than instruction.[1]

Because dual-career, single-parent, and wholly dysfunctional households have all increased, fewer grownups know young people well. Insufficient tissue connects youth with concerned adults. Young people often fall through the cracks. They easily become lost and invisible. They are known and influenced mainly by peers, and by industries that covet their money and seek to inculcate desired consumption habits. Usually they grow up anonymously but are not badly harmed, though sometimes they become menaces to society.

The lack of a productive connection to adults is not confined to any one type of youth. Those from busy and modestly successful families whose relatives are scattered across the country are one example. Another comes from isolated residential areas where appropriate peers or caring adults can be hard to find. The problem is more complicated for poor children or those from broken homes with few family supports; they often lack economic and emotional security, physical safety, constructive future dreams, and a decent home learning environment. A wide range of Americans consequently seek human relations that are not merely "professional." They want adults who will know children as individuals, care about them as individuals, and work with them as individuals. One source of these adults is school.

One example of how schools provide such attention is a small-scale (one hundred students), expensive ($5,000 per student), privately funded add-on program in a public high school with many low-income minority students. The key to encouraging students to graduate and go on to college is simply "costly, home-style attention." What they receive is a level of attention, consistency, and intensity that does not exist anywhere else in their lives. This is a low-tech effort. The program offers no curricular or instructional innovations at all, yet it seems largely successful in achieving its goals.

In regular two-hour afterschool meetings, students receive the services of an academic advisor, psychologist, social worker, career and college counselor, and outreach worker. They participate in activities ranging from community service, discussions of peer pressure, and preparation for the SAT. If their commitment slackens and they skip school, they are relentlessly pursued. Enrollees emphasize two themes: "They're constantly on you" and "They get to know who you are." Workers in the program emphasize its consistency, the accountability to which students are held, and the hard daily job of adult caring despite rebuffs. The program is something like a family. "I feel like a mother of 30 kids," one adult worker said. "Sometimes I think I care too much." What is impressive is not just the staff's technical expertise but their human skills: tremendous commitment, empathy with the population being served, and unusual resilience.[2]

Another task of personalization is increasing motivation to learn in a country where cultural incentives to learn are weak. Personal attention, to be sure, is not a necessary precondition for motivation. Many students do excellent work with good or less-than-good teachers carrying loads of 150 students. Able and self-directed students, especially when surrounded by peers like themselves and protected from disruptive influences, often learn well without being known well by teachers. But many American students come to school with none of these advantages.

Caring teachers can help disengaged, passive, confused, or discouraged students become connected to school and to learning. By making their commitments to students and subjects regularly visible, some teachers emerge as stimulating personalities who breathe life into learning. They get respect as role models or mentors. Students develop lasting interests through teachers' enthusiastic representations of subjects, or they develop interest in subjects because teachers show enthusiasm for the students. A few become actual apprentices. Positive relationships with their instructors can motivate students when other incentives fail. Personalization should not be confused with social work; it is directly linked to the promotion of academic learning.

The most striking finding of the first evaluation of the Coalition of Essential Schools, a large reform project based at Brown University, was the positive impact of personalization on students. Personal attention was part of the Coalition's program but by no means its most central idea. A high school teaching load of no more than eighty students was only one of nine principles advocated. Yet the

evaluation emphasized widespread student belief that small environments, informality, and "being known" by adults created more incentives to learn than the program's instructional or curricular
ideas. "Personalization builds bonds with an adult and motivates
students to invest in school work because they care more about that
teacher's opinion of them." High expectations pay off when consistently applied to students by adults who know them. The at-risk
program described earlier helps motivate the same way. A student
explained, "You need someone to say you can do it."[3]

Finally, personalization helps students learn by adjusting teaching to individual characteristics. Students are unique persons, their
differences should be understood and respected, and schools should
take those differences into reasonable pedagogical account. This
vast and difficult topic has many different layers. At the school level,
personalized *environments* require policies and practices that match
individual characteristics to institutional characteristics. The goal is
achieving the best fit between individual and school.

At the classroom level, personalized *instruction* further requires
that teachers learn in some detail the strengths, weaknesses, and
other educationally pertinent qualities of students. It requires that
students receive detailed feedback on their work; prescription
should be based on diagnosis. It also requires that teaching methods
take learner characteristics into account. Students should be known
well enough that curriculum decisions are appropriate. All this is
what "individualizing" education means in practice: considerable
one-on-one interaction between students and teachers.

The special needs movement of the past twenty years is the most
extensive American attempt to implement individualization on a
large scale. From the truism that each student learns differently
have emerged elaborate procedures to diagnose different "learning
styles," isolate types of learning disabilities, and design individual
education plans to remedy deficiencies. Large sums are directed by
law to these activities.

The movement has created a new class of teachers and specialists
trained in psychology and generally averse to the liberal arts tradition. They have pushed the idea of individualized instruction for a
limited but growing number of students further than it has ever
been pushed before. Even classic one-on-one tutorial instruction has

never pretended to determine instructional method by "learning styles" as revealed by psychological tests.

But almost all of this push has occurred on behalf of students with one or another serious (or at least measurable) learning problem. How the approach applies to the many students with no particular disabilities but who happen to learn in somewhat different ways is still unclear. Good teachers routinely adjust for slower or faster readers, verbose or quiet talkers, curiosity-seekers or grade-grubbers, penetrating or dull minds. It remains to be seen just how far individualization can be taken beyond these traditional diagnostic categories.

The long-term possibilities include more detailed diagnostic measures, more refined educational "treatments," and the vast potential of computer technology. Perhaps one day all students will have individual educational plans. Perhaps all will learn more in their own way and at their own pace in nongraded schools. Perhaps school traditions like the "senior class" will disappear. Perhaps the greatest promise of computer technology will be its ability, through interaction and massive data storage, to personalize instruction in ways teachers cannot. All this may require an educational organization very different from what exists in the industrialized world today. Yet even without these radical futures, often confidently predicted but never yet realized, schools can do far more to personalize education than they now do.

Barriers to Personalization

Personalization is much easier to advocate than to implement. Many if not most American schools contend that they already practice it. Their public commitment to take individualizing seriously has focused on increasing the variety of courses and programs, giving students and families wide choice over which they will select, and having schools remain largely neutral about the resulting decisions. But if these practices individualize, they usually do so in an anonymous way. They respond to student preferences without pressing adults to know more than a few students well. It is not easy to convert anonymous individualization into personalization. Why?[4]

In a large country where education is compulsory and universal through late adolescence, the greatest barrier to personalization is that students rarely experience it on a human scale. The schools they attend and the educational units they directly experience are too large, and the number of adults with whom they have productive contact is too small. The average size of urban high schools exceeds one thousand, and many of the most troubled ones are far larger. Even if big cities created dozens of small experimental schools, most youth would still attend big schools. The sheer dollar costs of changing this situation have stymied the most clever systemic reformers.

School size is sometimes a misleading indicator of how much individual attention students receive. Some large schools have organized themselves by smaller houses, clusters, or teams in which groups of teachers and students have extensive contact. But most have not, and often compound the size problem by grade-level organization. Public schools rarely span wide age and grade ranges (for example, K–12 or 5–12 combinations) where each grade is relatively small. Fewer than 4 percent of public school students attend such combined schools, and if rural schools are subtracted only 1 percent do. A student in a three-year junior high school of 750 students might well be in a grade of about 250, whereas a student in a K–12 school of 750 might be in a grade of about 58. The human scale is quite different, even though school size is the same.

After students leave the self-contained elementary classroom for the departmentalized world of middle and high schools, their connection to adults usually changes in two important ways. They now deal with many teachers for brief periods of time each day, teachers who carry heavy student loads. They also face the sudden disappearance of an adult specially charged with keeping track of each student's total academic and social development, a role formerly played by elementary teachers. Guidance counselors do not play this role; they have even larger loads than teachers, and their job descriptions stipulate that they spend most of their time on a few problematic students. These changes are formidable barriers to personalization.

The average number of students an urban public high school teacher instructs is about 117, and many teachers in bigger cities carry far larger loads. High student turnover compounds the problem because knowing students well takes time. Increasing personal attention for everyone requires reducing these loads, but even the practical compromise proposed by the Coalition of Essential Schools—80 students for each high school teacher—has so far not convinced many schools of its financial feasibility. The Coalition has since concluded that the 80:1 ratio is too large.[5]

An additional organizational reason teachers do not know students as well as they should is their preoccupation with classroom teaching. Public high school teachers devote roughly 82 percent of their time during school hours just to classroom teaching. Because reformers constantly stress teachers' need to work and plan together, planning is what they are likely to do if time is somehow freed up for new activities. The result is that most teachers have relatively little school time left to see students outside regular class meetings. The intense classroom scheduling of teachers and students is a large structural barrier against increasing opportunities for personal attention through conferences, office hours, and other unscheduled contacts.[6]

The scheduling pattern is well entrenched. Most public school teachers already feel overburdened—there is no time to add anything to their day—and union contracts too often legitimize these feelings and harden them into inflexible procedures. Taxpayers suspicious of the allegedly short workday and workyear of teachers may accept the idea of teachers' using time to plan with other teachers, since in other jobs adults often spend endless hours in meetings. But the value of using free time for more informal contact with students is harder to grasp.

Further, classroom instruction is itself somewhat sacrosanct. The idea of "time on task" is almost always applied to classroom tasks, not learning tasks undertaken anywhere else. In many schools and among many school reformers there is a tacit assumption that learning and sometimes even studying must occur in classrooms if it is to occur at all. Classroom instruction is also regarded as necessary for school safety and order; it serves a custodial and supervisory function that cannot easily be met in other ways. Thus tampering with the daily schedule to provide more opportunities for personal attention is fraught with peril.

All this assumes that personalization is universally applauded, and that the barriers to its extension consist of things like class size, teaching load, costs, and the organization of time. But additional barriers exist. Some regard personalization as a costly luxury or a form of coddling. After all, many students succeed in very impersonal schools. High-performing public schools in cities or suburbs are typically large institutions with high teacher-student ratios. They are not hothouses of nurturance. Students learn there not because teachers know them well, but because they are able and motivated. They are ready to take advantage of educational opportunities.

Why, then, need schools provide more than this? Personalization as nurturance can easily seem little more than another costly social service with an uncertain academic payoff—caring adults preoccupied with student self-esteem. Cost-cutting opponents can point to class-size statistics suggesting that long-range American trends toward smaller classes have not been accompanied by increases in student learning. The considerable research literature on class size has not shown that relatively modest (although extremely expensive) reductions make much of a difference on conventional measures of basic skills.

An even more subtle barrier is that teachers and students themselves sometimes resist personalization. Teachers with large loads are understandably wary of demands that they personalize more when no one stands ready to reduce the loads. Beyond this, the goal of knowing students well assumes that students and adults will want to know each other well. This is by no means always the case.

Students who are in school or in class against their will may regard efforts at personalization as hostile surveillance to be actively resisted. Adult commitment, in addition, is harder to build in schools than in families, extended families, or neighborhoods. The latter settings possess advantages of extensive prior individual knowledge and kinship attachments. Personalized teaching is not just a professional relationship in which technical expertise is dispensed by a service-provider; it is a human one based on genuine personal interest.

This interest may flag if teachers are afraid of students or simply do not like them very much. They may want to avoid them rather than know them. Such feelings are often understandable. Even typical adolescents can be unappealing—either excruciatingly passive or dangerously belligerent. And teachers must deal not just with typical students but with virtually all of them.

Recognizing these dynamics can be awkward for an occupation whose aspirations for true professional status in America have had only uncertain results. The admission that an important part of the teaching job does not depend upon technical instructional skill is difficult. It implies that the American tradition of teacher training may in part be flawed. Schools of education with their vast professoriate may feel threatened and hostile. To them, personalization may seem little more than unprofessional amateurism.

But it is unlikely that the public will ever finance the costly commitment to know all students well unless all students are regarded as worth knowing well. If all are not so regarded, as is the case at present, then reductions in school expenditures and teacher expectations can easily be justified. All attention can be concentrated conveniently on the minority of students who are designated as special for one reason or another.

Any insistence that teachers should or must connect with all students, that the effort to know them well is a moral imperative and failure to try constitutes professional dereliction, can be a loud danger signal to organizations committed to protecting teachers' rights and jobs. This is because a consequence of the position may be the claim that certain individuals or groups—for example, one gender, or one racial or religious or ethnic group—are better suited than others to reach and teach their own kind and should be given preferential treatment in hiring. It is just such reasoning, with a long and not entirely ignoble history in America, that the credentialized teacher certification process is designed to undercut. Personalization, in short, is a more complicated and controversial idea than it first appears.

Personal Attention as Independent-School Method

The heart of the independent-school method has always been individual attention. It is the centerpiece of the schools' claim to educational distinctiveness and a key means to promote both community and standards. Their basic design flows from the premise that knowing students well paves the way for good teaching, good learning, and a positive day-in, day-out community experience. They "must submerge nobody, no matter what the cost in time or labor." A teacher was certain that "whether they're strong, weak, or in the middle, every student is well known and well cared for." A principal was certain parents expected his school to "know their kid" above all else, a view confirmed by private school market research.[7]

The power of this idea continues undiminished across the decades in part because it is the least controversial claim private schools make. The traditions of "community" and "standards" each became vulnerable to charges of exclusivity, snobbism, and elitism. Over time they acquired more negative than positive connotations. Carefully and often artfully, the prep schools retained them but transformed their content to conform more closely to mainstream American values. Community was dissociated from homogeneous values and reformulated to embrace diversity. Standards were dissociated from cultural superiority and safely recast as hard work, AP, and personal best.

In contrast, individual attention never had to be reshaped to fit changing democratic realities because there was never overt hostility to the idea. Probably its most vigorous critics over the years were prep school students who felt adults knew and cared too much! Some students prefer to slip through the cracks. They don't want teachers saying, "Where's your English homework?" or "You can do better," or "Rewrite this paper," or "You shouldn't speak to another student in that way." They have long regarded personal attention as intrusion, and often it has been. But this has not been a serious criticism. Most families want more adult caring for their children, not less.

It is easier to assert a deep concern for each individual as a learner than it is to put in place mechanisms that implement the idea seriously. Personalization as prep school method pursues two somewhat different if greatly overlapping strategies. One strategy is to maximize the quality of human interaction within an educational community, especially between students and teachers. This strategy includes creating an ethic that high-quality relationships are crucial to successful educational communities, and creating schools small enough to function on a human scale.

The other strategy emphasizes mechanisms that match individuals to particular settings and approaches. The quest for a good fit between student and environment has consumed schools and parents alike. If individuals differ, and if good education should attend to those differences, then methods to perfect the fit should exist in addition to close teacher-student interaction.

Human-Scale Communities

Unless students are visible to adults as individuals with names and personalities, and teachers are similarly visible to students, personalization construed as human interaction is virtually impossible. Education on a human scale also requires that adults in a school community value personalization. Students must at minimum tolerate it. If enough do not want to be known, there are many ways to hide. Much of the prep school method is based on these notions.

Prospective independent-school students, for example, first get to know a school through individual interviews and individual tours led by student guides, even if school places are readily available. In the first days of school, interaction among students and between students and adults is encouraged by barbecues, camping trips, advisor meetings, teacher phone calls home, and the like. Key administrators work at learning students' names and faces as quickly as possible. One photographed new students to better connect names with faces. His goal was to address every student by name before students knew who he was, a powerful experience that virtually no student will ever forget.

Many schools have rituals where students are greeted each morning and afternoon by name and a handshake, and are expected to reciprocate and look the adult in the eye. "It's not just come by, but the child looks at you and says hello, and you call him by name." The head of a rigorous academic school would "not permit a kid to pass me in the hall without calling me by name. I tell 50 kids a day that I love them. The primary duty of a school is that every child be known and loved."

These simple rituals—"It's not something you have to think about, it's just what we do"—are meant in part to give students a sense that they are cared for and are full-fledged members of a community. They are equally intended to teach that personal attention is an active participatory process, a two-way street, an obligation of everyone. Students who are known by name in the hallway by most adults—"Everyone knows my daughter's name, even the teachers she hasn't had"—are being taught general responsibilities to interact with others inside and outside classrooms. A ninth-grader whose mind was on basketball rather than *Romeo and Juliet* understood that he would still be held accountable and would be called on. If he had pride in himself and had learned from school rituals he would be prepared for class.

The rituals at this particular school are designed to instruct teachers, too. Routine expectations include coming to school early, staying late, and sometimes showing up on Saturday mornings to give special help. Unusual faculty caring can become the stuff of modest school legends. When one student was ill a teacher arranged for her to participate in class discussions via a speaker phone he installed in his classroom.[8]

It is hard to escape the conclusion that this kind of interaction is less likely to occur in large school settings. A major indicator of human scale is the size of the school world students and teachers inhabit. Traditionally, school size has been the most common measure of a student's school world, and independent schools have always emphasized that they are smaller than the urban and suburban public schools that are their primary competition.

It is true that most independent schools doubled or tripled in size after World War II. They expanded in the 1950s because more qualified applicants wanted to attend. The rush to coeducation brought additional numbers in the 1960s through mergers or the addition of one sex or the other. And the rise of dual-career and single-parent families persuaded schools in the 1970s to add elementary grades downward to the preschool level.

Most needed to become larger if they were to have any chance of financing the broader programs parents and students wanted. The boys day school Browne & Nichols, for example, enrolled about one hundred and fifty students in grades 4–12 in 1950, with a senior class of twenty-nine. After expansion of each grade, a merger with the all-girls Buckingham School, and the addition of preschool through third grade, enrollment grew to about one thousand in the early 1990s.

Yet prep schools' growth over the years did not alter their reputation for smallness. One reason is that public schools and especially well-off suburban schools became even larger. Reformers such as

James B. Conant advocated in the 1950s larger consolidated public schools. Conant was not against individual attention, but against the small schools that in his judgment could not provide it. He argued that enlarged educational opportunities like better science labs and vocational guidance would be more effective instruments to individualize than close human ties in tiny but resource-poor schools. He hoped to professionalize individual attention, and thought only large schools could afford the programs, facilities, and services needed to do so.

Independent schools thus remain significantly smaller than affluent suburban public schools. The average prep school size in 1987–88 was 399 compared with 752 in affluent suburbs. In secondary schools, where student anonymity is usually more problematic than in elementary schools, the mean school sizes were 298 and 1,309, respectively. Independent schools managed to remain relatively small while growing enough to support academic and extracurricular activities usually available only in larger public schools. One of the most important reasons they retain a competitive advantage over suburban schools is their smaller size.[9]

Data on school size underestimate the smaller-scale environments most independent-school students experience. Prep school students are far more likely than public school students to attend combined elementary-secondary schools where the grade ranges are usually preschool–12 and sometimes 5–12 or 6–12. Sixty-two percent of all prep school students in 1991 attended combined schools as compared with 3.6 percent of public school students (only 1 percent if very rural schools are excluded). Even independent secondary schools usually include middle school grades. Their pattern is 7–12 or 8–12 instead of the traditional high school sequence of 9–12 or 10–12.

In combined schools the student's experience is on a more human scale even though the institution itself may not be tiny. Combined schools are usually characterized by smaller grades and other features that spread students out rather than concentrate them together. Human-scale environments do not automatically require small schools. In 1991, for example, the average size of a prep school twelfth grade was fifty-eight and an eighth grade forty-one. In 1987 only 3 percent of all prep school senior classes had more than two hundred students, and most of these were in large boarding schools. Eighty-four percent of senior classes were smaller than one hundred, and 63 percent of all seniors were in classes of fewer than one hundred.

The scale of the school world a prep school student experiences is further reduced by the practice of dividing combined schools into separate administrative units such as lower, middle, and upper schools. These divisions have their own leadership, organization, culture, and physical space. They are easy to understand and feel part of. Combined schools make students easier to know in an additional respect: the more grades in a school, assuming modest attrition because of residential relocation, the longer students are likely to stay and become familiar fixtures. They become "lifers." Prep school eighth-graders are much more likely than eighth-graders in privileged public schools to have spent five years or more in the same school.[10]

The Personal Match

The most direct way to match individuals with school environments lies in the original choice of school. An important step in personalizing education has already been taken after school selection but before attendance in a single class. Despite the growth of generic or standard independent schools, a significant variety of educational environments is available in the larger population centers. These include single-sex or coeducational schools, day schools or residential schools, progressive or traditional schools, schools with strengths in particular subjects, and schools for high-achieving or average children. School choice clearly enhances personalization.[11]

A less conspicuous way independent schools match individuals to environments emphasizes time as a dimension of learning. Although being left or held back a grade has usually been a stigma in America, prep schools have been relatively flexible in accommodating student differences by permitting or encouraging some to take more time to finish school. Ways to do this include deferring initial enrollment in kindergarten or first grade, repeating voluntarily as a "bonus year" an early or a transition grade (such as the ninth), or studying an extra year after twelfth grade prior to college (the "postgraduate" or "PG" year).

Many boarding schools, for example, have well-organized post-graduate programs to ease the school-to-college transition. These address maturational differences or academic difficulties in the most self-evident way. They give students more time to grow up and experience challenging subjects when they are older. But a thirteenth year of school is expensive in dollars and student time; hence it is rare. Students must get something they want from the extra time, such as college admission or financial aid (often in the form of athletic scholarships). Those who pay the bills must also have an incentive: admission to the right college, or the hope that students will meet minimum academic requirements to receive athletic scholarships. Having money or a special talent makes a bonus year at any level more likely.[12]

Perhaps no institutional effort at matching individuals to environments expresses more vividly the prep school commitment to personal attention than college counseling. The reason is freely acknowledged by most schools, though they sometimes wish it were otherwise. The clearest measure of student achievement in independent high schools is where seniors are accepted to college. It is a concrete, public, and highly valued outcome with immediate life consequences, not a general, long-term outcome hesitatingly attributed years later to school experiences. Since most high school graduates go on to college, the factor that connotes achievement is where they go. To educationally savvy America, college placement is the moral equivalent of performance on high-stakes national examinations in countries with centralized educational systems.

This is one reason independent schools are largely indifferent to how their students compare in academic achievement with students in other countries. Such measures do not much concern the constituencies to which they are accountable. Individual college acceptances do. Parents are not indifferent to learning, or to the arousal of serious intellectual interests, or to the formation of good character. But these results usually develop over a long time and have multiple causes, or else they appear with unpredictable suddenness for no apparent reason.

College placement, in contrast, is clear cut. Like winning or losing a championship game, it is a dramatic competitive event. It is celebrated or mourned. "This is really where it all ends up," a counselor said with resignation. "This is really the bang for the buck." An upper-school head made sure that her large counseling office was one of the first things a visitor saw just inside the school's main entrance. "That becomes part of our marketing package."

Until the 1950s, school heads did most college counseling themselves, although they rarely used that phrase, since their role was more directive than consultative. Even when the old College Board essay exams were still being used, the recommendations of heads were a crucial part of the admissions process, especially for students with borderline scores. They gave direct input to colleges and students about who colleges should accept and where students should go. The heads of some schools could exert leverage on colleges because they were important sources of tuition-paying students.

A headmaster might call a college and say, "I have twenty-three boys who want to go to your college. I think you should take these eighteen of them. I'll redirect the other five." Former students recalled how a headmaster with "incredible connections everywhere" would call them in one by one and tell them where they were likely to be accepted, predictions that usually proved correct. Frank Boyden of Deerfield Academy sometimes rode his buggy down to Amherst College and presented a list of students he announced would be enrolling there come September.[13]

Much of this changed dramatically after the surge of college applications in the 1950s. When the market for preferred colleges became a seller's one, heads spent more time reassuring students and parents that their lives were not over if they were not admitted to their first-choice college—and in any case it was not the schools' fault. "Counseling" then became a real and necessary activity, a specialized service involving varied techniques that school heads no longer had time to provide.

Two essential tasks had to be accomplished. First, families and students had to be taught that a wide variety of colleges were wholly respectable and conveyed no stigma of social or intellectual rejection. They had to understand and adjust to the new reality that Bates, Franklin & Marshall, Syracuse, and dozens of others were worthy options to Yale. Some re-education was essential if schools could ever hope to match student preferences with realistic possibilities. Even today many supposedly well educated families remain shockingly ignorant of the range of high-quality colleges and universities; they only know colleges they grew up hearing about.

Second, prep schools had to learn how to give students as large an edge as possible in the admissions race. They hoped, of course, that their traditional emphasis on high standards would impress colleges, as the NRO had aimed to demonstrate. But strong academic and extracurricular records were often insufficient. Many applicants to selective colleges had excellent but similar credentials. The key to a competitive advantage was to help applicants present themselves and be presented by their schools more effectively than others.

College counseling includes teaching families and students not merely about how college admissions "works" but, more important, about themselves. The ideal process encourages them to reflect on interests, preferences, and strengths that can lead to a more informed and mature student-college match. Great emphasis is placed on self-analysis, reality testing, information-gathering, and helping students take charge of the process, which schools still monitor closely.

It is routine, for example, for ninth-graders to be told that the academic programs they select should meet not only graduation requirements but the expectations of the kind of college they wish to attend. It is not uncommon for sophomores to take the Preliminary Scholastic Aptitude Test (PSAT) for practice, and then take it again as juniors. The point is not just to practice test-taking, but to acquire a sense of where one will likely stand on the Scholastic Aptitude (recently renamed Scholastic Assessment) Test taken later junior year and again senior year. It is also routine for schools to give juniors a thick packet of candid orientation materials about the whole process.

Presenting themselves effectively to a college is often the first anxiety-provoking task students must face. Much of the work of college counseling is designed to minimize silly student mistakes. One typical school-produced college guide, consisting of thirty-three single-spaced pages, made much common and uncommon sense. It emphasized, for example, that applications to second- or third-choice colleges should be taken just as seriously as those to first-choice colleges. Any hint that a college was regarded as a mere "safety school" (a place to fall back on if all else failed) would insult that college.

The guide stressed that an "early-decision" application—meaning students would commit themselves to attending a college if accepted there early—could boost the chances of those who were reasonable candidates to begin with. The guide also confirmed that being a "legacy" was advantageous—but that legacy usually meant that a parent had attended the college in question, not a sibling or another relative.

The guide noted that the most important part of an application was what students could control, the essays they wrote. Students write college essays themselves, but in virtually all prep schools they get feedback from teachers and counselors. Depending on school policies, the feedback may be general. "No, don't use it," or "Rip it up and start again." In others it may be much more specific although not as specific as comments on essays written for courses. Teachers might tell students, "You should proofread more carefully" when spelling or grammatical errors abound. Or they might ask questions that expose major weaknesses. "You say that your favorite subject is history but your worst grade was history. Shouldn't you deal with that apparent contradiction?" A student who rewrote college essays five times because of teacher feedback concluded, "It makes you mad, but they work very hard for us. It's unreal."

This written material is supplemented by group and individual meetings, usually held in the spring of junior year. The group meeting of parents (or parents and students) with college counselors is often the best-attended and best-planned school gathering aside from graduation. Everything is calculated to reduce anxiety, present the basic message about self-analysis, and convey reams of practical information. One school breaks parents into small groups to simulate a college admissions staff meeting. Each group gets three applicant folders and a mandate to decide in an hour which one candidate to admit. This teaches parents how complex and unpredictable the process is. It also gives them an idea of the school's limits in affecting admissions.

Lengthy individual sessions with juniors, parents, or both soon follow. Sometimes students write autobiographical essays to help clarify their goals and help counselors learn more about them. The process begins to focus on connecting information about self with information about colleges: by visiting them, reading about them, talking with representatives who often come directly to the school, or talking with teachers and counselors. By the spring of senior year, one counselor calculated, a typical student would have spent about eight hours in one-on-one college counseling. That is more tutorial-like time than students are likely to receive for any other single purpose.

The growth of "nontraditional" prep school students from families with no money or newly acquired money has given college counseling an added educational obligation: it must raise college sights by teaching students about the better colleges and universities. Privileged students learn about the higher education pecking order long before high school, but many able youth do not acquire this important lore on their own. They pass through high school with limited information on good colleges that might match their interests and have substantial financial aid to dispense. The function of effective college counseling is to widen the horizons not only of those who believe there is nothing beyond the Ivys, but also of those who have never heard of the Ivys.

The desired results of all these activities are tentative lists of colleges for each student to visit or think more about—lists that counselors can assess for realism. Do they include "stretches" or "reaches" (that is, desired long-shots), strong possibilities, and safety schools? If students' lists are wildly unrealistic or alternatively unambitious, all prep schools have methods to continue the educational process. One maintains a "black box" containing detailed school records of its students accepted at all colleges over a thirty-year period. It is easy to check grades, class rank, test scores, and major activities against one's own credentials. Opening the black box has been instructive to families and very helpful to the school.

Educating families and students benefits colleges, too. It enlarges the number of colleges deemed acceptable. The reputations and financial status of more than a few institutions have been enhanced by the fact that many independent-school graduates attend them. Educating families and students also reduces the number of applications to selective colleges that will surely fail. These colleges are grateful to schools whose tactful guidance eases their burden by eliminating weak candidates before they apply. Dean Bender perceptively attributed the higher Harvard acceptance rate of private compared with public applicants to prep schools' "more thorough pre-application screening."

Because the college counseling process informally screens students initially, and colleges know it, this becomes in itself a competitive advantage. Schools take steps to make themselves as well known to colleges as possible, especially respected colleges with little history of dealings with the school. When one college wait-listed an applicant the school believed to be a strong candidate, the college counselor called the college and learned that it knew nothing of the school or its program. The school urged that an admissions officer come visit. The next year the college accepted a weaker applicant for early decision.

Even so, one built-in prep disadvantage over typical public schools has remained. More students from individual prep schools are likely to apply to the same selective colleges in any year than from most public schools. The list of preferred colleges is fairly short, prep school families know it, and so multiple applications to the same colleges persist. This is another reason prep schools work hard to educate families about the larger world of high-quality American higher education. They want to spread their first- or high-choice colleges as widely as possible.[14]

The "school letter" is the most important document produced by schools in the college counseling process. Virtually all prep schools create a school letter about each senior, crafted as carefully as possible to present candidates in the most favorable but honest light. Gushing but unmerited praise is disastrous, for colleges soon know which school letters lack integrity or simply lack knowledge about how to communicate important material about a student. Many competent college counselors attempt to communicate personally to colleges "how I will try to represent the kids and what they can expect from me in the way of reporting." Competent counselors try to establish personal and continuing relations with college admissions officers, relations that come into serious play in cliffhanger situations where counselors' reputations and track records suddenly become relevant.

The school letter is a joint effort of many people, including students, whose autobiographical questionnaires or essays often reveal activities that may have escaped adult attention. At its best the letter is a small work of literary art, based on extensive input collected over the years from student folders and from direct queries made to faculty. Specific examples, direct quotes from teachers, and a story-line of some sort are woven together to create the best presentation possible. Most schools employ one or more college counselors who typically draft the letter. But the letters are usually reviewed by others—another counselor, the student's advisor, the upper-school head, or the school head.

In other schools, college counselors are the students' senior-year advisors—teachers who do counseling either as a paid add-on or with a slightly reduced teaching load. In one school seven teachers were college counselors. Each year their load was about ten seniors. The seven met together for two full periods a week all year to discuss each senior, and then to critique the letter drafts that each counselor wrote. In effect, each draft was edited by six people, some of whom were responsible for specific matters such as style, cohesion, and grammar. "Every letter is essentially okayed by the committee."

A research study which found that prep school AP students had lower academic aptitude than public school AP students also found, to the researchers surprise, that the same prep school students presented better student essays and school letters in their college applications than public school students. They determined this by means of blind ratings of the essays and letters by an outside panel. The study concluded with great understatement that prep school students, teachers, and counselors "devote more attention to putting the applicants' best foot forward."[15]

As late as 1959, Dana M. Cotton, a wise observer of prep schools and Harvard admissions, told an independent-school audience that the fairest decisions were made when college and school people sat down together and "exhaustively" discussed each candidate. "Faith in the recommendation of the school authorities and a mutual understanding of each others' problems are essential." In most instances this no longer happens. It is considered an unfair prep school advantage, because other candidates are not known well even in their own schools or because their schools are not known well to colleges. Most prep schools do not officially rank candidates, although the school letter allows discriminations among candidates to be made if schools want to make them. This, plus prep schools' propensity to discourage applications if they seem wholly unrealistic, suggests that the spirit if not the letter of Cotton's point still survives.

Prep schools remain active players in the college admissions process precisely because college counseling is so personalized and specialized. The prep school student, in a sense, has to pass muster not only by the colleges but by his or her own school. Especially near the end of the process, telephone calls are made for touch-and-go cases such as whether someone will clear the wait list. "One of the key elements of my job is getting on the phone," a counselor explained. Sometimes a school simply tells a college that a student will definitely enroll if admitted. Sometimes it advocates a student's case, or is asked its opinion.

Extensive personal attention in college counseling cuts both ways. A student's case may be better argued than it would have been otherwise, but prep schools have more knowledge of more students. Depending on the individual, schools choose just how hard they will argue a particular case. A prep school applicant often has to impress his own school almost as much as a college.[16]

The ultimate objective is "to make great matches and to convince parents that life is not going to end because they are not going to Stanford." Schools want each student to arrive at a short list of colleges of varying degrees of admissions difficulty, each of which the student would be content to attend. Schools want graduates to attend colleges of their choice and thus be, along with their parents, satisfied customers. It is to everyone's advantage to minimize disappointments caused by unrealistic expectations or ignorance of one's own preferences. The headmaster of the Hill School bluntly explained in 1957 that "by tactful guidance of the mediocre scholastic risk, we may even preserve a high percentage of 'acceptances to the college of first choice.'"[17]

Personal attention is the cement that glues independent schools together and energizes efforts to pursue ideals of community and standards. Knowing people well within human-scale institutions, and matching individuals to particular environments and experiences, are their most potent educational methods. Personal attention encourages, but never guarantees, decent communities. It brings maximum institutional pressure to bear on the crucial objective of college placement. And, as we will now see, it defines the teacher's role in ways that are somewhat different from the American educational norm.

9

The Role of the Good Teacher

Over many decades prep schools have embraced a distinct notion of the role of the good secondary and middle school teacher, including the ways good teachers influence individual students and where that influence happens. This notion emphasizes teachers more as personal exemplars or models than as experts in classroom method. Their impact comes more from personal attributes than from technical skills. In a sense, good teachers make sure students know them well for the same reason they get to know students well: to teach them effectively.

In contrast, the most influential approaches to individualizing education in the twentieth century are products of science and technology. Their goal is to make the process of matching students to educational experiences more scientific than the clumsy amateurism of, say, asking a student to repeat first grade or having a lengthy one-on-one conference after school. One such approach employs various tests to diagnose individual differences: vocational and academic aptitude tests, achievement tests as diagnostic and assessment tools, and psychological tests to uncover emotional disorders, learning disorders, and learning styles. Another approach stimulates individual interaction with learning materials without the constant presence of teachers. Over the years this has produced teaching machines, programmed instruction, and computer-assisted instruction.

Independent schools have generally kept a wary distance from both perspectives. They have embraced neither of them with the enthusiasm one would expect of institutions deeply committed to personalization as a defining tradition. Certainly they have not ignored diagnostic tests, computers, and the rest, but they do not celebrate them as crucial components of personalization, nor do they use them nearly so much as public schools do. Instead, they believe that teachers are or should be more like parents than physicians.

Porter Sargent's consumer guidebooks always emphasized that prep schools' main comparative advantage was "a richer and more inspiring influence of the strong and cultured personalities of the teachers directed toward the individual pupil." A leading school head after World War II argued that a teacher's "every contact" with a student communicated what the teacher "is and stands for as a person; his love of things of the mind, his integrity, his moral values." From the teacher's example the student would set his sights one way or the other. "In the last analysis he will probably not learn in any other way." Teachers were crucial role models for youth—living alternatives to cultural mediocrity.

When NAIS made a public statement on teacher education in 1963, it asserted that "the quality of the individual human being is the most important factor in the educational process, whether we talk about the teacher, the administrator, or the student." It followed that "effective teaching will depend less on the teacher's preparation than on his qualities as a person." A booklet designed to recruit college students to prep school teaching argued that "people are the single biggest factor" in whether a school was any good. This perspective gave great weight to the interest-generating or motivational role of teachers. One reason prep schools embrace one-on-one personal interaction as method is that it more directly confronts problems of student motivation than approaches originating from science and technology.[1]

A headmaster insisted that children need to be among teachers who "totally support the values and learning they sponsor." Some of the teachers' personal qualities should be avowedly subject centered, especially at the secondary level. What makes teachers effective is "incredible role modelling." They visibly demonstrate in their own lives that what they teach matters to them. "We have artists who teach art," one head pointed out. "They're not only 'teachers.' The dance teacher has travelled to Bali to study dance. The English department are all writers. Everyone has a passion for the material they teach." The hope is that if students see the passion, it will rub off on them. At their best teachers recruit students, not literally to take up a vocation (although that sometimes happens), but to take up a lasting personal interest.

Another desirable human quality for good teachers is liking students. One head emphasized that the faculty hiring process consciously sought out teachers who would be interested in "individuals, not just interested in teaching a group and relating to groups of kids." Another said that her school's greatest strength was the "individual teacher-student relationship."

These views all call attention to teachers' roles with individual students both inside and outside classrooms. Small classes provide opportunities—not guarantees—for one-on-one interaction conducive to modeling, mentoring, and exemplar relations. But classrooms are only the tip of the iceberg when the emphasis is on close teacher-student interaction. Much of the worklives of teachers and students occurs outside class; just as teachers do much of their teaching outside classrooms, students do much of their learning elsewhere, too.[2]

Small Classes

Small class size has always been the most publicized prep school method of providing personal attention. This is not surprising, given that it is the consequence of the school's smallness experienced most directly by students. Independent-school class size has long been roughly half that of privileged public secondary schools, and appreciably smaller than that of public elementary schools. The prep school averages have remained remarkably stable—about twelve students per secondary class in 1931, fifteen per class in 1958, thirteen per class in 1991.[3]

These dramatic numbers exert enormous power over what consumers of prep schools believe determines a good school. Independent-school students are significantly more likely to praise their teachers' interest in them, their relations with teachers, and the teaching itself than are students in privileged public or all public schools. Trustees visiting one prep school invariably came away cheering most about the "close knowing exchange back and forth with students in a smaller class. That is what they feel the clientele is really seeking."[4]

Everyone consistently mentions three virtues of small classes. Students cannot disappear or slip passively through the cracks. "They can see if you are spacing out," one student complained. "I fell asleep once and the English teacher used my name in all the examples. I woke up pretty quickly!" A once-shy girl explained that "people who might not speak get more opportunities to speak or it's more necessary for them to speak." She explained, "[Once I] got my voice I definitely made sure everyone heard it!" Beyond drawing out the reluctant or shy (a good example of how personal attention supports academic press), small classes make it possible for virtually everyone else to participate regularly and be heard.

Small classes also help teachers and students know one another better "as human beings." Voluntary interaction about academic substance, especially by reluctant, fearful, or embarrassed students, is more likely to occur if a comfortable relationship has initially been established. This implies not that the individuals are friends, but simply that the relationship is relaxed and friendly rather than tense or distant.

Finally, small classes enable teachers to focus on individuals as learners and, to some degree, to individualize instruction. Because students are known "intimately in the classroom, you know what the individual needs are and what the individual problems are so you can address them." An English teacher explained that she could establish after a few minutes, in a class of fifteen, who had done the reading and who hadn't, as well as what their different levels of understanding were. She determined, in effect, where everyone was— and therefore what the possibilities and limits of that day's class were. She could then make adjustments. In a much larger class she would be flying blind. In such a situation she thought she would probably dominate the class and limit discussion, just to make sure something positive happened.

At their best, creative schools and teachers capitalize on the opportunities presented by small classes to personalize education.

They do not just imitate group discussion methods—but with smaller groups (it is admittedly easier to have serious participatory discussions when class size is fifteen rather than twenty-five or thirty-five); nor do they just lecture to students—but with far smaller numbers in the lecture hall.[5] Instead, they use small classes to move toward a tutorial or one-on-one model of teacher-student interaction. They move toward the real promise of personalization.

One independent school, for example, organizes its twenty-one-class weekly schedule for English teachers so that every upper-school student receives a private twenty-minute "writing conference" once every two weeks. Each teacher has three regular classes that meet five times per week. Two are upper-school classes, one is from the middle school. Each class averages twelve students, so the total student load is thirty-six. Only upper-school students have writing conferences, meaning that twenty-four students must be seen individually every two weeks. In six extra full periods a week, a teacher can schedule twelve twenty-minute individual conferences. Thus all twenty-four upper schoolers have a writing tutorial every two weeks within an English teacher's twenty-one-class (fifteen plus six) weekly schedule.

Why all the trouble and expense for a twenty-minute individual conference twice a month? A teacher explained that small classes alone were inadequate to teach writing. "I need the kid in front of me." She could endlessly annotate students' written work, but half the time they didn't understand what she was saying. "You have to translate, so it's really important to look at a piece of writing and ask the student 'is this what you mean?'" On other occasions students needed to "talk through" a paper before they wrote it. She regarded the conferences as "incredible support," a classic example of implementing the idea of individualizing teaching. The school had capitalized on the potential of small classes by transforming class time into tutorials.

Yet it is counterproductive to canonize small classes to the degree that prep school publicists and prep school families have traditionally done. The idea of small classes as an educational panacea poses at least two major problems. One is their cost. The other is that their potential is rarely realized.

Small classes are prohibitively costly for public schools and an increasingly unacceptable cost for independent schools. If class sizes of thirteen to fifteen are essential for true individual attention, then most public school students will never experience it. There is little possibility of funding public schools at that level. Even many prep schools fear that they cannot further sustain the costs of small classes without narrowing their market to a dangerously small segment. A thoughtful administrator concluded that to continue "selling individual attention is going to hang us." Prep schools had trapped themselves by making small classes the centerpiece of their collective image. Increasing class size, as this administrator's school was of necessity beginning to do, was a no-win although inevitable move. It was viewed as betrayal by teachers who thought small classes were part of their contract, and by families who had been taught that small classes were the schools' biggest educational advantage.[6]

A closely related problem is that small classes in and of themselves do not often produce superior teaching or learning. Uncritical faith in them as a panacea ignores realities of instructional quality. The writing conferences just described are more the exception than the rule. The few efforts to look at what happens inside prep school classrooms suggest that their pedagogy is not different from that employed in comparable but larger college prep classes in public or other schools. Prep schools rarely exploit the possibilities of small classes in imaginative ways. If smallness provides opportunities for consistently superior classroom instruction, they are usually opportunities foregone.

Evidence on this point includes observations by veteran participants in formal school evaluations, data from student surveys, and data from classroom observations of research projects. An elaborate student survey in the 1970s comparing independent with suburban public schools, for example, concluded that although prep school students knew their teachers better because of smaller classes, the teaching in each school type was about the same. A more extensive study of sophomore opinion in 1990 suggests that prep school classes may "challenge" their students and press them to "understand" material (rather than recall facts) somewhat more than privileged public school classes, but they are less likely to push students to "try" as hard as they can. It is difficult to extract clear-cut classroom differences from this information.[7]

Classroom observations made in 1981–83 for A Study of High Schools permit comparisons between three independent schools and four public schools with ambitious college preparatory missions. This material reveals no prep school advantage in instructional technique. With classes of fifteen, teachers lectured as often and ran discussions with the same degree of skill as public school teachers with classes of twenty-five or thirty. The prep school teaching advantage was the presence of greater instructional consistency across the board. Public schools were much more likely than independent schools to have terrific and inept teachers working side by side. Prep schools had few truly bad teachers, but many average ones. They guaranteed more evenness in quality, especially in comparison with nonhonors or "regular" classes in other schools, but they by no means guaranteed consistently superior classroom instruction.[8]

That prep schools rarely capitalize on the opportunities of small class size is not really surprising. One explanation for a pattern of even but not consistently excellent instruction is that prep schools are more careful in original hiring, can rid themselves of very poor teachers more easily than public schools, but are reluctant to remove mediocre teachers who are useful. Their big mistakes are usually quickly identified. School heads take seriously responsible complaints that a teacher new to a school is unprepared, mean-spirited, or disengaged. They move in and make changes when changes are warranted.

But the schools typically lack the will to rid themselves of average or mediocre teachers with experience, especially those who serve the institution constructively in other ways. Some may be successful with one type of student but not others. Some may be effective in an extracurricular or administrative role that needs doing. Further, a decision not to keep an experienced teacher makes all faculty nervous because they realize that it could happen to them. Heads know how much effort and planning is required in declining to reappoint a teacher, and how backlashes can even threaten their own positions. Veteran mediocre teachers often have at least some parent, faculty, and alumni boosters. Given the choice, school trustees prefer keeping average teachers to lowered faculty morale or outright insurrection. They know parents are paying for happy environments. So heads proceed with great caution.

Another explanation for the infrequency of consistently outstanding prep school classes is that most teachers do not know enough about how to individualize classroom instruction. Small classes do not make teaching easier, although they surely ease problems of classroom control. From a teaching standpoint small classes can even be intimidating. The smaller the scale of teacher-student interaction, the more both parties are exposed. This is why formal tutorials scare students more than other instructional methods—there is absolutely nowhere to hide—and also why they scare teachers. Because small scale is rare, and because it is usually regarded as a virtue that automatically conveys educational benefits, there is virtually no tradition of professional development in relevant instructional skills. These include training in how to conduct one-on-one tutorials.

Further, the various ways small classes might be capitalized on to make an educational difference often require collective efforts to succeed. Making one-on-one tutorials routine and effective, or organizing individual students to work on their own, or orchestrating small groups of students to work productively together, usually requires institutional resolve. The writing conference tutorials could not easily have been established by individual teachers. The model required a collective school policy and effort, because the whole scheme assumed that a twice-monthly, twenty-minute conference was important for everyone and justified the expense of adding more English teachers than would otherwise have been needed.[9]

One final explanation for the absence of consistently good classroom teaching is simply that good teachers have discerned practical limits to what can be accomplished in classrooms. They see classrooms as only one setting for their work. A thoughtful teacher with only twelve students in a section realized she could do many things that the teacher of her daughter, enrolled in a public school with twenty students per class, could not do. She knew her students well, she thought, but she still taught them as a group. Everyone read the same books at the same time. This was not the same thing as individualizing programs based upon a diagnosis of learning characteristics peculiar to each one. She did not know how to do that. But she was also not sure that such a classroom approach was feasible, necessary, or desirable. She could give more satisfactory individual attention outside class.

Teachers' Work Outside Classrooms

The independent-school emphasis on personal attention, modeling, and exemplification as educational method encourages schools to maximize interaction between individual students and teachers. Much individual teaching and learning happens outside regular classroom instruction and its typical group format. The small-classes panacea places too much emphasis on classes; they are only the tip of the learning iceberg. They are but one of many places where students learn and teachers teach. Porter Sargent argued long ago that "the type of man or woman who has nothing to give the boys and girls outside the classroom is out of place" in the teaching profession. For him the ideal was the traditional boarding school teacher—the "triple threat" who taught, coached, and ran a dormitory.[10]

That role helped shape the notion of the proper role of day school teachers just as boarding school ideas influenced day schools in other ways. Teachers connect with students by arranged or spontaneous private conferences, by attendance and participation in nonacademic school events, by assuming the role of student advisor, and by providing elaborate written feedback on student performance.

Varied, out-of-classroom contact between students and teachers becomes possible not just because of belief in a conception of a teacher's or a student's proper role but because specific organizational features of prep schools enable teachers and students to connect more extensively. One crucial feature is the total student load of a teacher—the number of students a teacher is responsible for in all classes. This is a more decisive indicator than class size (although they are usually closely related) because it more accurately suggests how much time is actually available for a teacher to deal with each student. A college professor, for example, might teach eighty students in a course meeting three times per week. If she teaches only one course, which is sometimes the case, her total student load is only eighty even though her class size appears rather large.

In departmentalized middle and high schools, astounding differences exist between prep school teacher loads and those in other schools. The typical independent-school student load in the 1990s is around 60. Public school teachers in general, and in privileged suburban schools in particular, instruct twice as many students. Estimates vary between 120 and 113 students, with teachers in the most troubled urban areas often having larger loads still. Almost 90 percent of prep school teachers have student loads smaller than the 80-student objective espoused by the Coalition of Essential Schools.[11]

An equally important feature of school organization affecting out-of-class interaction is how much of a teacher's school day is spent outside regular classroom teaching. In general, prep school teachers have fewer classes per week than either privileged public school teachers or all public school teachers. Their traditional job description is four classes per day, meeting usually five times per week but sometimes four. Thus prep school teachers typically have about twenty classes per week, sometimes fewer but rarely many more. This is five fewer weekly classes, on average, than public school teachers. The prep teachers spend roughly 69 percent of regular school hours in classroom teaching, instead of the public school average of 82 percent. (Recall that in the English department schedule discussed above, teachers had only three regular classes per day, with the remainder of their weekly classload given over to individual conferences.)

As a result, prep school teachers usually have two or three "free" or unscheduled periods each day. This unscheduled time is rarely used to bring teachers together. In most independent schools professional development occurs informally whenever teachers talk about their work. Or it happens formally on days planned long in advance when school ends early or does not meet at all.

To the extent that courses do not always meet daily, students have more "frees" as well. This pattern resembles that in higher education. But unlike higher education, prep school teachers usually make their unscheduled time available to students. Given the group format of regular classes, students say, not surprisingly, that individual attention regarding coursework occurs far more frequently outside classes than within them. Less time spent in classroom instruction clearly does not reduce the total time spent on the job for independent-school teachers. Despite having many fewer students to teach, prep school teachers may actually spend more time on the job than public school teachers.[12]

How is individual attention practiced outside the formal classroom setting? Many schools build time into their schedules after the
regular day when teachers are predictably "on call." Such "extra
help," "tutoring time," or "afterschool study" periods (for example,
from 2:15 to 3:00 or 3:15 to 4:00) precede regular afterschool sports
and other student activities. These periods supplement the times
during the regular day when students and teachers happen to have
"frees" at the same time. They are the prep school version of office
hours. "I couldn't believe that faculty were in their offices with students just lounging and talking," was one teacher's first impression
of a prep school. "It seemed like such a normal part of life." When
she had been a student she had needed passes to go anywhere outside class.

It is hard to overestimate the value of built-in yet voluntary time
for out-of-class academic interaction. Students invariably praise the
"accessibility" and "availability" of teachers not only during structured times but during informal, incidental meetings, such as discussions over lunch or coffee in the cafeteria. A student explained
that after almost every class someone would ask a teacher, "Listen,
can I meet with you?" There was no shame in asking for help, and
teachers were completely willing to give it instead of saying, "Oh
that is my lunch break."

A mother recalled how her daughter, new to a private school, was
"struggling terribly" in biology. After much trepidation, she mustered the courage to admit apologetically to the teacher how little
she understood. They established when both had coinciding free periods, and he said, "I'll meet you out by that big tree on the front
lawn. Bring your biology book and we'll work on this and see if we
can't get it straightened out."

So on a gorgeous September day they sat under a tree and worked
on the problem. After about thirty minutes, much progress had been
made. The student turned to the teacher and said, "I'm really sorry I
took so much of your time. I really appreciate it, but I'll let you go
now." The reply was, "Absolutely not, Jessica. I want to get to know
you as a person. We have another half hour. Let's just sit and talk
and find out who Jessica is." As the mother told the story, the encounter was the "cement that glued [her daughter] to the school."
When Jessica told her parents the story that night, it glued them to

the school as well and elevated the biology teacher to near god-like status.

Stories like this make several points about the uses of individual attention outside classrooms. Like Jessica, most students who seek one-on-one teacher contact are concerned about "understanding" the material. It is this kind of academic problem—not questions about remembering facts, clarifying an assignment, or asking, "Will that be on the test?"—that drives students to the personal encounter. A physics student, for example, initially hated his course because the teacher "didn't teach." That is, he didn't lecture and ran the nonlab portion of the course as a seminar in which he asked questions to students sitting around a table. The teacher had seventh and eighth periods free for students to drop by, and one day this student finally mustered the courage to do so. "I was there by myself."

He told the teacher that he had done his homework and gotten all the right answers. But, "You know what? I don't understand a thing that I did." He could recite definitions, but couldn't explain what they meant beyond the words in the definition. So the teacher went to the chalkboard and started asking questions—the subject was centrifugal force. After nearly half an hour, progress had been made. The student began to see how "the acceleration points it toward the center." He felt much better when he left. "He doesn't give you the answer. He makes you think. I thought that was good." This kind of teaching, to students who find it easier to memorize definitions than to understand concepts, relies on the back and forth nature of conversation. The teacher's job is to figure out just where the student is at sea and lead him to dry land. In this case, it took a large block of one-on-one time that normally could not be spared from the regular class.

Another problem is that students are often reluctant to seek individual attention. They feel embarrassed, exposed, and unsure that teachers really want them to impose on their busy lives. The availability of teachers does not ensure that students will drop by. An administrator remarked that it was especially hard to get ninth- and tenth-graders to go to teachers for help and that better students were more likely to seek extra help because they were more confident. Jessica assumed from her prior experience that asking for help was an admission of stupidity and that teachers didn't have time to give it. The physics student was afraid of being exposed as a mere memorizer. His defensive strategy was bluntly to admit at the beginning that he didn't understand. The conference could start with that fact clearly on the table, instead of ending with it as a humiliating conclusion. Thus a major task of teachers in prep schools is not only to make themselves accessible outside the classroom, but also to create conditions where students will risk going to them for help.

Teachers have many incentives to do this. They generally believe out-of-class academic contact is a "vital part of the curriculum" and an essential way to cope with problems of individual puzzlement that inevitably arise in group classes. One teacher felt comfortable telling a struggling student in class that she couldn't help her much at that moment. But she could say, "When is your free period? Let's get together and we'll talk about it." The ability to say that helped move the regular class along. Teacher and student knew that time would be available to work on the problem together.[13]

But how are reluctant students encouraged to take the initiative? If students are clearly failing, extra help can be mandated. But in the cases cited, where one student's struggles were unknown because it was early in the semester and the other's were well disguised because he got the right answers, it was important to nudge them toward seeing teachers voluntarily. In many cases teachers simply make the first move. One explained, "Sometimes kids don't understand that they need to insist on extra help or extra attention. Not only do you give it to them but you insist that they take it."

Whether a teacher-initiated move is successful, or whether students make the move to approach teachers on their own, depends frequently on incidental or casual contact with students somewhat removed from academics. If students and teachers know each other in a variety of settings, some of the formal barriers between them can collapse and individual discussions about student work can become more frequent. Each becomes more approachable to the other. Casual contact is thus a powerful dimension of personal attention. It can be as simple as "the five-minute walk over to the gym, when we talk a bit, laugh, bip and bop, no big deal, but it's important, and goes on a lot, thank God."

Or it can be the result of the multiple roles teachers continue to play in prep schools. An American History teacher got to know many of his students better because he accompanied them on a school trip during spring break and was also their lacrosse coach. He recalled that on a camping trip with students, "sitting in the raft with a bubblehead helmet and a lifevest on, getting thrown out of the raft—everybody has an opportunity to mix it up with the kids. That really is very valuable."

It is to de-professionalize and humanize relations that prep school teachers often make great efforts to attend and sometimes participate in student afterschool events. "I want to go to the play so I can show up in the hallway and say to a student, 'You did a great job.'" A French teacher made a point of attending wrestling matches of a student who wasn't working hard and made sure he knew she was there. After he pulled out a victory in the last thirty seconds, she wrote him a note asking that he show the same intensity in French that he showed in the match. He "started turning," and the teacher knew that the small rapport emanating from her attendance had made an impact.

A college counselor who persuaded a father to allow his daughter to attend the college of her choice even though it was expensive (as he had permitted his sons to do) would never have had the opportunity had he not wandered over to watch her lacrosse game. The father was watching too and the conversation about college spontaneously ensued. This kind of teacher effort is enormously important, a parent thought, because "that's what connects the kids to the place. The faculty doesn't seem to end in the classroom."

Advising Students and Preparing Written Comments

Beginning in middle school, when school becomes fragmented and departmentalized, prep students are assigned "advisors." They are regular teachers, not trained counselors. Advising loads are always relatively small, generally ranging between six and fourteen students. When teachers advise, the load can be spread across the faculty and kept manageable. One of the basic differences between teacher roles in prep and most public schools is that an assumed part of the prep school job is student advising. The advising role is very different from the tradition of guidance counseling, which emerged in public education in the 1920s and has removed class-room teachers to this day from formal advising responsibilities.

"Counseling" is a separate public school profession with its own traditions, entrance requirements, and support associations. Public schools have few counselors, and the guidance counseling profession has never wished to define its mission as general advising. Instead, guidance moved from an initial concern for vocational guidance, to an emphasis on psychological counseling, to a more recent focus on tasks such as college counseling, monitoring the cases of troubled students, or managing the educational plans of students eligible for mandated special needs programs.

The teacher's advising role, in sharp contrast, emphasizes a strategically placed person clearly responsible for knowing most of what is important to know about a few individuals. All students have a designated adult with whom to identify. In the fragmented world of middle and secondary education, the advisor is expected to be the "main connecting point," the "synthesizer," the "filter," the "go-between," the "first point of contact," the "key person," and the "advocate" for each student. If prep schools attempt to know students well, the advisor is accountable for knowing a small group best. The advising system is the schools' most formal mechanism to provide a safety net ensuring that no one falls through the cracks. Schools tell parents that their key contact person is the advisor, and tell teachers the same thing.

Because the teacher-advisor role is uncommon in American public schooling, its centrality as an established and routine part of the prep school teacher's job needs elaboration. There is no absence of informal advising in American education. Many students in all schools find on their own a teacher who becomes a special confidante or information source. Why, then, is it so important to formalize the role, especially given that these advisors hardly ever receive any formal training and do not regard themselves as either therapists or learning specialists? What their expertise consists of is often very unclear.

The broadest answer is that advisors bring institutional accountability to the notion of individual attention. The existence of the role, with its various specific obligations, forces faculty who perform it to take seriously the totality of a student's development even when it progresses without profound emotional or academic crises. The role also officially legitimizes the belief that all students are "entitled to have an adult." For those who are shy, do not wish to impose, or wish to remain invisible, the advising system signals that one-on-one time is set aside just for them, that they are not bothering anyone or asking for special help by using the resource. Like many other independent-school procedures, advising systems make it easier for students to connect with adults and harder for students to avoid them.

The mechanics of advising vary from school to school. Students may stay with the same advisor for several years or change annually. Their ability to choose advisors varies, although opportunities always exist to switch. Sometimes a large percentage of the faculty advises at least a few students, and sometimes a small group of faculty assumes the responsibility year after year. These details are far less significant than what advisors do. Their work is broken down by activities with all their advisees together, often called advisories, and meetings with individual students.

Regular group advisory meetings usually include some combination of information-giving (deadlines that must be met), small group discussions of whatever is of moment at the school (theft, community service), social activities away from school (bowling or roller skating or lunch), or simply sitting around eating doughnuts. Although group advisories may be useful for these purposes, few believe they are the heart of the system. What counts most is the knowledge teachers have of individuals and the quality of the advisor-advisee relationship.

The advisor's job is to be the one adult responsible for synthesizing into some comprehensible picture disconnected data about a student from teachers, coaches, and the student. For example, Eric's Algebra teacher knew he hadn't done homework for several days. But Eric's advisor also knew he had consecutive lacrosse games and rehearsals for the school musical every night until 11 P.M. for a week. Further, the advisor knew from conversations with many teachers that Eric's confidence wasn't sufficiently developed for him to tell this to the math teacher, in hopes of getting a break but at least explaining the situation. Instead, Eric's *modus operandi* was to show up in class silently without his work and hope nobody noticed. In this case the advisor's role was to "run interference" by explaining the situation to the Algebra teacher and telling Eric that he should both hone his communication skills and better organize his time.

Sometimes advisors schedule conferences with students if a problem needs discussing. More often contact is initiated by students knocking on the door. One advisor who delighted in the role thought she saw four or five of her eleven advisees almost every day for a minute or an hour. "Maybe it's, 'I can't fit these classes in,' or 'I can't get along with this teacher,' or 'I can't get up in the morning.' Who knows? But I'm somebody who will listen and say, I hear you, and let's work towards a solution." Part of an advisor's expertise is just being there.

Sometimes listening to advisees and communicating with other teachers is all that is needed. A seventh-grader had been hinting for weeks to her advisor that all was not well at home. One day she announced that her father had moved out the night before. Teacher and student had a supportive talk, and all the child's teachers were instantly notified that she might be preoccupied. In all these examples, genuine concerns are at stake, but they are concerns that experienced teachers can address, helping the students immensely by providing support and communication. Their skills are not highly technical—they are rather like parenting skills—but are very important.

In some instances advisors encounter situations that require more expertise. When one advisor learned that an eighth-grader had gradually stopped speaking in all of his classes, he realized something was amiss and arranged for a full conference with the student's parents and his teachers. The teachers recommended a battery of learning disabilities tests, which the parents rejected as completely unnecessary. When the pattern persisted, another staff meeting was called and the parents relented. Here was a narrow academic matter where the advisor quickly realized that he was in over his head. His role was to aggregate information from many teachers, perceive a possible problem, and arrange a meeting where the relevant people could talk it through. When parents cry uncontrollably or when a parent refuses to speak to an advisor on the phone because the other parent is in the room, advisors recognize that the family dynamics are probably beyond their competence to deal with. They seek referral help, but have already played a strategic role in problem identification.

Another crucial part of the advisor's role is to synthesize feedback about students for parents and advisees. In some schools advisors meet in thirty-minute individual conferences several times a year with parents, or with parents and their children, to assess the child's progress. Parents expect oral reports, the opportunity to ask questions in person, and a "real dialogue around a specific student." Advisors also make group presentations to parents on back-to-school night in the fall. They lead discussions of advisees when each one is reviewed before the entire school faculty, a procedure that sometimes occurs as often as four times a year. Advisor feedback is to parents as well as from them, to the faculty as well as from it. All this is part of what personal attention means.

One way advisors give feedback is to summarize the situation of each advisee in a paragraph mailed home usually two or three times a year. These summary comments are in large part based on one-paragraph written comments prepared by all the student's teachers two or three times a year. The argument for written comments, both course-specific and summative, is that they supplement letter or number grades to give a fuller picture of progress and problems. Letter grades alone have very limited value as useful feedback. How much, after all, is there to be learned from the single letter "B"?

Writing a paragraph forces teachers to think about a student, synthesize ideas, look for patterns, and communicate information in ways that both inform parents and affect student behavior. Like advising, preparing written comments is one more extension of the independent teacher's role with few parallels in public schools. The comments are another formal and public mechanism that projects a school's commitment and accountability to individual attention.

Good written comments require much time and hard work. Because students and parents take them very seriously, they are among the most politically sensitive documents independent schools produce. Students often like them because they can mute parental reaction to poor performance. "If I get a bad grade, at least my parents know why." A father could be shown "that this is what happened and this is what you're going to improve on and this is what I'm doing well in." Parents want comments to be individualized and insightful. They are a symbol of what tuition buys. Many carefully scrutinize them for tone, interpretation, and prognosis. They look closely at grammar, spelling, and style. All become evidence of a teacher's and a school's competence. What can they learn about their child?

Schools want comments to be constructive and useful, so they frequently apply quality control with almost the same care devoted to the school letter sent to colleges. Even teachers with the best of intentions can write poor comments that undercut their purpose. Several experienced adults often read comment drafts before they are sent out. Common problem areas are carefully checked: bad grammar, misspelled student names, a formulaic tone, or an excessively negative assessment. Many schools have guidelines on what a good written comment looks like: balance, accentuating the positive, mention of movement over time, specific examples to justify a point or a grade, concrete suggestions for improvement, ordinary-language descriptions of learning habits. Although quality control sometimes falters, the schools try hard to minimize embarrassing or insensitive slips.

The actual content of written comments varies greatly. Some focus exclusively on academic performance. One English comment simply identified a problem. "She knows how to organize her paper but she still does not apply grammatical structure." Comments also attempt to teach important distinctions. Some begin with praise for a student's being well prepared, knowing the right answers, and doing well on daily quizzes where memorizing material is important. But then the comment notes difficulty in connecting facts, using information to answer broad and fresh questions, and generalizing. The student fares less well on longer tests because she or he doesn't "understand the material" or "get the concept."

The hope is that such remarks will help students and parents grasp the distinction, and that students will seek out teachers privately to learn more about what they mean by understanding material or getting concepts. Sometimes, especially with bright students, comments raise the reverse issue: students who understand large concepts can be careless with details and supporting evidence.

Good written feedback like Sam's comment embodies much of the independent-school tradition of personal attention and of the extended role of teachers outside classrooms. Sam's middle school social studies teacher was not only a comment writer but an advisor. He corrected daily homework and longer papers and attended to the latter closely enough to note in his comment how one paper in particular was well and carefully edited. Much of this teacher's work was done outside the classroom. His small student load enabled him to work as he did and to sense the puzzling change in Sam's behavior.

The personal attention Sam received was directed primarily toward a clear academic purpose. The tight link between personalization and academics gave focus to the teacher's remarks. The warning that class silence could breed mental softness and the personal "And I miss your voice" ending were both aimed at increasing class participation and taking the work of thinking more seriously. The purpose of the comment was to change Sam's behavior, to motivate him. The teacher's attitude was caring and his manner friendly, but the tone made clear that he was neither a buddy nor a therapist.

Like most expressions of personalization, Sam's comment was the product of an institutional commitment. Along with advising and the creative use of unstructured teacher time, it was developed and sustained by collective action and was not just a voluntary act by an individual. A father recalled when an eighth-grade teacher of his daughter's had quoted a sixth-grade written comment to demonstrate to her just how much she had improved. "I was amazed that they would even keep the comments, much less refer back to them." Personalization is not a vague ideal but a schoolwide expectation implemented by clear procedures.

Student loads must be kept to manageable numbers or the idea of personalization is unrealistic. Schools must deliberately appoint faculty who enjoy working with the kind of young people the school attracts. Without this attitude teachers might write cold or perfunctory comments and subvert the comments' role in furthering open communication and student motivation to engage in school. Sustaining a system of high-quality written comments, itself just one part of a commitment to personalization, requires multiple policies affecting faculty hiring, teaching loads, and comment quality control.

Parents like Sam's mother often mention their delight that comments are "about what kind of person my child is and not just about how he is doing in the course." What moved her most was the respect and concern permeating the warm and graceful comment. Sam's problem, if he had one, was the kind of problem that sensitive and experienced teachers see all the time. Sam was a good student slowly tuning out of participation for one of an endless number of preadolescent reasons. The written comment was a tool to alert him to what was happening and to use personal concern as a motivator to bring him back to the rough and tumble of class discussion.

Written comments are not reserved for special occasions like handling academic or personal crises, or bestowing praise for high achievement. What was striking about the strongly positive reaction of Sam's mother was the rather ordinary situation the comment addressed. Sam's teacher had perhaps—or perhaps not—received an early warning signal, even though Sam seemed neither passive nor withdrawn. Yet the signal was enough to trigger thoughtful feedback to all concerned parties.

Americans are conditioned by the media to see schooling issues in terms of extremes—profound crises like student violence or perhaps mainstreaming the emotionally disturbed, or dramatic triumphs like sports championships or science contest victories. But most students experience their developmental bumps and hurdles more quietly, perhaps like Sam. They do not need the expertise of those who deal with the great extremes of sadness, anger, or ambition.

For this reason, the less dramatic knowing, caring, and daily hard work of Sam's teachers have such strong appeal. The human connections they attempt to forge confer educational benefits in many ways. These connections also sustain the larger school community as well as impress upon students basic community standards such as decency, hard work, and participation. In this way personal attention permeates every effort to build community and sustain standards. It is a good starting point to make good schools.[14]

CONCLUSION

Lessons from Privilege

Schools are virtually the last democratic line of defense against negative forces that lavish enormous funds on inculcating anti-educational values in youth. The central job of schools is to emancipate the young not just from ignorance but from a sterile pop culture of mental passivity. Because anti-educational pressures are deep and insistent, schools must be especially purposeful. They must consistently stand for—model daily—the power of knowledge and thoughtfulness.

Schools must also stand for decent relations among the young and between the young and their teachers. This, too, challenges much of the world outside schools, but there is nothing wrong with challenging that world when it is indecent and anti-educational. More schools need the courage to define themselves proudly as places apart from mass culture, defenders of children's safety, and cultivators of their intellects. Schools cannot fairly claim the support and respect of society without performing this role.

Public schools must be purposeful but not exotic, partisan, or narrowly exclusive. Independent education suggests that the bases for effective educational communities can be broad and deep. A longing for a basic school ethos of "be nice and work hard" is widespread. Perhaps this is not the most ambitious ideal imaginable, but, when carried out with seriousness, it is a responsible countervailing force against education's adversaries.

A related lesson is that a school's students and families greatly affect its possibilities. Recognition of this fact heightens the attention and respect schools owe students and families. Because pro-education families wield enormous power over education, it is in the immediate self-interest of schools to nurture them. The day-long care of their children from early childhood through adolescence, for example, is one of the most attractive services single-parent or dual-career families receive from independent schools.

The most promising approach to making student-body composition a positive school asset is the increase of school-choice programs within public education. This is a private school lesson many public schools have already learned. Choice is no longer pursued just by residential relocation or pushing for the right teachers; choice is today publicly celebrated at the school level—except where it involves private schools or cross-district dollar transfers. It is a useful way to help assure minimum student commitment to school.

Most of the new choice options do not have meritocratic admissions standards. The country is not witnessing the expansion of elite exam schools like Bronx Science or Boston Latin. The entrance standard is, rather, student (and often family) commitment to the school or subschool. This entrance standard is selective, but only very modestly so. It is similar to what pertains in most private school admissions where meritocracy is rare but student commitment to learning is expected.

Like most prep schools, public schools of choice value "diversity" when it is accompanied by the agreement that participants have clear obligations to school that must be met if membership in the school community is to continue. Unbridled diversity unaccompanied by any basic value agreement is largely a failed idea. Students who consistently disrupt an educational community—and they are relatively few—should be removed from that community to more restrictive environments.

Perhaps the idea of public boarding schools can be revived. Shaping a network of such schools—they would have to be small and would be very hard to staff well—is not beyond the experience of several existing small and specialized boarding schools. But a successful boarding experience usually depends on a degree of voluntary participation. If attendance at such schools were to become near-incarceration, the independent-school tradition would be of less use than, say, the military tradition during the existence of the draft. Americans paid for the draft, however, because they valued national security far more than the extensive but ancillary educational services accompanying it.

The quality of a school's internal freedom depends to no small degree on the success of its external accountability. Prep schools gain a sense of true independence only after they have convinced society that they are deserving of it. Because they are guaranteed no money or freedom, they must always deal in the social marketplace. They must raise funds, attract students, keep state and federal regulators away, get students into serious colleges, avoid scandal. This process—coping with perpetual jeopardy—creates the identity and loyalty that give the best of them an added boost of daily energy. Public schools seeking freedom from central bureaucracies must understand that the productive energy they value comes not from freedom alone but from the accountability or jeopardy that should be freedom's natural companion.

Often each constituency of adults within a school has a separate domain of authority and thus exerts real leadership. But in a good school constituencies also feel pulled toward common institutional loyalty and mutual dependence. This sense of loyalty and dependence derives in part from the practical reality of private-sector independence—the school is their own and must survive by their collective efforts. But it also derives from vital traditions that make everyone proud to be a member of the community. Pride sustains community.

There is no substitute for strong leadership by prep school principals. School heads can make a mark because governing boards want them to and give them authority over crucial matters such as faculty appointments and continuations. Prep schools are lucky because there are relatively few alluring jobs to drain off their best talent, whereas public schools are hurt by numerous opportunities for gifted educators to leave schools and children. How to stop this little-noticed brain drain is unclear.

There is no substitute for strong leadership from trustees and governing boards. They must be educated about weighty fiduciary and ethical responsibilities. Second-rate boards quickly produce second-rate schools or systems. The politicizing of many public school-board elections, along with the tendency of single-issue or ambitious zealots rather than wise moderates to seek office, has severely damaged many public school districts. The only practical response is for advocates of the public interest to spend as much money and energy on school-board elections as do advocates of special interests.

There is no substitute for strong leadership from teachers. The considerable authority wielded by private school heads, compared with most of their public school colleagues, is paralleled by a similar authority wielded by private school teachers. Collectively, they have much more control over curriculum policy than public school teachers. Individually, they run their own classes not merely more independently but with crucial decision-making power over such issues as the creation and revision of reading lists. This is one of many work conditions that keep those who love both children and subjects in prep schools despite lower salaries and longer work days.

Without being unusually able, most students can learn far more than most schools typically demand of them and far more than they think they can learn. Prep schools have taught this lesson about average students for decades. It is no news that very able students do well in all but the poorest schools. The news is that when everyone must be treated equally because everyone is paying the same high price, privilege begets an ironic democracy of broad access to academic opportunities and press. All students, not just top-track students, can be given challenging and worthwhile educational tasks as well as reasons to work hard on them.

American education offers more opportunities than incentives, in stark contrast to the rest of the industrialized world. Prep schools show just how powerful incentives are for schools and for students. Teachers and administrators must also have good reasons to work hard if they are to succeed with a broad ability range.

Sometimes incentives to work hard at learning rub off on students simply by membership in a particular school community. Its educational values, rituals, and the positive attitude of its teachers toward learning are so strong and consistent that few students can escape the school's magnetic lure. But this is rare. More typically, prep schools do not create student incentives where none at all exist, but build on and exploit for purposes of learning the incentives students already possess at varying levels of commitment.

The incentive to gain admission to desired colleges (or desired secondary schools) is a fundamental family and student incentive that prep schools attempt to mobilize. College "domination" over schools is less intrusive today than it once was. The most selective colleges care more about aptitude than learning, and the least selective care about attracting enough students to survive. But college influence over prep schools, if not exactly domination, is still real. On balance it is a constructive force because of its impact on student incentives.

AP courses, for example, have probably brought more challenging academic experiences to more students than any other single reform in recent American high school history. In addition, most prep schools emphasize the distinction between meeting their minimal graduation requirements and the more demanding student programs that competitive colleges seek. What is most instructive about prep school incentives and the role of colleges and the College Board in channeling incentives toward learning is how rare other incentives are in American schooling.

Most young Americans lack incentives to learn. The greatest barrier to building new incentives for students to work hard is the fact that "receiving" organizations such as colleges and businesses fail to create them. These organizations typically remain on the sidelines, blaming schools for not motivating students while doing nothing themselves.

Whenever incentives to work hard are raised as an issue, discussions become polarized around where power to create incentives and academic standards should reside in a democracy. The prep school tradition suggests that it is not necessary to choose between the extremes of rigid state or federally mandated standards and those set entirely by individual schools. The polarizing disputes between those who trust only experts at the top and those who trust all schools equally do not have to occur. A balance of power is possible, and the prep school tradition provides a good example.

Cooperative and voluntary intermediary agencies like the College Board have provided external accountability without heavy-handed regulation. Prep schools are free to create curricula and teach as they wish largely because colleges hold them accountable. Thoughtful and voluntary external assessment, as represented (with admitted imperfections) by the old College Board essays and the current AP examinations, raises the stakes (the results are respected and have consequences) and legitimizes the educational process (students are compared against a national standard). Teaching and learning become easier when teachers and students work together toward a common end. The whole system works because there are incentives for colleges, schools, and students to make it work.

Prep schools attempt to promote high standards for average college-bound students through a variety of educational practices. One is a lean and demanding curriculum designed for all. Each student, regardless of ability, struggles with much the same basic academic studies. The less proficient tend to work harder, and though some do not succeed as well as others, the effort they expend is still valuable. They learn more than they would have learned otherwise, do not permanently abandon important fields of thought at too early an age, and gain time for serious interests to be eventually aroused.

A somewhat different approach accepts the idea of fixed abilities and seeks to build on areas of greatest student strength. It may seem surprising that notions of standards based on a common and demanding experience for all can coexist peacefully with notions of standards emphasizing an individual's personal best. They do coexist in good prep schools because the coursework is not dumbed down. Prep schools are usually unwilling to fail students who are doing their best as long as they are struggling with challenging material.

This admittedly slippery but workable notion of standards suggests how deeply imbedded in American educational culture independent schools are. Many do not step on the educational gas as rapidly as schools in other countries because they do not need to. Like all social institutions they make the compromises they need to make. They do what needs to be done to secure admissions to American colleges and keep American parents happy. In most cases this is academically more demanding than what other schools with similar students require, but academic demand and high standards are relative terms that must be understood in an American context.

Prep schools are rarely hotbeds of intellectual curiosity, as distinct from academic achievement, because this quality is weakly rewarded by most colleges and by the adolescent prep peer culture. This is frustrating to many. Prep students spend much time on sports and other nonacademic activities in part because they know colleges value excellence in these activities, and also value the energy and wide-ranging interests indicated by extensive participation in them.

Personal attention within small-scale environments is a potent educational method and a logical demand of an educated public on all its schools. Knowing kids well is not sentimentality, as independent-school families have long been aware, but a tool to entice students into greater academic engagement than would have otherwise occurred. Personal attention, at the least, can reduce anonymity and increase connectedness to a caring community. Close contact with teachers who exhibit passion for their fields can be a strong motivator for students in a country with weak traditions of commitment to learning. Personal attention also means knowing students well enough to be able to take special learning characteristics into account.

The most important prep school method of personalization is simply the attitude that it should permeate all aspects of school life. Every student (and teacher) is assumed to be worthy of both respect and special attention. If this belief is lacking, any mechanisms to implement it will be subverted. Simple practices like addressing students by name attempt to teach that knowing and respecting each other are school expectations. More concretely, independent schools are small, or at least broken down into small-scale settings within a larger institution. Teachers are responsible for far fewer students than most teachers in other schools. The average load of about sixty students per teacher in independent high schools is one of the most telling statistics in American education. In addition, schools that include many grades reduce age segregation, promote cross-age student and teacher activities, and increase adult knowledge of students because the students are (barring attrition) in the same setting for more years.

Some of the most dramatic instances of personal attention occur outside formal classes, and together they suggest a distinct vision of the teacher's role. Although classroom work by teachers and students is usually crucial to the success of a good course of study, it is never the entirety of a good course. Much of the real work by teachers and students happens elsewhere. Student-teacher connections outside classes, through conversations or teacher feedback on student work, are often the most individualized and educationally significant academic contacts students and teachers have. All schools should recognize this practical reality and increase both opportunities for unstructured teacher-student interaction and time for teachers to give students thoughtful personal feedback. Advising systems and written comments are formal mechanisms to accomplish this, but less formal interaction is at least as productive.

Implementing these practices in most public schools often requires extra money to reduce student-teacher loads and always requires teachers to play multiple roles. Personal attention is neither financially nor psychologically easy. There are only a few ways that schools with routine loads of 100–120 students (or more) for each teacher can progress toward personal attention without unrealistic infusions of new money.

One possibility is that more large schools will reorganize themselves fully or partly into smaller subschools with teams of faculty responsible for no more students than they can know well. For this to work in an entire school the curriculum would have to be reduced notably to maximize faculty involvement and minimize arcane courses with small enrollments. Even without this radical step a portion of a school or a grade could be deliberately arranged so that all students had at least one experience with small classes where teachers knew them by name.

Another possibility is that interactive computer technology might become a successful revolution in education, in contrast with other ballyhooed but failed technological revolutions starting with filmstrips in the 1930s. The special promise of emerging computer technology is the possibility of customizing instructional methods, content, and feedback to students in more powerful ways than teachers alone are likely to do.

Behind these possibilities is the issue of commitment. Lack of money is not the only barrier to personalization. Every teacher right now could stay late two days a week to hold open office hours.

Every teacher and administrator right now could take on eight or ten student advisees and become committed to knowing each one well. Classes right now could meet less frequently, freeing teachers to meet with individual students and students to work on their own. When schools are not making some of these efforts, a commitment to the idea of knowing students well is usually lacking. If teachers and administrators feel overworked, underappreciated, comfortable with their existing roles and routines, or alienated from the students they are expected to know well, change is unlikely even when it need not cost much.

These specific "lessons" from private schools together suggest three broad themes that Americans concerned with high-quality schooling might remember. The first is that prep schools at their best do very little that is truly surprising. The prep school tradition rests much more on experience and common sense than on research or scientific discovery. This book reveals no dramatic educational secrets. Thus, for example, commitment and passion in adults help arouse commitment and passion in young people whom they know and respect. A sense that schools are truly special communities often changes the adults and students who join them. Their greatest resource is people, though the importance of economic resources invested fully in schools should not be underestimated. Incentives to perform well are crucial energizers for students and teachers, and in part must come from the larger society outside schools.

This list of almost self-evident qualities could go on. But we must never diminish these basic ingredients of good schools whenever the latest fad rolls over us. Fads are easy to put into place; someone will always have a package or a gimmick to sell. The enduring qualities of good schools are harder to secure without time and commitment.

Second, the prep school tradition is, in fact, traditional. It is true that independent education can take pride in many educational innovations. "Progressive" education, for example, got an enormous boost from a few independent schools early in the twentieth century. But the heart of the tradition is a joint concern for decent character and academic literacy; it is not very trendy. What keeps this tradition from becoming dusty and anachronistic is not only the respect most Americans have for these two basic goals but also the prep schools' commitment—a democratic one in the best sense—to pursue them for a very broad range of student aptitudes.

Third, what is perhaps most humbling about the prep schools' best efforts is how they reveal education as an uncertain, unpredictable, and mysterious process. Even excellent schools cannot guarantee miracle cures, magic methods, or quick fixes. They do not invariably produce educated individuals or decent individuals. They sometimes fail miserably or, more often, do not meet their own hopes or those of parents. Independent education, because it contains so many advantages, demonstrates the frailty of all schools more convincingly than do less advantaged schools.

Thus independent schools put the difficulty of the national schooling enterprise in useful perspective. Many factors besides school affect human growth. Developing good skills, knowledge, values, habits, and interests in a person may be even more difficult than performing open heart surgery. Working in schools is tough and intellectually complex under the best of circumstances. It is always a struggle, a process never finished. It demands more dignified treatment than Americans have ever given it. Prep schools have no magic bullets, but they have many sensible and usable ideas. They also, with few exceptions, invest uncommon dignity in the work they are about. This is lesson enough.

Appendix

Notes

Index

APPENDIX

Sources and Methods

My objectives were to identify significant features of the independent-school tradition and to explore how they might shed constructive light on important issues confronting all American schools. Learning about the independent-school tradition required analyzing very different materials. Given their endless quantity and variety, they could only be sampled. The multidisciplinary strategy of consulting unusually broad sources was accompanied by the necessity to make hard choices about what to examine and what to pass up. Much valuable material for a complete picture of independent schools was ignored because it was not essential. My task was to write thematic chapters, not to conduct a comprehensive "study" of the development or present status of independent schools in the United States.

The sources fell into three broad classes. Written or historical sources included print and archival records spanning the past century: books, articles, reports, minutes, correspondence, and the like. Quantitative sources included several national databases with significant independent-school representation, as well as statistics regularly collected by independent schools themselves. Field studies sources included interviews of students, teachers, administrators, and parents in representative schools. Sources used in the text are identified in the Notes, except that field note citations are omitted for reasons of confidentiality. Taken together, the endnotes serve as a bibliography.

The print and archival record alone was vast. All independent schools have their own stories. Dozens go back to the early Republic, hundreds more are nearly a century old, and some have serious scholarly histories. Numerous organizations, membership associations, periodicals, and small foundations have surrounded them as a kind of support system. There was no dearth of written material reaching back to the late nineteenth century.

I read more than a hundred histories of individual schools, all issues of national independent-school journals, and articles about prep schools in educational and general periodicals. I examined the archives of the NAIS, now located in Washington, D.C., and the records of the College Entrance Examination Board in New York. The NAIS Archives contain records of its two predecessor organizations; the SEB dates from 1924 and the NCIS from 1943. I reviewed annual reports of Harvard College and Harvard undergraduate admissions from the beginning of the century to the 1980s in the Harvard University Archives. Whenever possible, I relied on existing secondary sources, such as histories of the College Board and well-researched histories of individual schools.

These retrospective materials, along with references from them that pointed the way to additional print literature, proved sufficient for my purposes. But they were still only a sample. I ignored entirely, for example, the records of several important organizations geared toward serving prep schools, such as the Educational Records Bureau. I consulted no archives of any individual school, and focused on Harvard for a higher-education perspective because of convenience, Harvard's importance to many prep schools, and its unusual influence (prior to the 1950s) on precollegiate secondary education. I used historical materials when they helped make a point, but have not written a history book.

Independent schools can be examined quantitatively more fully than ever before. Several large-scale surveys in the late 1980s collected significant questionnaire information from prep school students, teachers, administrators, and parents. Large educational surveys are nothing new, but independent schools had never been included in any serious way before. Although not expert in quantitative methods, I became familiar with four important databases and enlisted the help of more knowledgeable authorities.

One database was maintained by the prep schools themselves. In 1950, NCIS began to collect annual statistics from member schools on topics such as enrollments and tuitions. Over the years the effort expanded to include financial aid, financial operations, and minority enrollments. From time to time special statistical surveys were conducted on subjects such as black enrollment and coeducation. By the end of the 1970s, data from individual schools were computerized, making flexible longitudinal analyses possible.

The main strengths of NAIS statistics have always been response rates of nearly 100 percent and rigorous fact-checking. The main weakness is that content has quite naturally served practical administrative interests (for example, salaries, tuitions, enrollments). Data about the school experiences of teachers or students have not been collected. Further, some statistics are of dubious validity because individuals with incomplete information fill out the forms. NAIS statistics on students of color provided by administrators, for example, show fewer students of color than when students themselves designate their race. Nevertheless, NAIS statistics were indispensable to establishing various trends discussed in this book, such as those in Chapter 4 concerning diversity.

The second database was provided by the Admissions Testing Program of the College Board, as developed and administered for the Board by Educational Testing Service. For my purposes this database consisted of scores achieved by college-bound seniors on the SAT, along with responses to a Student Descriptive Questionnaire (SDQ) survey completed by most of these students. SDQ items include race and religious affiliation, parental income and education, course-taking patterns in high school, and prospective majors in college. Almost all prep school seniors take the SAT, renamed the Scholastic Assessment Test after this book was completed, and very large numbers of college-bound students in other schools do as well.

The Admissions Testing Program database for a given year offered three clear advantages. First, the public high school senior test-taking population was enormous, and the prep school group was the entire population of twelfth-graders. The latter was thus not a sample but a census. This meant that virtually every calculated statistic, even when disaggregated by race, gender, or SAT score, was quite accurate. Technical problems about statistical "significance" and overlapping "confidence intervals," which have long plagued surveys with relatively small samples, virtually disappeared.

Second, public school SAT-takers were in effect prescreened to resemble the prep school population on some important dimensions. The comparison was not between apples and oranges. Virtually all SAT-takers were not only college-bound but also bound for colleges that required the SAT. These were usually four-year institutions with some sort of entrance requirements.

Third, the ability to link SAT and SDQ data made it possible to ask questions pertinent to this project. In Chapter 7, for example, a central issue is whether the school experience of "average" college-bound prep school students differs from college-bound public school students of similar aptitude. The SAT, though hardly perfect, is a useful measure of aptitude for verbal and mathematical work. "Average" or "gifted" college-bound students in different school types can be broken out and linked to courses they actually took.

With these possibilities in mind, I obtained from the Admissions Testing Program and Educational Testing Service data on participants during the 1989–90 school year (called SAT:90 in the Notes). These included 41,172 NAIS school seniors and 85,286 public school seniors. The latter were a random sample constituting one-tenth of all public school seniors who participated in the Admissions Testing Program. From these two groups of college-bound seniors, SAT scores were available for 39,862 NAIS school seniors and 80,476 public school seniors.

Although the groups were similar in that both took the SAT, an additional subsample of "privileged public" school students was drawn from the larger one. These were seniors in the highest family-income category measured by the SDQ ($70,000 or more in 1990) whose parents both possessed bachelor's degrees. SAT scores were available for 5,649 of them. The privileged public subsample represented roughly 7 percent of all public school students in the 1990 Admissions Testing Program. Three comparison groups of college-bound seniors were thus available. One attended prep schools. Two-thirds of the general public school sample attended suburban, rural, and small city schools. The privileged public group overwhelmingly attended suburban high schools.

The third database was the National Education Longitudinal Study of 1988 (NELS:88), the most ambitious of several longitudinal studies sponsored by the National Center for Education Statistics (NCES). Its immediate predecessor, known as High School and Beyond (HSB), spawned several important quantitative studies of private schools. But these were studies largely of Catholic schools. Independent schools in the HSB sample were both small in number and unrepresentative. They were almost all "high-performing" schools with very selective student bodies. One objective of NELS:88 was to rectify this situation by including a significant number of NAIS schools. Having been asked by NELS officials to persuade NAIS schools to participate, I learned much about the NAIS sample. It seemed very representative of NAIS schools as a whole.

NELS:88 was designed to study the educational experiences of a representative sample of American eighth-graders in 1987–88. It was not a study of schools but of students, although the critical mass of eighth-grade samples (25 to 30 students per school) made it in fact a school-level study for eighth grades. Later on, too late for this project's timetable, the research design was altered to permit some school-level analysis for grades beyond the eighth. The basic idea of NELS:88 was to follow the same students at two-year intervals as they progressed through high school and beyond. The 1988 database consisted of separate questionnaires completed by each student, two teachers of each one, a parent or guardian, and the school principal. It also included an 85-minute test given to each student, consisting of 116 multiple-choice items in the fields of reading, mathematics, science, and history. The combined reading and math portion is Chapter 7's proxy for eighth-grade "aptitude."

The 1988 database included 1,425 eighth-graders from 63 NAIS schools (about 23 students per school), 16,771 public school students, and 2,831 students in Catholic and other private schools. As with the SAT:90 database discussed above, I created an additional sample of privileged public eighth grades (not eighth-graders). That is, I selected 1,425 students from the 63 public school eighth grades with the highest aggregate family "socioeconomic status" (SES). SES is a measure combining family income, parental occupation, and parental education.

When the eighth-graders became tenth-graders in 1990, 998 NAIS students from 87 schools continued in the database, along with 14,897 public school students. Deadlines and funding issues precluded extensive analysis of this 1990 First Follow-Up (NELS:90) and any analysis of subsequent ones. But I again constructed a privileged public school sample of 80 sophomore classes containing 570 students.

The great strength of NELS, besides its longitudinal dimension, is the variety of its questions and its participants. The survey of parents, for example, explores issues such as expectations and family income in much greater detail than the SDQ. The tenth-grade student survey asks many questions about individual and peer-group values. NELS will keep quantitative analysts busy for years.

By contrast, NELS:88 proved more problematic than SAT:90. One problem was that a fairly large prep student sample of more than 1,000 quickly became smaller once it was broken into groups according to race, academic aptitude, or gender. Then large differences between NAIS and other schools (particularly privileged public schools with equally small samples) melted away into statistical insignificance. Technical problems of significance were best avoided when the NAIS sample was never disaggregated. But in that case, observed significant differences were often banal or self-evident. The large aptitudinal differences between NAIS eighth grades and other eighth grades, for example, are not surprising. To confront the significance problem, I reported in the text large differences that may not have achieved technical significance, but that nonetheless seemed worth reporting because of their size, consistency, and inherent interest. I did this on several occasions, always making it clear in the Notes.

Another problem was that many NELS questions seemed confusing or so dependent on student background and school context that answers were suspect. For example, an important tenth-grade question that asked students whether courses were challenging, required them to understand, or required them to do their best confused thoughtful adults when asked what these questions meant to them. Students' perceptions of what "challenging" or "understanding" mean depend on their previous school and life experience with such abstract ideas. As another example, tenth-graders were first asked how much homework in total they did per week in all courses, and then were asked to break out homework time subject by subject. Not surprisingly, the sum of the subject-by-subject answers far exceeds the initial total amount answer. It is not clear which one is closer to the truth. Despite these caveats, NELS proved useful on many key points and surely would have proven even more useful with more resources and time. This database remains a major asset for independent education. The use of its base year here only skims the surface.

The fourth database, and at times the most frustrating, was the Schools and Staffing Survey of 1987–88 (SASS:88), also sponsored by the NCES. The focus of SASS:88 was adults who work in schools rather than students who attend them. It gave special emphasis to issues of teacher supply and demand. But it was also a fruitful source of information about teacher and administrator attitudes and working conditions, survey data available nowhere else and especially germane to the issues of morale and governance discussed in Chapter 3. Separate attitude surveys were administered to teachers and principals, and additional surveys for administrators addressed school demographics and teacher supply and demand. What was especially attractive about SASS:88 was its size. More than 12,000 schools and 67,000 teachers were surveyed in a complex, stratified sample. Nearly one-fourth of NAIS member schools were reported to be in the sample—220 schools—and nearly 900 NAIS teachers.

But there were early warning signals that all was not well. An early SASS published report claimed, as one of many examples, that NAIS schools assigned less homework than any other public or private school type. Very extensive discussions with NCES over a two-year period eventually produced a reanalysis of the NAIS sample. It turned out that 30 percent of the purported NAIS schools were schools with no NAIS affiliation. They were also schools wholly unrepresentative of NAIS schools. Cooperation from NCES eventually removed these schools from the SASS:88 database used in this book.

The final SASS sample of 149 NAIS schools and 549 teachers is accurate and representative. Representativeness is defined by my personal examination of each school in the sample against various characteristics of the entire NAIS school population (size, grade level, gender mix, location, and so on). As with the other databases, I broke out a privileged public school comparison group consisting of 243 public schools and 1,341 teachers in those schools. Public schools in this subsample were suburban, had no federal educational services for the poor, and had the smallest number of students eligible for free lunch. Administrators reported that 72 percent of students in these schools were college-bound.

Except for the NAIS statistics, all the technical work on the SAT:90, NELS:88, NELS:90, and SASS:88 databases was carried out at the Harvard Computing Center by two senior Harvard doctoral students in educational statistics. Anne Chase was responsible for NELS:88 and NELS:90; Nelson Treece took charge of SAT:90 and SASS:88. Their work was supervised in part by Faith Dunne of Dartmouth College. Our working relationship involved my writing memos and having conversations about which issues needed exploration. They then did the number-crunching and analysis, to which I responded, often with puzzlement about their arcane world. They then came back with clarifications and more analysis.

The last main procedure was to conduct field work in ten independent day schools. The field work took place during 1991–92, after I had identified the book's three main themes. The protocols were therefore quite focused and not open-ended. The field studies were brief. They were entirely devoted to individual and group interviews. Each school visit was the equivalent of two person-days, meaning ten interview sessions per school. As explained in Chapter 9, there were no classroom observations. All interviews were tape-recorded, and analytic field notes for each one were written by the project's field researchers, Robert L. Hampel, Barbara S. Powell, and myself. The most interesting interviews were fully transcribed. Although the names of people and schools are disguised in the text, all vignettes are accurately depicted. No composites or invented dialogue are used.

I first observed three of these schools ten years before as part of the research for an earlier project, A Study of High Schools. They were the Bishop's School, in La Jolla, California, Buckingham Browne & Nichols School, in Cambridge, Massachusetts, and Colorado Academy, in Denver. The main selection criteria for the other seven schools were representativeness and convenience. (Boarding schools were excluded from the field studies but by no means from the rest of the research.) For logistical reasons a second San Diego–area school was added, Francis Parker School, along with another Denver school, Kent Denver School. Pingree School was added, a coed school north of Boston that began as a girls school in 1961, and also Winsor School, an older Boston girls school that has remained single sex.

Three schools from the Philadelphia-Baltimore region were included, one of the epicenters of American independent education. William Penn Charter School, in Philadelphia (founded 1689), and Germantown Academy, northwest of the city (founded 1759), are by far the oldest of the ten schools. Yet they are also among those that most directly face the changing demographics of independent-school populations. The much younger Gilman School, in Baltimore, is the historical progenitor of the country day school movement. It remains all boys technically, but its curricular arrangements with surrounding girls schools suggest that a school can be single sex without giving up easy educational contact with the opposite sex.

Nine of the ten were combined schools. Six were pre-K–12, and three were 5–12, 6–12, and 7–12. Only Pingree was a 9–12 high school. Eight were coed, two were single sex. Total school size ranged from 230 to more than 1,000. The median size of senior classes in 1991 was 66, with a range of 38 to slightly more than 100. In addition to these field studies, I conducted separate interviews with key figures in the national independent-school community. I consulted additional field notes from the database of the Stanford University Center for Research on the Context of Secondary School Teaching. Field notes from independent and suburban schools collected during 1981–82 for A Study of High Schools were reexamined.

My writing task was to integrate retrospective, quantitative, and field study material as seamlessly as possible. I have tried to avoid producing a history book, a numbers book (there are deliberately no tables), or an ethnography. My efforts were geared toward keeping the research apparatus as much in the background as possible, while still demonstrating that the arguments advanced have multidisciplinary research support.

Notes

Abbreviations

IS	*Independent School*
ISB	*Independent School Bulletin*
ISEBAR	*Independent School Education Board Annual Reports* (NAISA)
NAIS	National Association of Independent Schools
NAISA	National Association of Independent Schools Archives
NCR	*National Council of Independent School Reports* (NAISA)
NELS:88	Database from National Education Longitudinal Study of 1988
NELS:90	Database from 1990 First Follow-Up of NELS:88
SASS:88	Database from 1987–88 Schools and Staffing Survey
SAT:90	Database from 1990 Scholastic Aptitude Test and Student Descriptive Questionnaire
SEBAR	*Secondary Education Board Annual Reports* (NAISA)

Introduction

1. Excellent recent studies examine the most numerous types of private schools—Catholic schools and conservative Christian schools. See Anthony S. Bryk, Valerie E. Lee, and Peter B. Holland, *Catholic Schools and the Common Good* (Cambridge, Mass.: Harvard University Press, 1993); and Alan Peshkin, *God's Choice: The Total World of a Fundamentalist Christian School* (Chicago: University of Chicago Press, 1986). The standard general studies of prep schools are Otto F. Kraushaar, *American Nonpublic Schools: Patterns of Diversity* (Baltimore and London: The Johns Hopkins University Press, 1972); and Leonard L. Baird, *The Elite Schools: A Profile of Prestigious Independent Schools* (Lexington, Mass., and Toronto:

Lexington Books, 1977). Kraushaar's ambitious inclusion of virtually all kinds of private schools dilutes his analysis of prep schools, whereas Baird's survey research focuses largely on Northeastern boarding schools.

1. The Vulnerability of Educational Communities

1. Esther Osgood, "Report of the Executive Secretary," *SEBAR 1951–1952,* pp. 10–12.

2. Bill Carter, "A Cable Challenge for PBS as King of the Preschool Hill," *New York Times,* March 21, 1994, p. 1.

3. David Riesman, *Constraint and Variety in American Education* (Garden City, N.Y.: Doubleday Anchor Books, 1958), pp. 137–140.

4. The idea that schoolwide educational beliefs can have a potent "effect" received a large research boost from the 1979 study *Fifteen Thousand Hours* by Michael Rutter and his British colleagues. They made educational community into a distinct and separate causative factor. By cleverly labeling it "ethos" instead of, say, climate or atmosphere, they emphasized the educational dimensions of community (such as clear goals, consistency of practice, homework done) instead of the human relations dimensions of decent communities. Elementary school reform efforts like the "effective schools" movement also promoted this idea. Contemporary reforms like Theodore R. Sizer's Coalition of Essential Schools value both aspects of community. Coalition schools should be decent places with an atmosphere of unanxious expectation, but also places with an unmistakable intellectual focus. See Michael Rutter et al., *Fifteen Thousand Hours* (Cambridge, Mass.: Harvard University Press, 1979). The platform of the Coalition was first enunciated in Theodore R. Sizer, *Horace's Compromise: The Dilemma of the American High School* (Boston: Houghton Mifflin, 1984).

5. Charles Merrill, *The Walled Garden: The Story of a School* (Boston: Rowan Tree Press, 1982). The positive virtues of "a place apart" in our hurried society, as distinct from the conventional negative stereotype of school as isolated ivory tower, were first suggested to me by Cesar L. Barber in his senior chapel address, "A Place Apart," given at Amherst College, May 18, 1956, Amherst College Archives.

6. The orderly nature of independent schools is fully documented in all the databases explained in the Appendix. Although not a significant problem, theft of valuables like cameras is usually cited by students as their greatest safety concern.

7. David Aloian, "Gilded Youth, Gilded Schools," *ISB* (October 1969): 6. The argument that the "experience itself" is the main product of prep schools was also thoughtfully made about the same time by another well-known headmaster, in Edward T. Hall, "Two Heads Are Better," *ISB* (October 1968): 13.

8. Report of the Day School Group, in *SEBAR 1940,* p. 40; "Religion in Boys Schools," *Private School News* 8 (March 1932), pp. 1–2; Robert Danforth Cole, *Private Secondary Education for Boys in the United States* (Philadelphia: Westbrook Publishing Company, 1928), p. 105. A similar study in 1948 found no decrease in

required chapel or religious instruction, in *SEBAR 1947–1948,* p. 42. Samuel S. Drury of St. Paul's is quoted in Nelson W. Aldrich, Jr., *Old Money* (New York: Alfred A. Knopf, 1988), p. 149; Allen Hackett, *Quickened Spirit: A Biography of Frank S. Hackett* (New York: Riverdale Country School, 1957), pp. 151–152.

9. Allan V. Heely, *Why the Private School?* (New York: Harper & Brothers, 1951), pp. 207, 192–193.

10. Eugene S. Wilson, "Religion in the Independent School," *ISB* (November 1952): 4–7. Wilson's concern reverberated inside NCIS circles for years. See NCIS Executive Committee Minutes, April 16, 1953, p. 3, NAISA, and Francis Parkman to Laurence Springer, January 24, 1961, NAISA. His observation that prep school graduates were not superior in moral character is confirmed by his Amherst colleague at the time John Esty, who later was a headmaster and then president of NAIS. Interview with John C. Esty, Jr., July 22, 1991.

11. Paul Chancellor, *The History of The Hill School, 1851–1976* (Pottstown, Penn.: The Hill School, 1976), p. 87; Aldrich, *Old Money,* p. 158; Frederick S. Allis, Jr., *Youth from Every Quarter: A Bicentennial History of Phillips Academy, Andover* (Hanover, N.H.: University Press of New England, 1979), pp. 646, 657–660. Current data on school religious affiliation come from NAIS, data on eighth-grade religious courses from NELS:88, data on seniors' religious affiliation from SAT:90, and data on sophomores' commitment to religion from NELS:90. These quantitative sources and the "privileged public school" subsamples are described more fully in the Appendix. An overview of religion in the schools just prior to the 1960s is Earl G. Harrison, Jr., "The Teaching of Religion in Independent Schools," *ISB* (May 1962): 55–60. On voluntary religion being good for religion, see Rev. Robert L. Hammett, "Is It Worship When You Have To?" *ISB* (February 1970): 6–9.

12. For a ringing defense of sports as character-building see Charles D. Wardlaw, "Administration of Physical Education," *Private School News* 7 (June 1931), pp. 7–8. Data on sports participation are from SAT:90. NELS:90 shows the same pattern of participation for high school sophomores.

13. For a critical prep school view of team sports as character education see Joshua L. Miner and Joe Boldt, *Outward Bound U.S.A.* (New York: William Morrow and Company, 1981), pp. 52–59.

14. The intellectual context for these changes was a powerful conception of developmental "stages," as represented by such key figures as Erik Erikson (who popularized the idea of "identity") and Lawrence Kohlberg, who claimed that morality could be understood as a psychological process. Both were astute popularizers as well as creative thinkers, so their ideas were quickly absorbed by prep schools eager for authoritative guidance. Heely, *Why the Private School?* pp. 171–187; National Council of Independent Schools, *Some Inquiries Helpful in Appraising Mental Health in a School* (Boston: NCIS, 1952), NAISA; *NCR* 36 (December 1955): 12; Cary Potter, "College Drop-Outs: Our Responsibility," *ISB* (October 1965): 18; Alphonse J. Palaima, "The Bright Boys," *ISB* (February 1966): 13–15; John C. Esty, Jr., "The Lamp of Learning—Not the Shoehorn," *Rostrum* 1 (September 1965): 3–4.

15. Fred M. Hechinger, "Sex Education Program," *New York Times,* July 10, 1966, p. 1; Cary Potter, *Annual Report of the President 1970–71* (Boston: NAIS, 1971), pp. 6–8.

16. See Miner and Boldt, *Outward Bound U.S.A.,* and Thomas James, *Education at the Edge: The Colorado Outward Bound School* (Denver: Colorado Outward Bound School, 1980); *ISEBAR 1961–1962,* pp. 67–68.

17. Robert M. Sandoe, "Here We Are—What Do We Do Now?" *ISB* (December 1975): 6; Richard Katz and David Kolb, *Outward Bound as Education for Personal Growth, Working Paper 322–68* (Cambridge, Mass.: Alfred A. Sloan School of Management, M.I.T., 1972).

18. Harvard Knowles and David Weber, "The School Community as a Moral Environment," *IS* (December 1978): 13–15; Lee M. Levison, *Community Service Programs in Independent Schools* (Boston: NAIS, 1986). NELS:90 data suggest that most prep school sophomores rarely participate in voluntary service, but the fraction that do is larger than students from other school types.

19. The classic essay that propagated the Boyden legend is John McPhee, *The Headmaster: Frank L. Boyden, of Deerfield* (New York: Farrar, Straus and Giroux, 1966). An excellent biography of Mrs. Hinton and her school is Susan McIntosh Lloyd, *The Putney School: A Progressive Experiment* (New Haven and London: Yale University Press, 1987). Heely, *Why the Private School?* pp. 74–75, 104; John S. Iversen, Jr., "Do I Dare to Eat a Peach?" *ISB* (February 1969): 6.

20. John F. Gummere, "Report of the Chairman of the Executive Committee," *SEBAR 1957–1958,* p. 8.

2. The Family School

1. Coleman was not the first social scientist to argue that students were an important cause of school effects. For example, the argument that attending school only with blacks had negative effects on blacks was a famous part of the 1954 *Brown* desegregation case, awkward as the argument seems today. James S. Coleman et al., *Equality of Educational Opportunity* (Washington, D.C.: U.S. Government Printing Office, 1966), pp. 183, 325.

2. Edward Yeomans, *The Shady Hill School: The First Fifty Years* (Cambridge, Mass.: The Windflower Press, 1979), pp. 1–11; Allen Hackett, *Quickened Spirit: A Biography of Frank S. Hackett* (New York: Riverdale Country School, 1957), pp. 56–59; Jean Parker Waterbury, *A History of Collegiate School, 1638–1963* (New York: Clarkson N. Potter, Inc., 1965), pp. 102–122.

3. Report of the Day School Group, March 1, 1940, *SEBAR 1939,* p. 67; R. A. McCardell, ed., *The Country Day School: History, Curriculum, Philosophy of Horace Mann School* (Dobbs Ferry, N.Y.: Oceana Publications, 1962). Prettyman is quoted in Harold S. Wechsler, *The Qualified Student: A History of Selective College Admission in America* (New York and London: John Wiley & Sons, 1977), pp. 148–149. James B. Conant, *Education and Liberty: The Role of the Schools in a Modern Democracy* (Cambridge, Mass.: Harvard University Press, 1953), p. 33.

4. Porter E. Sargent, *A Handbook of the Best Private Schools* (Boston: Porter Sargent, 1915), pp. xxiv, xxi; *Sargent Handbook, 1938–39,* p. 65; Frank D. Ashburn, "The Headmaster's Letter," *ISB* (October 1973): 30. The Sargent handbooks are still published annually, but have been toned down. Vigorous and opinionated consumer guides to private schools have usually failed. The market so far has been too small and too geographically segmented by day schools to support a higher-education type of guidebook industry. See Joan Barrett and Sally E. Goldfarb of the *Yale Daily News, The Insider's Guide to Prep Schools,* 1979–80 edition (New York: E. P. Dutton, 1979).

5. John S. Iversen, Jr., "Do I Dare to Eat a Peach?" *ISB* (February 1969): 5; John Hoyt Stookey, "An Optimistic View of the Independent School Market," *IS* (December 1980): 7.

6. Bradford McE. Jacobs, *Gilman Walls Will Echo: The Story of the Gilman Country School, 1897–1947* (Baltimore: The Gilman Country School for Boys, 1947), pp. 7–12; Shirley K. Kerns, "The Country Day School Movement," *Harvard Alumni Bulletin* 42 (May 10, 1940): 972–974; Frank S. Hackett, "The Country Day School Movement," in *Sargent Handbook 1924–25,* pp. 15–17; Mrs. Francis K. Carey, quoted in *Private School News* 2 (October 25, 1926): 1; *Sargent Handbook 1918,* pp. 37–38; Robert Danforth Cole, *Private Secondary Education for Boys in the United States* (Philadelphia: Westbrook Publishing Co., 1928), p. 21; *Sargent Handbook 1915,* p. xxiv. The best study of the first generation of boarding schools remains James McLachlan, *American Boarding Schools: A Historical Study* (New York: Charles Scribner's, 1970).

7. Early comments on the more explicit social service functions of prep schools include Frederick C. Calder, "The School as Family," *ISB* (October 1972): 5, and David Fleishhacker, "Should You Care about Day Care?" *IS* (December 1980): 16–17. The comparative statistics regarding how students spend time on after-school activities, homework, television watching, and outside reading are drawn from NELS:88 and NELS:90.

3. Governing Independent Communities

1. The idea of "jeopardy" as private school benefit as well as burden was first suggested to me by Donald Erickson.

2. Roger W. Riis to Hart Fessenden, June 18, 1942, NAISA.

3. The College Board annual reports changed the word "private" to "independent" in 1938. On the Pennsylvania issue see NCIS, "Minutes of Meeting of the Executive Committee," February 13, 1946, and October 29, 1946, NAISA. On how legislative threats created, for example, the Connecticut Association of Independent Schools, see *NCR* 15 (June 1950): 7.

4. The wartime directive distinguishing between public and private schools was a major issue at the first meeting of NCIS, held at Brooks School in Massachusetts. "Minutes of the First Meeting of the National Council of Independent Schools," August 10, 1943, NAISA. On St. Paul's see Francis V. Lloyd, Jr., "The Law and the Private Schools," *ISB* (February 1949): 7–8. On state legislation affecting private

school teacher certification, see NCIS, "Minutes of the Committee on the Relations of Independent Schools and Higher Education," April 1, 1952, p. 4, and October 28, 1952, p. 2, NAISA.

5. On federal regulation, see NAIS memos to schools on ERISA, for example, John P. Downing to Heads of Schools, May 21, 1976, and memos regarding the effect on school musicals of the Copyright Revision Act of 1976 and the effect on school bus safety standards of the Motor Vehicle and School Bus Safety Amendments of 1974, in John C. Esty, Jr., to School Heads and Business Managers, July 21, 1978, and July 21, 1978. On the concern of heads over federal intrusion, see Thomas Read, "Special Study for NAIS," (February 1976), Part G, p. 10. On student rights and the problems of litigiousness, see Cary Potter to Heads of Schools, September 15, 1969; *NAIS Report of the President* (March 6, 1975), p. 5; and Cary Potter to Heads of Schools, April 9, 1976. All of these are in NAISA.

6. Porter E. Sargent, *A Handbook of Private Schools 1932–33* (Boston: Porter Sargent, 1932), pp. 30–32, 45–46; *Sargent Handbook 1933–34*, p. 13; *Sargent Handbook 1929–30*, pp. 45–46. The assets and some faculty of the Country Day School were merged with those of Rivers School in 1940, a newer institution that managed to survive.

7. On the professionalization of school marketing, see *The New Marketing Handbook for Independent Schools* (Boston: Boarding Schools, 1987) and T. Griffith, *The Audiovisual Marketing Handbook for Independent Schools* (Boston: Boarding Schools, 1987).

8. Barbara Hadley Stanton, *Trustee Handbook,* sixth ed. (Boston: NAIS, 1989), p. 67.

9. Elizabeth B. Hall, "The Vanishing Headmistress," *ISB* (October 1966): 40; Edward T. Hall, "Two Heads Are Better," *ISB* (October 1968): 14; *Private School News* 1 (November 20, 1925), p. 8.

10. The opinions of principals and teachers used in this discussion come from SASS:88. This database provides the largest available independent-school teacher and principal samples on internal governance issues. The very strong authority of prep school heads compared with both public school principals and their own governing boards is apparent in an early SASS publication, *Detailed Characteristics of Private Schools and Staff 1987–88* (Washington, D.C.: National Center for Education Statistics, December 1991), pp. 14–18. Extensive SASS reanalysis undertaken for this project (and the source of all SASS percentages cited in the text) does not change the large differences noted in that report.

11. Since salaries increase annually, dollars cited in books are always behind the times. But the patterns themselves are quite stable. These data come from *NAIS Statistics: Tuitions and Salaries 1990–91* (Boston: NAIS, 1990), pp. 16, 25. Public school teacher salary data were provided to NAIS by the National Education Association. Administrator data were provided by Educational Research Service, Arlington, Virginia. An analysis of 1987–88 data yielded similar results. See Arthur G. Powell, "The Conditions of Teachers' Work in Independent Schools," in Milbrey W. McLaughlin, Joan E. Talbert, and Nina Bascia, eds., *The Contexts of Teaching in*

Secondary Schools: Teachers' Realities (New York and London: Teachers College Press, 1990), pp. 130–131.

12. *Trustee Handbook* (1964), p. 35; *Trustee Handbook* (1970), p. 36; Bruce McClellan, "Hidden Agenda—What Are Trustees Made Of?" *IS* (May 1978): 30; *Trustee Handbook* (1974), p. 56; *Trustee Handbook* (1989), pp. 41, 16, 20, 5. Linda Gibbs of NAIS and others have pointed out that boards are by no means uniformly supportive of retreats and other forms of self-evaluation. See Linda M. Gibbs, "Overview of Results: NAIS 1991 Survey of Board Chairs," *NAIS Leadership Forum* (Winter 1992), p. 2.

13. On pushy parents and the tendency of independent schools to discourage actively their involvement in formal governance, see Susan Moore Johnson, *Teachers at Work: Achieving Success in Our Schools* (New York: Basic Books, 1990), pp. 47, 94–95, 100.

14. The percentages are from SASS:88. The point about peer influence on the prestige of schoolteaching has often been made in personal essays by young teachers applying to a summer institute at the Klingenstein Center for Independent School Education, Teachers College, Columbia University. See also Johnson, *Teachers at Work,* p. 52, and Pearl R. Kane, *The Teachers College New Jersey Survey: A Comparative Study of Teachers in Public and Independent Schools* (New York: Department of Educational Administration, Teachers College, Columbia University, 1986).

15. Comparative data on morale are from SASS:88.

16. The survey data are from SASS:88. The "run their own business" quote and the observation about faculty disagreements in academic schools are found in field notes and faculty debriefings dated May 12, 1989, and April 23, 1990, in the Stanford Teacher Context Center. See also Johnson, *Teachers at Work,* pp. 274–275, 51, 132–133.

17. The survey data are from SASS:88. Johnson, *Teachers at Work,* pp. 204, 181, 206, 209; *Trustee Handbook* (1970), p. 13; John C. Littleford, *Faculty Salary Systems in Independent Schools: A Sequel* (Boston: NAIS, 1984), p. 2; *NAIS Statistics: Tuitions and Salaries 1990–1991* (Boston: NAIS, 1990), p. 18; S. Arbuckle, "Conceptual Memo," January 26, 1990, p. 1, Stanford Teacher Context Center. The 1970s editions of the NAIS *Trustee Handbook* mentioned student involvement in decision-making, but dropped those sections in later revisions when student unrest subsided.

18. The point about heads's safely giving teachers authority is made in John E. Chubb and Terry M. Moe, "Politics, Markets, and the Organization of Schools," paper presented to the American Political Science Association (1985), pp. 37–38; *Trustee Handbook* (1980), p. vii.

4. Diversity and Community

1. Frederick J. V. Hancox, "Report of the Chairman of the Executive Committee," February 16, 1935, *SEBAR 1934,* p. 15; Rev. Norman B. Nash, "Postwar Changes in the Schools," *ISB* (January 1947): 50.

2. Claude M. Fuess, "Free Enterprise in Education," speech to the Association of Independent Schools of Greater Washington, D.C., October 21, 1952, pp. 7–9, NAISA. The most savage sociological critique is remarkably positive about the formal education delivered by prep school teachers and curricula. The authors argue that the nefarious workings of boarding schools—the training of a ruling class who lose their souls in the process—are mainly carried on by the other students. They emphasize the power of student-body composition used for evil ends. See Peter W. Cookson, Jr., and Caroline Hodges Persell, *Preparing for Power: America's Elite Boarding Schools* (New York: Basic Books, 1985).

3. *Private School News* 7 (March 1931), p. 2; Frederick S. Allis, Jr., *Youth from Every Quarter: A Bicentennial History of Phillips Academy, Andover* (Hanover, N. H.: University Press of New England, 1979), p. 616. Allis's thorough scholarship exposed discriminatory practices far less flagrant and mean-spirited than those at hundreds of other independent schools whose written histories ignore the issue entirely. The ironic price serious schools like Andover pay for supporting scholarly institutional histories is that people sometimes read them. This is one reason few serious school histories exist. On quotas, see the report of three eminent heads, Frank D. Ashburn, Wilson Parkhill, and Herbert W. Smith, "Preliminary Report of [NCIS] Watching Committee on Relation of Quota Policy to Freedom from Taxation," February 1946, and "Minutes of the [NCIS] Executive Committee," February 13, 1946, NAISA. On independent schools open to blacks, see Robert U. Jameson, "Independent School Slants," *ISB* (February 1948): 19–20, and Mira B. Wilson, "Colored Students Are an Asset," *ISB* (February 1949): 12–13. The one-third estimate for 1960 is based on the first NAIS survey of black enrollments, conducted in late 1966.

4. In 1970 alone, fourteen of the twenty-one NAIS schools founded were Southern. See Zebulon Vance Wilson, *They Took Their Stand: The Integration of Southern Private Schools* (Atlanta: Mid-South Association of Independent Schools, 1983), pp. xv–xvi, 2–5. Data on school foundings are based on the 1983 NAIS membership. They include schools eager to join soon after their founding, and generally represent more stable and ambitious schools. "Southern" states are defined as the eleven states of the Confederacy, plus the four slaveholding states in 1861 that did not secede (Maryland, Delaware, Kentucky, and Missouri). The District of Columbia is also included.

5. Conant's 1952 speech to the American Association of School Administrators was widely reported at the time, widely praised by public school spokespeople, and bitterly denounced by independent and Catholic officials. It was one of only four addresses over a lifetime that Conant reprinted in his autobiography. For the speech and some prep school reaction, see "Unity and Diversity in Secondary Education," in James B. Conant, *My Several Lives: Memoirs of a Social Inventor* (New York, Evanston, and London: Harper & Row, 1970), pp. 665–670; "Minutes of the NCIS Executive Committee," April 22, 1952; John F. Gummere, "Report of the Committee on Public Relations of the National Council of Independent Schools," June 21, 1952; "Minutes of the NCIS Executive Committee," June 30, 1952, all in

NAISA. Also Kenneth C. Parker, "Our Schools and the Public," *ISB* (November 1952): 16–18. Conant's social thought is developed in "Education for a Classless Society: The Jeffersonian Tradition," *The Atlantic Monthly* 165 (May 1940): 593–602; James B. Conant, *Public Education and the Structure of American Society* (New York: Bureau of Publications, Teachers College, Columbia University, 1946); and James B. Conant, "The Dilemma of American Education," speech to AASA, March 5, 1947, Conant Papers, Harvard University Archives. On Roxbury Latin School see Conant to Roger Ernst, November 1, 1944; Roger Ernst, "Memorandum of Phone Conversation With JBC," November 4, 1944; Henry W. Holmes, "The Roxbury Latin School," February 13, 1945, all in the Henry W. Holmes Papers, Harvard University Archives.

6. The Orphan Annie strip appeared on March 3, 1947. On the moral and intellectual fallibility of prep school students see, for example, Wayne Davis [editorial], *Private School News* 1 (January 20, 1926), p. 4, and Calvin Trillin, *Remembering Denny* (New York: Farrar, Straus and Giroux, 1993), p. 41. On the educational merits of student heterogeneity, see James McConaughy, "Report of the Elementary Schools Committee," March 1, 1941, *SEBAR 1940*, pp. 82–83; William R. Wood, "Strictly from the Curbstone," *ISB* (April 1948): 6; Harold Howe II, "The Need for Entangling Alliances," *ISB* (May 1967): 16; and Joan E. Talbert, "Conditions of Public and Private School Organization and Notions of Effective Schools," in Thomas James and Henry M. Levin, eds., *Comparing Public and Private Schools, Volume 1: Institutions and Organizations* (Philadelphia: The Falmer Press, 1988), pp. 184–186.

7. On early financial aid policy, see Thomas F. Morrison, "A Study of the Granting of Financial Aid in the Member Schools of the Secondary Education Board" (1943), NAISA; *SEBAR 1942*, p. 22; Isabel Boyd Proudfit, "A Parent Looks at the Independent School," *ISB* (November 1949): 14. On economic diversification and meritocracy, see William S. Piper, Jr., "Public Relations for Independent Schools," *ISB* (April 1945): 5; John F. Gummere, "The Case for Private Schools," *ISB* (May 1951): 30; *NCR* 17 (December 1950): 9. On how meritocracy could dampen the image of exclusivity, a lesson private higher education also learned well, see Francis Parkman, "The Problems and Future of the Independent Schools," in American Council on Education, *Long-Range Planning for Education* (Washington, D.C.: American Council on Education, 1958), p. 55.

8. The most successful collective effort to help financial aid promote economic diversity in the 1950s was not an organization to raise money but an organization to standardize how aid should be dispensed. The 1957 School Scholarship Service, modeled on a similar organization for colleges, advanced the idea that aid should be awarded on the basis of need, and provided a single method to calculate it. It added some fairness and rationality to decision-making that had been, and to some extent remains, idiosyncratic. Richard W. Day, "The Independent School in 1975," *ISB* (May 1965): 15; *NCR* 3 (May 1947): 7. Family-income data are drawn largely from NELS:88. On financial aid sources see *NCR* 33 (March 1955): 1–4 and *NCR* 36 (December 1955): 4. On the national scholarship idea see Francis Parkman,

"Memorandum of Meeting of Public and Independent School Representatives at William Penn Charter School, October 18, 1954"; NCIS, "A Proposal for a National Scholarship Program on the Secondary School Level" (January 1956); Eugene S. Wilson to Frank Boyden, John Kemper, and William Saltonstall, March 2, 1961; Francis Parkman to Eugene S. Wilson, April 7, 1961. All these are in NAISA.

9. Although they never expected to receive benefits themselves from plans such as tuition tax credits, some prep school leaders worried that financially shaky schools, especially Catholic schools during the 1970s, would fail unless the government intervened. For reasons of politics as well as principle, it was important that a diverse community of nonpublic schools survive. Such a community, of which the independent schools were but one small part, ensured that American private schooling would not be class-based and would be almost as diverse as public education. It is no surprise that NAIS in particular believed in strengthening the community of diverse private schools, and took the lead in establishing an umbrella association, the Council for American Private Education. In the late 1970s, NAIS also moved warily toward grudging support for tuition tax credits, qualified by elaborate eligibility requirements to ensure that privileged students would never benefit. The trick was to avoid offending both nonprivileged private schools who wanted federal assistance and public education organizations adamantly opposed to it.

Throughout all this, the prep schools resented bitterly the apparent betrayal of their interests by private higher education. They had hoped for a natural political alliance between the two private sectors. They did not see that their lingering ties with exclusivity, the growth of the public suburban pipeline to colleges, and the political impossibility of distinguishing between religious and secular private schools would all cause private higher education to abandon them whenever important public-policy issues arose. See Consortium on Financing Higher Education, *Sources of Undergraduate Grant Aid at the COFHE Institutions 1988 to 1990–91* (Cambridge, Mass.: COFHE, November 1990), pp. 7–8; *NAIS Annual Report, 1970–71,* pp. 11–14; Cary Potter to Heads of School, April 12, 1972; Cary Potter to School Heads, November 18, 1977; *NAIS Annual Report, 1977–78,* p. 8; John C. Esty, Jr., to Heads of Schools and Board Chairmen, July 21, 1978, all in NAISA.

10. Fairly reliable national statistics on independent-school financial aid were first collected in 1950 by the National Council of Independent Schools. See *NCR* 17 (December 1950): 9, and *NCR* 25 (March 1953): 7–8. Family-income statistics are drawn from both NELS:88 and SAT:90. On direct grants to undergraduates in prestigious colleges, see Consortium on Financing Higher Education, *Sources of Undergraduate Grant Aid at the COFHE Institutions 1988 to 1990–91,* Table 7, p. 3.

11. The first statistics on faculty children appeared in *NCR* 56 (December 1959): 8. One reason data on tuition remission to faculty children were reported at all was to stress that the practice was financial aid and not added faculty compensation. The latter might be treated as taxable income by the Internal Revenue Service. Between the end of the 1950s and the end of the 1960s the number of all aid recipients who were faculty children rose from 18 percent to 23 percent. The portion of all financial aid dollars received by this group increased from 20 percent to 24

percent. A clear majority of students receiving full scholarships were faculty children. Even in 1990, when racial minorities were equally preferred, faculty children constituted more than 20 percent of aid recipients and received more than 22 percent of all aid dollars.

None of this discussion intends to minimize the large variation in how individual schools approached economic diversity and how successful some were in achieving it. A few major donors cared—Phillips Exeter received a single $5 million gift in 1965 just for financial aid. Equally committed but less wealthy schools experimented with sliding-scale tuition policies. In the early 1990s NAIS mounted a "Pricing and Affordability" project to tackle affordability from the opposite angle. Instead of seeking new aid sources, it asked how expenses and thus tuition could be reduced.

12. Interview with Cary Potter, November 2, 1989; "Summary of Conversation with the Fund for the Advancement of Education, June 17, 1963," NAISA. On the escalation of the civil rights movement in 1963, see Carl M. Brauer, *John F. Kennedy and the Second Reconstruction* (New York: Columbia University Press, 1977), pp. 230–274. On collaborative programs in general and A Better Chance in particular, see Edward Yeomans, "New Developments in Summer Programs," *ISB* (December 1965): 26–30, and *"No Reason . . . Except Faith": Ten Years of ABC* (Boston: A Better Chance, Inc., 1974). On the difficulty of recruiting black students see Wilson, *They Took Their Stand,* p. 12, and John D. Verdery, "We *Wanted* Negro Students," *College Board Review* 47 (Spring 1962): 15–19. Data on black patronage of prep schools are from SAT:90. Of college-bound black and white seniors enrolled in public and independent schools, 7 percent of black students with family incomes above $70,000 attend prep schools, compared with 10.4 percent of whites and 14.4 percent of Asian Americans. These data do not include students in Catholic or other private schools.

13. Despite the impressive moral commitment of many educators who worked tirelessly to bring black youth to white schools, the fairly speedy acceptance of their labors owed much to a pragmatic recognition that prep schools could no longer exclude by race without facing harsh legal consequences. In 1970, for example, the Internal Revenue Service announced that it would deny tax-exempt status to private schools practicing racial discrimination—a ruling that NAIS supported and that helped achieve full nondiscrimination as a criterion for NAIS membership. In 1978, an impatient Carter administration attempted to add affirmative action quotas and guidelines of the sort common in higher education to the IRS definition of school nondiscrimination. This was considered rigid and intrusive by NAIS. It was killed largely and ironically by a huge letter-writing campaign by activists from the emerging "religious right." See Jeremy A. Rabkin, "Taxing Discrimination: Federal Regulation of Private Education by the Internal Revenue Service," in Neal E. Devins, ed., *Public Values, Private Schools* (London, New York, and Philadelphia: The Falmer Press, 1989), pp. 133–157. Also Cary Potter to Heads of Schools, April 22, 1974, and John C. Esty, Jr., to Commissioner of Internal Revenue, October 18, 1978, NAISA.

Minority enrollment trends are drawn mainly from four early special surveys conducted by NAIS for the 1966–67, 1969–70, 1971–72, and 1975–76 school years, all in NAISA, and for later years from the annual published NAIS statistics. Financial aid trends were obtained by integrating these minority surveys with annual NAIS financial aid statistics. On racial preferences see Dwight H. Horch, *How Parents Finance Private School Costs* (Princeton, N.J.: School Scholarship Service, 1986), pp. 6, 8. Unlike the estimates used in the text, the 1990 NAIS statistics report that only 12.7 percent of prep students were persons of color. I have instead relied on the SAT:90 database, where prep school seniors individually indicate their racial identification. The NAIS statistics are rough estimates made by school officials, include only a few racial groups, and do not report others. Interestingly, both databases report the same percentage of African-American students. All other categories in the SAT database show more persons of color than the NAIS figures. Although NAIS statistics do not permit financial aid breakdowns by racial groups, it is clear from SAT data that African-American prep school families remain considerably less affluent than either Asian-American or Hispanic-American families.

14. SAT scores are for the high school class of 1990. I regard Scholastic Aptitude Test (as the SAT was called until the mid-1990s) scores as a useful if rough and imperfect indicator of learned and innate capacity to do academic work requiring verbal and mathematical abilities. The SAT indicates in the main what students bring to high schools, not what high schools "produce" in students. SAT results should be attributed to habits acquired through family and community upbringing, to elementary schooling, and to innate ability. The scores reported in this and subsequent chapters combine scores on a verbal and a math test. The minimum score on each test is 200 and the maximum 800. The lowest possible combined score is thus 400 and the highest 1,600. Doing "very well" on the SAT is here defined as a combined score on the verbal and math sections of 1,200 or above out of a possible 1,600—roughly the top 17 percent of all individuals taking the SAT. For more information on SAT:90 see the Appendix.

15. Robert Coles is quoted in David Mallery, *Negro Students in Independent Schools* (Boston: NAIS, 1963), pp. 51–55. For the integrationist headmaster see Wilson, *They Took Their Stand,* p. 130. On separatism and black identity see William L. Dandridge, "Black Reflections on the Independent School: An Overview," *ISB* (December 1970): 9–10; William R. Link, "Black Youth, Black Nationalism, and White Independent Schools," *ISB* (October 1969): 14–15; Allis, *Youth from Every Quarter,* pp. 627–628; David Mallery, "Four Black Students Talk about School," *ISB* (December 1970): 11–13; Robert Sam Anson, *Best Intentions: The Education and Killing of Edmund Perry* (New York: Random House, 1987), p. 161. On the black experience in boarding schools see Richard L. Zweigenhaft and G. William Domhoff, *Blacks in the White Establishment: A Study of Race and Class in America* (New Haven: Yale University Press, 1991), pp. 7, 40–41, 43, 66–67. The NELS:90 survey asked 1990 high school sophomores how closely two statements about race applied to their schools: "Students make friends with students of other races and ethnic groups" and how OK was it to "make racist

remarks." Tolerant attitudes were widely held in all school types examined, with the prep school responses slightly more tolerant but not enough to be considered statistically significant.

16. The annual membership directory of a major private school association, the Secondary Education Board, began in the late 1940s to report male-female enrollment data by individual school. The 36 percent figure was obtained by aggregating information provided by 308 schools in 1949–50. In 1950 the NCIS began to collect similar data with similar results. See *NCR* 17 (December 1950): 8. On girls' College Board exam participation see *Thirty-Eighth Annual Report of the Secretary* (New York: College Entrance Examination Board, 1938), p. 24. On the sometimes different functions of boys and girls schools, see Millicent C. McIntosh, "The Girls Schools and College Entrance," *ISB* (November 1946): 31, and Adele Q. Ervin, "Public Relations in Girls' Secondary Schools," *ISB* (May 1952): 12–13. For the earlier trend toward single sex, which converted many previously coed New England schools, see *Private School News* 7 (June 1931), p. 5. On single-sex justification see Mary Frances and Homer E. Barnes, "The Value of Parallel Education," *ISB* (November 1950): 18.

17. A useful overview of student unrest is Alan R. Blackmer, *An Inquiry into Student Unrest in Independent Secondary Schools* (Boston: NAIS, 1970). On its relation to coeducation see Lillian Radlo, "Boys and Girls Together (?)," *ISB* (December 1969): 12. On student preferences for coeducation see Leonard L. Baird, *The Elite Schools: A Profile of Prestigious Independent Schools* (Lexington, Mass., and Toronto: Lexington Books, 1977), pp. 34–35. For the Andover debate see Simeon Hyde, Jr., "The Case for Coeducation," *ISB* (December 1971): 20–24; Allis, *Youth from Every Quarter,* pp. 669–682; and Susan McIntosh Lloyd, *A Singular School: Abbot Academy, 1828–1973* (Andover, Mass.: Phillips Academy, 1979), pp. 409–450. The gender statistics are from special NAIS surveys as well as the regular NAIS annual statistics. A perceptive account of the decline of women in prep school leadership positions is Elizabeth B. Hall, "The Vanishing Headmistress," *ISB* (October 1966): 39–41.

18. Jean S. Harris, "Let's Hear It for Coeducation, Folks," *ISB* (December 1973): 5–7. Harris later achieved public notoriety for her role in the death of the "Scarsdale Diet Doctor" and her work with young mothers in prison.

19. Lloyd, *A Singular School,* p. 412; Carol Gilligan, *In a Different Voice* (Cambridge, Mass.: Harvard University Press, 1982), and Carol Gilligan, Nona P. Lyons, and Trudy J. Hanmer, eds., *Making Connections: The Relational Worlds of Adolescent Girls at Emma Willard School* (Troy, N.Y.: Emma Willard School, 1989). A gender sourcebook for prep school educators that emphasizes its educational rather than legal, athletic, or sexual aspects is Anne Chapman, *The Difference It Makes: A Resource Book on Gender for Educators* (Boston: NAIS, 1988). The course-taking patterns are drawn from SAT:90. A thoughtful and balanced inquiry was conducted by Andover on the early consequences of coeducation there. It concluded that gender is only one relevant variable. Whether able girls attend science and math classes with very able boys or just boys is, for example, an important factor in whether

girls persist in those subjects. See Kathleen M. Dalton, *A Portrait of a School: Coeducation at Andover* (Andover, Mass.: Phillips Academy, 1986). Despite these complexities, in late 1991 Emma Willard School launched an expensive and sophisticated advertising campaign asserting clear-cut research support for single-sex education. Interesting quantitative research by Valerie Lee on the impact of girls schools was not yet available when this manuscript was finished.

20. The survey data come from NELS:90. Words like "roughly," "around," and "significant" are used deliberately in the text as signals to readers. They indicate directions that may not be technically significant, usually because of small samples, although the raw data differences are extremely large and of significant interest. Robert Coles, *Privileged Ones* (Boston: Little Brown, 1977), p. 413.

21. Richard W. Mechem, "Independence for Education 2: A Public School Comment," *ISB* (October 1967): 24–26. See also William D. Geer, Jr., "Old Myths and New Realities," *ISB* (May 1974): 5–7.

5. Student Incentives and the College Board System

1. The revival of interest in comparative or international education, occasioned by America's preoccupation with the test scores of its teenagers compared with teenagers in other industrialized countries, has clearly demonstrated the cultural basis of many educational incentives. See, for example, Max A. Eckstein and Harold J. Noah, *Secondary School Examinations: International Perspectives on Policies and Practice* (New Haven and London: Yale University Press, 1993), and Harold W. Stevenson and James W. Stigler, *The Learning Gap: Why Our Schools Are Failing and What We Can Learn from Japanese and Chinese Education* (New York: Summit Books, 1992). On American education see Richard Hofstadter, *Anti-Intellectualism in American Life* (New York: Vintage Books, 1962).

2. The American literature on the subject is vast. Psychologists and teachers typically speak of "motivation," whereas policymakers and economists use the word "incentives." For a general overview see Arthur G. Powell, "Motivating Students to Learn: An American Dilemma," in Susan Fuhrman and Jennifer O'Day, eds., *Rewards and Reform* (San Francisco: Jossey-Bass, 1996).

3. Research on school-to-work transitions suggests that American employers value school achievement much less than employers elsewhere. James E. Rosenbaum and Takehiko Kariya, "From High School to Work: Market and Institutional Mechanisms in Japan," *American Journal of Sociology* 94 (1989): 1334–1365.

4. Charles W. Eliot, "Liberty in Education" (1885), in *Educational Reform* (New York: The Century Company, 1898), p. 131.

5. Frank S. Hackett, "The Country Day School Movement," in *A Handbook of American Private Schools 1924–25* (Boston: Porter Sargent, 1924), p. 15.

6. On college admissions, see Harold S. Wechsler, *The Qualified Student: A History of Selective College Admissions in America* (New York and London: John Wiley & Sons, 1977). For the College Board I have relied mainly on the *Annual Reports of the Secretary,* consulted in the Board's Archives in New York, and on two

complementary histories. Claude M. Fuess, *The College Board: Its First Fifty Years* (New York: Columbia University Press, 1950), is a memoir by a longtime head of Phillips Academy who directly experienced many of the issues under discussion. John A. Valentine, *The College Board and the School Curriculum* (New York: College Entrance Examination Board, 1987), is a more scholarly account by a longtime Board staff member. The 1885 Andover quote is from Fuess, p. 7. The word "system," which came from Carl Brigham of Princeton, is from Valentine, p. 48.

7. Data about private school candidates for College Board examinations are taken from various *Annual Reports of the Secretary* of the College Entrance Examination Board. See also Porter E. Sargent, *A Handbook of the Best Private Schools* (Boston: Porter Sargent, 1915), p. xx; *Private School News* 7 (October 25, 1930), p. 15; A. W. Craig, "Why Independent Schools Need to Have a Well-Planned and Well-Executed Program of Religious Instruction," *ISB* (February 1946): 5.

8. "Views of Associate Secretary," *Thirty Third Annual Report of the Secretary* (New York: College Entrance Examination Board, 1933), p. 8; Valentine, *The College Board*, p. 48.

9. Thomas S. Fiske, *Twenty Seventh Annual Report of the Secretary* (New York: College Entrance Examination Board, 1927), p. 1; Allan V. Heely, *Why the Private School?* (New York: Harper & Brothers, 1951), p. 105.

10. Richard M. Gummere, "Twenty Years Onward, or the Next Two Decades in Secondary Education," *SEBAR 1940*, pp. 12, 6; Claude M. Fuess, "Free Enterprise in Education," speech to the Association of Independent Schools of Greater Washington, D.C., October 21, 1952, p. 9, NAISA; Arthur S. Roberts, "Report of the Chairman of the Executive Committee, March 8, 1947," *SEBAR 1946*, pp. 28–29.

11. *Definition of the Requirements, Edition of December 1934* (New York: College Entrance Examination Board, 1934), pp. 7–14, College Board Archives.

12. Nicholas Murray Butler, *First Annual Report of the Secretary, College Entrance Examination Board of the Middle States and Maryland* (New York: College Entrance Examination Board, 1901), p. 20.

13. Ashburn is quoted in *NCR* 5 (December 1947): 3. Farrand is quoted in Fuess, *The College Board*, p. 68; F. J. V. Hancox, "Report of the Chairman of the Executive Committee, February 15, 1936," *SEBAR 1935*, p. 15.

14. Bradford McE. Jacobs, *Gilman Walls Will Echo: The Story of the Gilman Country School 1897–1947* (Baltimore: Gilman Country School, 1947), pp. 59–61.

15. Arthur S. Roberts, "Report of the Chairman," March 8, 1947, p. 28; Richard M. Gummere, "Twenty Years Onward," p. 12. See also W. S. Litterick, "The Faith We Live By," *ISB* (May 1947): 22; J. DeQ. Briggs, "Letter to Editor," *Harvard Alumni Bulletin* 34 (February 19, 1932): 620; Frederick Winsor, "Letter to Editor," *Harvard Alumni Bulletin* 34 (February 19, 1932): 619; F. A. Shaw, "Letter to Editor," *Harvard Alumni Bulletin* 34 (February 19, 1932): 620; *English Examination, June 16, 1941* (New York: College Entrance Examination Board, 1941), pp. 29–30, College Board Archives.

16. Fuess, *The College Board*, pp. 85, 63; Valentine, *The College Board*, p. 29.

17. Jacobs, *Gilman*, p. 60.

18. Fiske, *Twenty Seventh Report,* p. 10; *Forty Second Annual Report of the Secretary* (New York: College Entrance Examination Board, 1942), pp. 5–6; *Forty Fourth Annual Report of the Secretary* (New York: College Entrance Examination Board, 1944), p. 8; *Thirty Fifth Annual Report of the Secretary* (New York: College Entrance Examination Board, 1935), pp. 35–36.

19. The SEB lacked the financial and organizational commitment to external assessment that energized the College Board. It had no outside readers. Completed examinations were simply shipped off for scoring to whichever secondary schools candidates wished to enter. In 1928, for instance, a New York City boy took the SEB examinations for St. Paul's School in New Hampshire, given at St. Bernard's School in Manhattan. After completing the test, he taxied over to the Buckley School, also in Manhattan, where he took exactly the same examination, this time for admission to the Hill School in Pennsylvania. The two New York schools that administered the examinations sent both off to the respective secondary schools for grading. When the SEB learned of this strange event, its response was not to suggest a single process of external scoring, but to recommend that candidates bring carbon paper to the test centers.

In reality, SEB was a small, shoestring operation that was comprised mainly of Eastern boarding schools and their elementary feeder schools, which were a minority even within the small world of independent education. To the extent that the SEB grew and flourished, the reasons lay less with its examinations than with the fact that it served almost by accident as the first reasonably national association of independent schools. F. J. V. Hancox, "Report of the Chairman of the Executive Committee, February 15, 1930," *SEBAR 1929,* p. 13; Howard T. Smith, "Report of the Chairman of the Executive Committee, October 1927," *SEBAR 1927,* p. 13; Frederick H. Osgood, *Report of the Annual Conference of the Secondary School Examination Board, October 31, 1925* (Boston: Secondary School Examination Board, 1925), p. 9, NAISA.

20. McGeorge Bundy, quoted in "The American Dream at Groton," public television documentary, October 1988; Wayne E. Davis, "Editorial," *Private School News* 6 (June 1930), p. 4; Frederick Winsor, "Is Harvard Too Hard on the Undergraduates?" *Private School News* 7 (November 25, 1930), p. 5.

21. Herbert Smith, "Commission on Relations with Higher Education, April 21, 1948," National Council of Independent Schools, p. 4, NAISA; Henry W. Bragdon, "The College Entrance Examination Board Test in Social Studies," *ISB* (January 1947): 19.

22. Thomas S. Fiske, *Nineteenth Annual Report of the Secretary* (New York: College Entrance Examination Board, 1919), p. 7; James B. Conant, *My Several Lives: Memoirs of a Social Inventor* (New York, Evanston, and London: Harper & Row, 1970), p. 427; Robert Danforth Cole, *Private Secondary Education for Boys in the United States* (Philadelphia: Westbrook Publishing Co., 1928), pp. 131–133; H. T. Smith, "Report upon the Curriculum Study, February 25, 1933," *SEBAR 1932,* p. 42.

6. The Collision of Standards and Meritocracy

1. Claude M. Fuess, *The College Board: Its First Fifty Years* (New York: Columbia University Press, 1950), pp. 154–158, 67–68; John Stalnaker, *Forty Fifth Annual Report of the Executive Secretary* (New York: College Entrance Examination Board, 1945), pp. 25–26; Millicent C. McIntosh, "The Girls' Schools and College Entrance," *ISB* (November 1946): 31.

2. It was common knowledge that prep school students as a group did not need or value high college grades as much as their public school comrades, because their future lives did not depend as much upon them. They had worked hard in school to pass college admissions examinations. Once they were admitted, good grades for many had little future value. By perfecting social skills instead, the "gentleman C" preppie was often acting rationally. See C. N. Greenough, "The College," *Harvard Annual Reports 1923–1924,* p. 47, Harvard University Archives; L. T. Spencer, "College Achievement of Private and Public School Entrants," *School and Society* 26 (October 1, 1927): 436–438; Wayne E. Davis, "Editorial," *Private School News* 6 (June 1930), p. 4; Delmar Leighton, "The College," *Harvard Annual Reports 1934–35,* pp. 129–130, Harvard University Archives; Carl C. Seltzer, "Academic Success in College of Public and Private School Students: Freshman Year at Harvard," *Journal of Psychology* 25 (1948): 419–431; F. S. Von Stade, Jr., "Freshman Year," *Harvard Annual Reports 1953–54,* pp. 193–194, Harvard University Archives.

3. Thomas S. Fiske, *Fourteenth Annual Report of the Secretary* (New York: College Entrance Examination Board, 1914), p. 12; *Thirty Third Annual Report of the Secretary* (New York: College Entrance Examination Board, 1933), pp. 3–4; *Thirty Sixth Annual Report of the Secretary* (New York: College Entrance Examination Board, 1936), pp. 16–19; *Thirty Seventh Annual Report of the Secretary* (New York: College Entrance Examination Board, 1937), p. 9.

4. John M. Stalnaker, *Forty Third Annual Report of the Executive Secretary* (New York: College Entrance Examination Board, 1943), pp. 23–24; Stalnaker, *Forty Fourth Annual Report* (1944), p. 26; Henry Chauncey, *Forty Sixth Annual Report* (1946), p. 5; Henry W. Bragdon, "The College Entrance Examination Board Test in Social Studies," *ISB* (January 1947): 19; Frank Bowles, *Forty Eighth Annual Report* (1948), p. 60; William H. Cornog and William C. Fels, in *Fifty Second Annual Report of the Director* (1953), p. 42.

5. James B. Conant, *My Several Lives: Memoirs of a Social Inventor* (New York, Evanston, and London: Harper & Row, 1970), pp. 128–138, 417–432; Richard M. Gummere, "The Independent School and the Post-War World," *ISB* (April 1943): 5; W. J. Bender, "Committees on Admission," in *Harvard Annual Reports 1952–53,* pp. 104–106, Harvard University Archives; W. J. Bender, "Committees on Admission," *Harvard Annual Reports 1953–54,* p. 239, Harvard University Archives; McGeorge Bundy, "Who's Going to Get to College?" *Harvard Alumni Bulletin* 58 (April 7, 1956): 510.

6. Herbert Smith, in National Council of Independent Schools, "Commission on Relations with Higher Education," April 21, 1948, p. 4, NAISA; Frank Ashburn, at "National Council of Independent Schools Annual Meeting, July 6–7, 1950," p. 3, NAISA; Frank Ashburn, *NCR* 5 (December 1947): 3; Thomas F. Morrison, "Can Schools Uphold Their Standards?" *ISB* (May 1942): 26–27; Louis Zahner, "Composition at the Barricades," *ISB* (May 1960): 4–5; Hart Fessenden, "The Tail of the Dog," *ISB* (February 1946): 17–18.

7. Arthur S. Roberts, "Report of the Chairman of the Executive Committee," March 9, 1946, *SEBAR 1945*, p. 7; Frank Ashburn, *NCR* 5 (December 1947): 4.

8. Esther Osgood, "How Independent Are the Independent Schools?" *ISB* (January 1945): 13; "Report of the Recording Secretary," *SEBAR 1946*, p. 31.

9. Secondary Education Board, *Definition of the Requirements for 1954*, NAISA; "Special Meeting of Elementary and Secondary Schools," March 8, 1946, *SEBAR 1945*, pp. 28–34.

10. Arthur S. Roberts to Hart Fessenden, February 6, 1947; Roberts to Fessenden, February 21, 1947, NAISA.

11. Paul W. Lehman, "Letter to Editor," *ISB* (January 1959): 26; Edward T. Hall, "What Price Competition?" *ISB* (January 1957): 8; Thomas J. Copeland, "A Junior School's Reaction to the New Admissions Program," *ISB* (April 1958): 50; Wilbur J. Bender, "The Top-One-Percent Policy: A Harvard Look at the Dangers of an Academically Elite Harvard," *Harvard Alumni Bulletin* 64 (September 30, 1961): 21–25.

12. Concern at the national association level for curriculum, teaching, and standards was somewhat altered by the merger of the two major independent school associations—SEB and NCIS—in 1962 to form NAIS. SEB from its inception had been much more a "teachers" than a "headmasters" group. When the two organizations joined, NAIS style and leadership came to resemble the perspective of school heads, although it did not entirely neglect curriculum policy and practice. See Arthur S. Roberts, "Report of the Chairman of the Executive Committee," March 8, 1947, *SEBAR 1946*, p. 28; "NCIS Executive Committee Minutes," February 8, 1961, NAISA; Wellington V. Grimes to Colleagues, October 1970, NAISA.

13. Jack Higgs, "Foundations on the Rocks," *ISB* (May 1961): 62; Paul Swain Havens, "The Old School Tie," March 8, 1952, *SEBAR 1951–52*, p. 36; John A. Lester, G. F. Cherry, O. F. Shepard to Members of the General Curriculum Committee, December 17, 1928, Secondary Education Board Bureau of Research, NAISA; Max McConn, "Progressive Experimentation in Secondary Schools," February 25, 1933, *SEBAR 1932*, pp. 34–36.

14. Allan V. Heely, *Why the Private School?* (New York: Harper & Brothers, 1951), p. 70; Robert Kelley, "The Unfinished Agenda of the Independent School," *ISB* (January 1962): 9.

15. Francis Parkman, "The Problems and Future of the Independent Schools," *Long-Range Planning for Education* (Washington, D.C.: American Council on Education, 1958), pp. 52–58; Francis V. Lloyd, "The Era of Authoritarian Headmasters," *ISB* (April 1965): 44.

16. On the SSAT see Benjamin T. Whitman, "The Evolution of the Secondary School Admission Test Board (1957–1983)," Unpublished doctoral dissertation, Teachers College, Columbia University, 1991.

17. There is yet no full history of AP, despite its more than forty years of existence. Two useful accounts are John A. Valentine, *The College Board and the School Curriculum* (New York: College Entrance Examination Board, 1987), pp. 79–91, and Frederick S. Allis, Jr., *Youth from Every Quarter: A Bicentennial History of Phillips Academy, Andover* (Hanover, N. H.: University Press of New England, 1979), pp. 549–554. The Kemper and Kenyon projects were supported by the Fund for the Advancement of Education. The first AP examinations were given in May 1954 to students in twenty-seven schools, ten of which were independent. On AP as a prep school marketing strategy, see John D. Davies, "But, Mr. Bender—," *Harvard Alumni Bulletin* 64 (March 17, 1962): 465. Data on recent participation can be found in the annual *AP National Summary Reports* published by the College Entrance Examination Board. The data on prep school sophomores who planned to take AP courses come from NELS:90.

18. Warren W. Willingham and Margaret Morris, *Four Years Later: A Longitudinal Study of Advanced Placement Students in College* (New York: College Entrance Examination Board, 1986), p. 21.

19. On AP course difficulty compared with college instruction, see Edwin H. Dickey, "A Comparison of Advanced Placement and College Students on a Calculus Achievement Test," *Journal for Research in Mathematics Education* 17 (March 1986): 140–144, and Eric Wimmers and Rick Morgan, "Comparing the Performance of High School and College Students on the Advanced Placement French Language Examination," *French Review* 63 (February 1990): 423–432.

20. These percentages are rough order-of-magnitude estimates as explained in the Appendix. Data were obtained from actual rather than statistically weighted SASS:88 teacher survey responses. The samples are 549 teachers from 149 very representative NAIS schools, and 1,341 teachers from 243 privileged public suburban schools. It was possible to identify undergraduate colleges attended by all 1,890 teachers. Using various college consumer guides, I constructed two lists of "highly selective" and "selective" private liberal arts institutions. (Only 60 of the 96 selective liberal arts colleges turned out to have even one graduate in either teacher sample.) The central campus state universities were selected from states where at least one NAIS school exists, and include several institutions in states with more than one recognized central campus (for example, California and New York). Once the three lists were constructed, I counted how many teachers from each sample attended the institutions on each list.

21. Eric Rothschild, *Teacher's Guide to Advanced Placement (AP) Courses in United States History* (New York: College Entrance Examination Board, 1991).

22. *A Student Guide to the AP Mathematics Courses and Examinations* (New York: College Entrance Examination Board, 1991), p. 7; *Contact* [Kent Place School] 5 (October/November 1991): 7.

23. Carl Brigham, "Views of Associate Secretary," *Thirty Third Annual Report of the Secretary* (New York: College Entrance Examination Board, 1933), pp. 12–13.

24. Among the vast body of material AP produces to validate its efforts and assist students and teachers—including detailed booklets on why particular essay answers were scored as they were—see *The College Board Technical Manual for the Advanced Placement Program* (New York: College Entrance Examination Board, 1988) and *The AP Reading: An Introduction for Applicants* (New York: College Entrance Examination Board, 1992).

25. *Baltimore Morning Sun,* January 7, 1992, p. 8B.

26. Richard W. Day, "The Independent School in 1975," *ISB* (May 1965): 15. In the early 1990s the College Board began experimenting with an AP-like program with broader appeal.

7. The Challenge of Average College-Bound Students

1. For a fuller treatment of accommodations to most students and of "specialty shops" for students at the extremes, see Arthur G. Powell, Eleanor Farrar, and David K. Cohen, *The Shopping Mall High School: Winners and Losers in the Educational Marketplace* (Boston: Houghton Mifflin, 1985), chaps. 1–3.

2. Louis Auchincloss, *The Rector of Justin* (Boston: Houghton Mifflin, 1956), p. 44; Thomas Donovan, "Some Platitudes That Bear Repetition," *ISB* (January 1965): 25.

3. The public schools' score advantage was short-lived. By the late 1960s independent schools surpassed them. In 1990 the average independent-school SAT score was 1,054 compared with 899 in public schools. All SAT material is from SAT:90. See also "NCIS Executive Committee Minutes," October 27, 1950, pp. 4–5, NAISA; Henry S. Dyer and Richard G. King, *College Board Scores No. 2: Their Use and Interpretation* (New York: College Entrance Examination Board, 1955); Joshua A. Fishman, *1957 Supplement to College Board Scores No. 2* (New York: College Entrance Examination Board, 1957).

4. The NRO was one of the first projects of the NCIS. The main beneficiaries were schools whose graduates attended a variety of colleges unfamiliar with prep schools and their grading practices. Schools with long-established college feeder patterns got little boost from the statistics, so many Eastern prep schools never joined NRO at all. The membership eventually included suburban public schools also eager to counter college admissions policies that gave excessive weight to class rank or aptitude scores. See *Fifth Annual Report: National Registration Office for Independent Schools, 1949* (Chicago: Commission on the Relation of Independent Schools with Higher Education, 1949), NAISA. On the founding and development of NRO, see "Summary of the Verbal Report of Mr. Herbert Smith, Francis Parker School, Given to the Heads of Private Schools of Wisconsin on November 14, 1942, at the Milwaukee University School"; Herbert B. Barks to Herbert W. Smith, December 8, 1942; "NCIS Executive Committee Minutes," February 14, 1944; W. L. W. Field, "Notice to Members of the [SEB] Committee on Public Service, May 31, 1944"; "Minutes of the Second Annual Meeting of the NCIS," Harvard Faculty Club, August 2–3, 1944; "About the National Registration Office for

Independent Schools, 1945–46," n.d.; "NCIS Minutes of the Executive Committee," October 29, 1946, p. 2; *NCR* 2 (December 1946): 3; NCIS "Scrapbook," September 15, 1950. All are in NAISA. Interview with Wellington V. Grimes, December 13, 1989.

5. After only five years the NRO report was 310 pages long and included nearly 4,000 student records from 124 schools. NCIS hoped in vain that considerable research use would be made of NRO data. The notable exception was analysis done by the young educational psychologist Benjamin S. Bloom. See *NCR* 53 (June 1959): 2, and Benjamin S. Bloom and Frank R. Peters, *The Use of Academic Prediction Scales* (Glencoe, Il.: The Free Press, 1961). *Forty Sixth Annual Report of the Executive Secretary* (New York: College Entrance Examination Board, 1946), p. 56; James W. Wickenden to Cary Potter, May 24, 1971; Cary Potter to James W. Wickenden, May 26, 1971, NAISA.

6. Priscilla L. Vail, *Smart Kids with School Problems* (New York: E. P. Dutton, 1987).

7. Course-taking data are from NELS:88. They combine parent reports of what eighth-graders are studying with reports from the students themselves.

8. James H. Grew, "A Quantitative Investigation of Foreign Language Study," *ISB* (April 1958): 7–8.

9. Evidence of the long-standing independent-school tilt against science and toward the humanities can be found in the Student Descriptive Questionnaire (SDQ) college-major predictions of independent and public high school students, published annually by the College Board. See also Warren W. Willingham and Margaret Morris, *Four Years Later: A Longitudinal Study of Advanced Placement Students in College* (New York: College Entrance Examination Board, 1986), pp. 17, 24, 36. Harvard College's wise observer of such matters reports that Eastern boarding schools have often been effective at dissuading even Asian Americans with strong science aptitude from college interest in science. Interview with Dean K. Whitla, October 25, 1990.

10. Data on high school course-taking are from SAT:90.

11. Willingham and Morris, *Four Years Later*, pp. 17, 37. This project studied a large sample of AP students in 1979 who attended selective liberal arts colleges in the early 1980s. A substantial number of independent-school graduates were included and broken out for analysis. This is one of few studies that link SAT scores directly to AP scores, and hence is a valuable comment on prep school access to AP by ability.

12. This analysis rests on NELS:88. Some data are taken from Kenneth R. Rasinski and Jerry West, *Eight [sic] Graders' Reports of Courses Taken During the 1988 Academic Year by Selected Student Characteristics* (Washington, D.C.: National Center for Education Statistics, July 1990). The proxy for academic "aptitude" is a composite score on reading and math tests administered to all students in the NELS:88 sample. Because the population sampled represents all eighth-graders, the aptitude range is far wider than that represented by college-bound seniors who take the SAT. This is why it seems reasonable to define "average" college-bound eighth-graders as those who score below the top tenth but are still in the top half. Those in the

bottom half would score well below "average" on the SAT were they ever to take it at all.

13. National secondary school data on the relation of course-taking to student aptitude are from SAT:90. These are more authoritative than NELS:88 data, which were used for the eighth-grade analysis. The former sample is far larger, issues of statistical significance do not exist, and the SAT indicator of "aptitude" is much better than the brief NELS test. "High-aptitude" students are defined as those with combined SAT scores exceeding 1,200.

Why does this discussion emphasize "participation" instead of "achievement," when America cares so much about achievement? One reason is that schools, parents, and students consider participation an important and concrete outcome on its own terms. Another reason is that assessing student achievement in secondary academic subjects is not an easy research task. It is harder to measure than a basic elementary competency like reading. AP examinations are virtually the only curriculum-driven achievement tests widely used in American public and prep schools. But only a minority of students take AP exams, and most are not average students. Moreover, linking AP and SAT scores was far too costly for this project to attempt. The College Board Achievement Tests (renamed "Subject Tests" in the 1990s) are not an adequate substitute because they are insufficiently curriculum driven.

14. Information about homework comes from student surveys in NELS:88 and NELS:90. SAT:90 has no information on homework. Readers should be aware of an important statistical point. Although the four-hour-per-week homework "advantage" of the prep school average student over privileged public schools is very significant statistically, the within-prep-school difference between the top tenth and the rest of the top half is a strong tendency that just misses technical significance because the NELS sample sizes are relatively small. (The mean hours of weekly homework reported are 9.55 hours for the top tenth, 12.52 hours for the next four deciles.) Because the tendency is strong and wholly consistent with student interviews, I have chosen to report it.

15. Harold J. Corbin, Jr., "Cautions, Causes, and Cures: Pressures and the Young," *ISB* (January 1964): 71; Edward T. Hall, "Keepers of the House," *ISB* (May 1966): 13–16; George H. Hawke, "In Our Elementary Schools: Abnormal Pressure upon Normal Children," *ISB* (December 1966): 14–16; Edith B. Phelps, "Big Angry Questions," *ISB* (December 1967): 8. Dean Bender saw the irony that prep schools which had dramatically increased the quality of student bodies simultaneously experienced a steady decline in applicants accepted to Harvard. See W. J. Bender, "Admission and Scholarship Committees," *Harvard Annual Reports 1959–60*, p. 235, Harvard University Archives. The "rats" analogies are from Edward S. Hall, "What Price Competition?" *ISB* (January 1957): 6–7, and Charles Merrill, "Avalanche," *ISB* (December 1969): 20.

16. William Huntington Thompson, "Reading for Today," *ISB* (February 1949): 5; John B. Bigelow to the Editor, *ISB* (April 1949): 15; John McGiffert, "Reading for Today: A Rebuttal," *ISB* (April 1949): 2.

17. William R. Link, "Needed: A New Humanism," *ISB* (May 1970): 18–19; Douglas Heath, "Education for 1984," *ISB* (October 1969): 8–9. Sympathy for this critique of academic learning and for the moral superiority of youth permeate two important prep school studies of the time: Otto F. Kraushaar, *American Nonpublic Schools: Patterns of Diversity* (Baltimore and London: The Johns Hopkins University Press, 1972), and Leonard L. Baird, *The Elite Schools: A Profile of Prestigious Independent Schools* (Lexington, Mass., and Toronto: Lexington Books, 1977).

18. Cecily C. Selby, "Trust and Tradition: Evolution and Entropy," *ISB* (December 1970): 6. A female teacher unsympathetic to the erosion of academic standards attributed much of the change to an influx of young male administrators motivated by draft evasion. They were generally more liberal, trendy, and unintellectual than women. Susan O. Bishop, "Where Have All the Headmistresses Gone?" *ISB* (October 1974): 23. A succinct overview of prep school change caused by the 1960s is John Chandler, Jr., "Entering the Eighties," *IS* (February 1980): 7–9.

19. Higher education curiously resisted this turnabout. The teacher who worked in Africa scorned the colleges' continuing abdication of responsibility for school improvement. Unwilling to put any academic press on schools but wanting to be perceived as constructive anyway, higher education adopted politically attractive but usually ineffectual proschool policies. School-university "partnerships," for example, were safe ways to assert an interest in schools without real effort to change student habits or teaching practices. On the resurgence of academic values, see Bishop, "Where Have All the Headmistresses Gone?" p. 23; Frances O'Connor, "Creating Our Own Futures," *ISB* (October 1975): 6; Edward T. Hall, "An American Headmaster in an African School," *ISB* (February 1976): 49–52; Richard A. Hawley, "The Good-Bad Class," *ISB* (February 1976): 58; Edward M. Kennedy, "A New Coalition of Commitment," *IS* (May 1981): 33.

20. On Japanese willingness to take seriously the American bromide that all students can learn, see Harold W. Stevenson and James W. Stigler, *The Learning Gap: Why Our Schools Are Failing and What We Can Learn from Japanese and Chinese Education* (New York: Summit Books, 1992).

21. One reasonable way slow readers learn to read faster is to do lots of reading. Although experts, tutoring, and coping skills have an important place in managing learning disabilities, students with these or any learning problems must realize that they will have to work harder than other students if they want to succeed. This is the only way. I am grateful to Jeanne Chall and Priscilla Vail for pointing out to me the necessary relation between hard work and overcoming learning handicaps.

8. The Power of Personal Attention

1. Milbrey W. McLaughlin and Joan Talbert, with Joseph Kahne and Judith Powell, "Constructing a Personalized School Environment," *Phi Delta Kappan* 72 (1990): 230–235.

2. Peter Marks, "Turning around Troubled Students, Intensively," *New York Times*, April 14, 1994, p. B1.

3. Gerald Grant et al., "Report of the Committee on Evaluation of the Coalition of Essential Schools," September 1, 1988, pp. 17–18, author's possession.

4. Arthur G. Powell, Eleanor Farrar, and David K. Cohen, *The Shopping Mall High School: Winners and Losers in the Educational Marketplace* (Boston: Houghton Mifflin, 1985), chap. 4.

5. Susan P. Choy et al., *Schools and Staffing in the United States: A Statistical Profile, 1990–91* (Washington, D.C.: National Center for Education Statistics, 1993). This updates the original SASS:88 database utilized in earlier chapters.

6. The 82 percent figure is calculated from SASS:88, excluding time when teachers reported "absence" from school.

7. Carl G. Wonnberger, "Quo Vadimus?" *ISB* (May 1956): 3. One market research study found that students rated a "caring and concerned faculty" the most important attribute of a good private school. It was slightly more important than the faculty's teaching ability. Sanford Roeser, "School Selection Factors: What Research Tells Us," *The New Marketing Handbook for Independent Schools* (Boston: Boarding Schools, 1987), pp. 24–26.

8. Interview with Rev. F. Washington Jarvis, October 1989. For an argument that these rituals and habits are not possible in large schools, see Douglas H. Heath, "Survival? A Bigger School?" *ISB* (May 1972): 14.

9. The "wealthy suburban" public school size of 752 is drawn from SASS:88. These are suburban schools with no Chapter One services and the minimum number of free-lunch services for the poor. The average size of all suburban schools then was 638, and of all urban schools 656. It is not surprising that large schools were often in well-off suburbs. Smallness was less valued in the 1950s, when the nuclear family, the mother as homemaker, and the stable neighborhood were still taken for granted as major sources of personal attention. In addition, these schools were assumed to be safe, orderly, and relatively homogeneous. Their size did not seem especially important. Susan P. Choy et al., *Schools and Staffing in the United States: A Statistical Profile, 1987–88* (Washington, D.C.: National Center for Education Statistics, 1992), p. 10.

10. Independent-school statistics are taken from 1987–88 and 1990–91 NAIS data. These correspond with SASS statistics collected for those years and permit comparison with "wealthy suburban" public schools in SASS:88. I examined senior class size in 1987 using NAIS statistics. The data on attrition in the five years before eighth grade are from NELS:88. About a third of prep school students had been in the same school for at least five years, compared with about 11 percent of students in privileged public schools. Students in Catholic and other private schools showed even less school attrition than the prep eighth-graders.

11. This advantage is a double-edged sword. Good schools often reinforce family values and thus sustain them in the outside world. But bad schools are often bad because they do exactly the same thing. The perfect school match may seem perfect only because it reinforces family preferences that are themselves anti-educational to many citizens. This is one reason school choice is so controversial.

12. Lynda Richardson, "Deciding If It's Time for Kindergarten or Time to Wait a Year," *New York Times,* July 20, 1995, p. C4. Postgraduate or "PG" programs have played crucial roles in readying athletes for the Ivy League and Division I college sports, and readying students for the service academies. But it is also important to understand the relatively small impact of innovations that attempt to manipulate the time variable. Despite a few other examples described earlier (such as a regular one-year foreign language course spread out over two years), neither independent schools nor public schools have experimented much with more radical forms of personalized self-paced instruction. Courses last a year, a semester, or a trimester. Senior year (or sixth form) remains intact. There are no incentives to challenge these regularities, and every incentive (predictable tuition income and teacher job routines, school loyalty as exemplified by class and grade solidarity) to keep things as they are.

13. Interview with John C. Esty, Jr., July 22, 1991. On the symbiotic relation between heads and college admissions officers, see Robert Hampel, *The Last Little Citadel: American High Schools since 1940* (Boston: Houghton Mifflin, 1986), pp. 32–35.

14. W. J. Bender, "Admissions and Scholarship Committee," *Harvard Annual Reports,* 1959–60, Harvard University Archives, p. 236.

15. Warren W. Willingham and Margaret Morris, *Four Years Later: A Longitudinal Study of Advanced Placement Students in College* (New York: College Entrance Examination Board, 1986), p. 17.

16. Dana M. Cotton, in *SEBAR 1958–59,* p. 53.

17. Edward T. Hall, "What Price Competition?" *ISB* (January 1957): 6.

9. The Role of the Good Teacher

1. The headmaster who spoke of teachers as exemplars was Andover's John Kemper. Yet under his prodding the independent-school community took teacher education more seriously in the 1950s and 1960s than it had before. Most of this new interest had little to do with confidence in extant teacher-education programs. In the 1950s perceptive headmasters realized that the rapid growth of suburban public schools, along with the increase in size of most independent schools, created a serious prep school teacher recruitment problem. It was unwise to reject all teacher education, since appropriate teacher education might be a powerful recruiting method. The growing Master of Arts in Teaching programs shared much private school distrust of teacher education and emphasized study of the liberal arts disciplines and supervised teaching. Kemper urged prep schools not to ally with hardline opponents of teacher education. They should issue constructive policy statements, recruit when possible from M.A.T. programs, and develop internship programs of their own. A positive position would also help damp down state insistence that prep school teachers be certified just like public school teachers—a demand that some states might impose if prep schools seemed wholly contemptuous

of the very idea of teacher education. Porter E. Sargent, *A Handbook of Private Schools, 1930–31,* (Boston: Porter Sargent, 1930), p. 25; Frederick S. Allis, Jr., *Youth from Every Quarter: A Bicentennial History of Phillips Academy, Andover* (Hanover, N. H.: University Press of New England, 1979), p. 644; *NAIS Report No. 5* (June 1963): 5–6; NAIS, *Teaching in the Independent School: A Career* (Boston: NAIS, ca. 1963); "NCIS Executive Committee Minutes," February 10 and April 8, 1954, NAISA.

2. Frank H. Wallace, "What Children Need from Teachers," *ISB* (May 1976): 66.

3. Class size estimates are from *Private School News* 7 (May 1931), p. 17; Robert D. North, "A Report on the Advanced Placement Program," *ISB* (January 1958): 6; and the 1990–91 enrollment statistics of NAIS.

4. Data on student attitudes toward teacher-student relations are from NELS:88 and NELS:90.

5. Whether it is possible to have a "good discussion" in a class of between twenty-five and thirty students depends entirely on what is meant by a good discussion. If one means a sustained conversation around serious issues, with some students participating and most others attentive, then the field notes of A Study of High Schools contain examples of good discussions with classes in the high twenties. If a good discussion means that virtually all students directly participate in a noncontrived way, hardly any good discussions were ever observed after class size reached twenty.

6. The extensive literature on the relation of class size to achievement has not especially helped the cause of prep school administrators who wish to increase class size modestly in order to cut costs and make schools more affordable. The research may be inconclusive in some respects, but it does not prove that small prep school classes have no value. The usual definitions of achievement are exceedingly narrow, and the research does not address the many reasons small classes are desired by families apart from scores on basic skills tests. For recent research confirming the value of smaller classes for younger children learning basic skills, see Frederick Mosteller, "The Tennessee Study of Class Size in the Early Elementary Grades," in *The Future of Children* 5 (Center for the Future of Children; Summer-Fall 1995), pp. 113–127. For the downside of the long up-down relation private school administrators have had with the "small classes are better" issue, see John Chandler, Jr., *Report of the President, March 6, 1964* (Boston: NAIS, 1964), p. 8; and Peter Aitken et al., *Access and Affordability: Strategic Financial Perspectives for Independent Schools* (Washington, D.C.: NAIS, 1994), pp. 93–111.

7. Thomas Read, "Challenges for Independent Schools in the 1990s," March 20, 1989, NAISA; Leonard Baird, *The Elite Schools: A Profile of Prestigious Independent Schools* (Lexington, Mass., and Toronto: Lexington Books, 1977), p. 125. The questions on understanding, challenge, and trying hard are from NELS:90. Student opinion surveys on the quality of classroom teaching are very tricky to interpret since most students have nothing with which to compare their experience. Ambitious prep school students might be aware that they are trying less hard than some

ideal, since their basic orientation is work and achievement. But they still might be trying harder than other students.

8. The 1981–82 field studies for A Study of High Schools emphasized life in classrooms. That and other research suggested that large instructional differences would not be found between prep school classrooms and comparable college prep classrooms in public schools. Therefore, a major field studies decision for this book was not to collect additional classroom data. The totality of "courses" as experienced by students, not just the classroom part of the course, became the focus. See the Appendix and its counterpart in Arthur G. Powell, Eleanor Farrar, and David K. Cohen, *The Shopping Mall High School: Winners and Losers in the Educational Marketplace* (Boston: Houghton Mifflin, 1985), pp. 325–332.

9. On this point see Carl G. Wonnberger, "Let's Examine the Independent School," *ISB* (February 1948): 14.

10. Porter E. Sargent, *Handbook of Private Schools, 1924–25*, p. 17.

11. NAIS first collected data on secondary-teacher loads in 1986, when the reported median was 63. In subsequent years the average ranged between 50 and 60. In 1991, departmentalized middle school teachers (grades 6–8) taught on average 40 students, whereas K–5 teachers taught on average 17. SASS:88 data show an average independent-school secondary load of roughly 61 students, compared with 118 students in privileged public schools and 120 in all public schools.

12. The classic load of about 20 classes per week is substantiated by historical studies, teacher surveys, and contemporary interviews. For example, John DeQ. Briggs, "The Teacher's Load," *ISB* (February 1967): 27; and SASS:88. Although data from SASS:88 clearly indicate that independent-school teachers spend less time in classrooms than public school teachers, these data also indicate that out-of-classroom work by prep school teachers makes up for their fewer in-class hours. Their aggregate work week does not seem significantly longer than that of public school teachers (although any "minutes-per-student" analysis would show much greater time given to individual prep school students). On the other hand, a small but thorough study (responses were obtained by interviews, not by questionnaires) of 172 public and private school teachers in New Jersey concluded that independent-school teachers have longer work weeks in spite of having smaller student loads. Public school teachers spend slightly more time in classroom instruction than independent-school teachers, slightly less time on school duties unconnected to their regular teaching (coaching, monitoring study halls), and considerably less time on out-of-classroom activities connected to their teaching (planning, correcting student work, meeting individually with students). This last difference—independent-school teachers reported spending 5.5 hours a week more on such activities than public school colleagues—explained the longer independent-school teacher work week. See Pearl R. Kane, *The Teachers College New Jersey Survey: A Comparative Study of Public and Independent School Teachers* (New York: Department of Educational Administration, Teachers College, Columbia University, 1986), pp. 37–41.

13. One-on-one teaching is usually easier for teachers when students come to them with a particular question or puzzle. This frames the conversation, and allows

the teacher to concentrate on how to help a student "get it." It is harder when the primary burden of framing the interaction falls on the teacher, which is the case for most tutorials. Then the teacher must first figure out what is important to discuss and where a discussion might productively go. In this more open-ended situation, the teacher's competence as an authority who knows all the answers—let alone all the questions—is much less obvious. One overlooked reason one-on-one teaching is rare is that it is difficult and threatening. It is no accident that its frequency increases when student and teacher commitment to learning is also high.

14. Sam's mother, a member of a parent focus group, brought a copy of the written comment to the meeting to give to me. She had carefully highlighted in blue the last one hundred words so I would not fail to see this concrete evidence of how the school provided personal attention to her son.

Index

4.00